W9-AUU-215

remembering

CHARLIE

DOUBLEDAY

remembering

CHARLIE

A Pictorial Biography

J E R R Y   E P S T E I N

D O U B L E D A Y

NEW YORK LONDON TORONTO SYDNEY AUCKLAND

4-6-89

253 9946

N28-30.00

Published by Doubleday, a division of
Bantam Doubleday Dell Publishing Group, Inc.
666 Fifth Avenue, New York, New York 10103

"Doubleday" and the portrayal of an anchor with a dolphin are trademarks
of Doubleday, a division of Bantam Doubleday Dell Publishing Group, Inc.

Library of Congress cataloging-in-publication data applied for

ISBN 0–385–262825

No photograph in this book may be reproduced without permission

Copyright © 1989 by Jerry Epstein

All rights reserved.

PICTURE CREDITS
The majority of photographs of Charlie Chaplin, Oona and family in
Switzerland and in London between 1953 and 1977 by Jerry Epstein; others
by Oona Chaplin, Charlie or guests. Most stills from the Chaplin films
supplied by the Bubbles Company. Other credits: Grigori Alexandrov p.160
top right, Marcus Blackman p.47 *bottom right, Daily Express* Newspapers
p.191, p.208, London *Daily Mirror* p.10 *top,* Loomis Dean/*Life* magazine
p.41, p.57 *bottom right,* Yves Debrine p.119 *top,* J.R. Eyerman/*Life* magazine
p.68, p.70, Raymond Heil p.123, Florence Homolka p.92 *right,* p.94, Angus
MacBean p.158, Museum of the City of New York p.27, National Film
Archive p.63 *bottom,* p.85, p.88, p.95, p.99, p.131, p.133, pp.168–9, p.181
right, p.185 *top right,* p.188 *bottom right,* p.199 *top left, top right* and *bottom
right,* p.214, p.217 *top right,* p.222 *top left,* p.224 *top right,* Jerome Robinson
p.54, p.74, W. Eugene Smith/*Life* magazine p.83, p.86, p.92 *bottom left,* p.93
right, p.97, p.100, p.101, Wolf Suschitzky p.140.

Designed by Simon Jennings, Alan Marshall,
Laurence Bradbury and Roy Williams
Typeset by Bookworm Typesetting, Manchester
Printed and bound by Printer Industria Gráfica s.a., Barcelona

FOR OONA
Through her friendship she has
enriched my life

AND FOR HER EIGHT CHILDREN
In the hope that this book will tell them more
about their father

"If something survives from the 20th century, that something will probably be Charlie Chaplin; that emblem, that solitary man, who fought back and brought to the world a great beauty."

(Freddy Buache, Curator of the Swiss Film Archive)

CONTENTS

PREFACE

Recently, as I was straightening out my workroom, a friend came across the multitude of photographs I had taken over the years of Oona and Charlie Chaplin and their family. "These pictures should be published!" she said excitedly, "They're beautiful. They show a wonderful side to Chaplin that the public should see." I was preoccupied at the time, and dismissed it from my mind.

A short time later, during a visit to Oona Chaplin in Switzerland, we were looking at some other photos of the family. "Your pictures are still the best," she said. I then asked her if I could have them published. "I don't think Charlie would have minded." "No," she replied. "He loved your pictures."

That was the beginning of this book. Fortunately, I always gave the negatives to Oona and she methodically filed them away. If I'd kept them, I think they would have been scattered and lost over two continents.

After my decision to do the book, Oona had the negatives printed; flew to London and, in two large valises, presented me with what seemed like thousands of pictures. We went to work immediately. Knee-deep in photographs, we separated the good from the bad.

The late publisher Norah Smallwood told me that interesting text is just as important as pictures. But what should the text be? Someone suggested that Oona's eight children tell me how they saw their father. I thought it was a great idea. But I discovered that children don't know their parents that well; they had very little to say. I tried another angle – speaking to people who knew Charlie – but there was a sameness about their comments.

Other friends suggested that the text should be the story of my association with Chaplin. I was dead set against it. I loathe people who, after working for someone famous and becoming close friends with the family, disclose what went on behind closed doors.

However, after some arm-twisting I realized that the only personal thing I could reveal about Oona and Charlie, was that of two people very much in love. I was making a mountain out of a molehill. My enthusiasm grew.

But I was shy of doing the actual writing. I approached Geoff Brown, the deputy film critic on *The Times* in London. He was keen to do it.

For six months Geoff taped my stories and anecdotes, then wrote a chapter. It was good, but it didn't sound like me and I felt since the book was to be written in the first person it had to have my voice.

Geoff then said, "If you want the book to sound like you, write it yourself and afterwards I'll help with the editing." I still didn't want to do it; I had a screenplay to finish with Simon Callow. But it was Oona who finally convinced me. "*You* must write it," she said. "It has to be in your words." She sounded just like Charlie talking to me. That did it.

I wrote the first chapter. Then I would edit, shift, reshape and edit again. (I felt like Charlie, cutting one of his films). Each editing made me recall more. So the re-editing process started over again.

When I was exhausted, Geoff would go over my work and recommend further cuts. Then I would go over his edits, sometimes reinstating what I felt were the "juices".

Things that kept me away from Charlie – in the theater, films, television and film packaging – I've eliminated. Only when there were humorous incidents or anecdotes involving people like Errol Flynn, Eddie Constantine or Hitchcock, did I include them.

I never bothered Oona for further information and in turn she never interfered with the writing of the book. She never saw the completed text until it was ready for publication.

I have refused to pontificate on or try to analyze Charlie's character. Who am I to do this? But, as in a good film, the best way to know a person is to throw him into a situation. And that's what I have done. Charlie is seen as I knew him – in action.

So let me share with you the thrills, tensions and joys of my thirty-year association with the cinema's greatest artist, Charles Spencer Chaplin. And hopefully, through the text and photographs, you, the reader, will get to know Charlie Chaplin better, as actor, film-maker, husband, father and friend.

Jerry Epstein

CHARLIE 1 AND ME – THE BEGINNINGS

ABOVE: The London *Daily Mirror*, September 20th, 1952. Charlie's being banned from America made front-page news throughout the world.

BELOW : As a child, Charlie lived at the end of Methley Street, South London, next to a slaughterhouse and a pickle factory.

On September 5th, 1952, Oona and Charlie Chaplin were about to leave Hollywood for New York with their family on what was to be a fateful journey. The following week, they would sail to London on the *Queen Elizabeth* for the opening of *Limelight*. We had just completed the film, and were making the final trims. Charlie was as excited as a schoolboy – *Limelight* was to be his greatest triumph.

In the evening, Charlie and I drank coffee at Googie's, a small café on Sunset Boulevard. At the time, the FBI and the House Un-American Activities Committee were hounding him for alleged Communist sympathies; he was also being accused of practically every sin under the sun by the Hollywood columnists Louella Parsons and Hedda Hopper. But Charlie cast all his problems aside and waxed rhapsodically about his love for America. "I could never have found such success in England. This is really the land of opportunity!"

The next morning, Saturday September 6th, as they left the editing room, Charlie insisted that Oona go to the Bank of America with him – to put her signature on a joint account, just in case anything happened to him. Oona did not want to do it. Nothing was going to happen.

Luckily, he insisted. Nine days later, in the mid-Atlantic, a cablegram arrived on the *Queen Elizabeth* from US Attorney-General James McGranery, revoking Charlie's re-entry permit. He could only return to the US if he applied as an ordinary immigrant, passing through Ellis Island. Even then he would be held for hearings, to determine his suitability for admission. This was happening to the man who had helped to create the American movie industry, one of the most famous people in the world. Even in deepest Africa, they knew the name and silhouette of Charlie Chaplin.

I was in a state of shock when I heard the news on the radio. All the headlines blared "CHARLIE CHAPLIN REFUSED RE-ENTRY TO THE U.S." I didn't know how to reach him. I called Arthur Krim, the President of United Artists, in New York, and he helped reassure me that everything would be all right. Little did I know at the time that the revocation of Charlie's re-entry permit would affect us both for the rest of our lives.

During the last five years, the Chaplins had become a large and important part of my life. I ran the Circle Theatre, a pioneer theater-in-the-round in Los Angeles, and Chaplin's son Sydney was among the actors. From 1947 to the end of 1950, Chaplin directed and advised me on plays. We became close friends. When *Limelight* moved into production in 1951, I was offered a job as his personal assistant.

The day after those shock headlines, the *Herald Examiner,* a Hearst journal, serialized his life story. And what a story it was – the original rags to riches drama. Chaplin's early life rivaled Oliver Twist's. He grew up in the slums of South London, where he was born on April 16th in 1889. Both his parents were music-hall artistes: his father, Charles, was a comic singer; mother Hannah was a soubrette. Charles Sr deserted the family, and later died an alcoholic at thirty-seven. Worn down by the effects of abject poverty and malnutrition, Hannah lost her mind. When Charlie led her to hospital, the local children threw stones. She later spent years being shunted in and out of asylums.

Without a mother, young Charlie and his elder brother Sydney were temporarily placed in a Dickensian workhouse. On Christmas Day, the inmates were given oranges. Charlie had never seen an orange before, and didn't know it was something to eat. He never forgot how the fruit's bright color stood out against the drab workhouse walls.

When Hannah was released, the family stayed in dingy lodgings – with a slaughterhouse and a pickle factory for neighbors. But food was still scarce. Sydney would queue for free soup at the local Mission while Charlie stayed home. He had to: the boys only had a single pair of shoes between them.

The past preyed on Chaplin's mind for the rest of his life. Years later, in the 1950s, when I joined him in London, he had me drive him round his old haunts in my car. He seemed to need these trips into his past to replenish his spirit. He'd point out The Three Stags pub on Kennington Road, where he last saw his father alive. We'd drive past the

CHARLIE (ENCIRCLED), AGED EIGHT, AT
HANWELL SCHOOL (1897).

OONA AND CHARLIE AT BANKEND, SOUTH EAST LONDON, WITH ST PAUL'S IN THE DISTANCE (1959).

OONA AND CHARLIE AT BANKEND, SOUTH EAST LONDON, WITH ST PAUL'S IN THE DISTANCE (1959).

gates of the Lambeth workhouse, in silence. We'd see where Hannah was committed, and walk to the door of the family garret at 3 Pownall Terrace (I took photographs of Charlie standing outside), and the various music-halls where he performed.

Some evenings, with Oona seated in the back of my Hillman Minx, he'd guide us down dark, foggy streets, half-lit by gaslight and still suffering from the effects of the Blitz. We were deep in the heart of Jack the Ripper country. Hearing footsteps behind us, it was easy to imagine the Ripper stalking through. Once, my car stalled, and we couldn't wait to get out of there – even Charlie!

Other days we drove to Wapping, Stepney, Canning Town and Hackney – still impoverished areas, but now dotted with high-rises. These monstrosities depressed Charlie; to him, they were like prison blocks, unfit for family life. We took another trip to Southend, where he had first seen the sea as a child. On arrival he immediately bought cockles from a stand on the beach – just as he did as a young boy. Smells and tastes were as important to him as places.

One chilly gray day, Oona, Charlie and I drove to Sheerness, and sat on a dirty deserted pebble beach huddled together in the cold, eating containers of cottage cheese. We were all shivering and miserable, but Charlie wouldn't admit it. For some reason he had a yearning to see Sheerness again.

During some nocturnal trips he'd sit quietly in my car, staring out of the window at the streets and houses. He'd give me brisk traffic directions – "Turn right!", "Left here", and God forbid if I went the wrong way. Then suddenly he'd say, "That's the flat Sydney and I moved to after he came back from the seas." At other times I'd stop the car; he'd hop out and peer through people's windows, masking his face, curious about how they lived. He never tired of those trips down Memory Lane.

As a child, Charlie had been forced to dress in odds and ends. At one time he wore stockings cut down from his mother's red tights – the local lads referred to him as "Sir Francis Drake". But the Charlie I knew was always an immaculate dresser. In Hollywood he wore white slacks and a tweed jacket; he'd come to the Circle in cream-colored spats, which looked strange even then. He loved the thought of his butler giving him two clean handkerchiefs every morning – one for his breast pocket, one for his trousers. To Charlie, that was the height of luxury.

But with all his present wealth he couldn't get used to the idea of wearing a clean shirt every day: he had to wear it just one day more – a hangover from his childhood.

Charlie had a persistent fear that one day he would go insane, like his mother. He felt the condition was hereditary. Hannah's own mother, too, had been committed to an asylum. As a child he saw the effects of drink and poverty on other music-hall entertainers apart from his parents: he was horrified when his mother brought home a derelict colleague from the halls, Eva Lester, giving her a good bath, a few spare clothes and several shillings. As he grew older, Charlie brooded about the famous comedians of his youth who ended their days in poverty and despair. It was a recurring nightmare of his. "What would have happened to me," he said to me one day, "if I hadn't gone to America?"

When Charlie was nine, the Muses called. He joined the Eight Lancashire Lads at the Theatre Royal, Manchester, clog dancing up and down the country, and playing cats and dogs in pantomime. Afterwards, he went back to school, but he was itchy for work. So he took odd jobs, as an errand boy in a naval shop, a printer's helper, a glassblower, and a newsboy for W. H. Smith the newsagents. His first break came along in the theater when he portrayed Billy the messenger boy in William Gillette's dramatic version of *Sherlock Holmes*; he toured the play for nearly three years, then appeared in the West End. Years later, when he directed at the Circle, he would impress us by reciting the entire text from memory.

Top: The Karno troupe *en route* for America in 1910. Charlie in the center, with the life-preserver, and his understudy, Stan Laurel, on the far left.

Bottom: Charlie in San Francisco during Karno's American tour – the first time he was given top billing.

Charlie's real breakthrough came with Fred Karno, then Britain's Number One music-hall impresario, known to all his employees as "The Guv'nor". First, Sydney joined Karno's troupe; two years later, in 1908, Charlie appeared at the Paris Folies Bergères in Karno's *Mumming Birds*. Debussy saw the show and asked to meet him. "You are instinctively a musician and dancer," Debussy told Charlie.

In 1910, Karno took the troupe to the United States, in a revue called *The Wow-Wows*. His understudy and room-mate was a Lancashire lad, Stanley Jefferson – later to find fame as Stan Laurel. While touring, Charlie studied the cello and began to educate himself. He was determined to improve his lot. Charlie soon fell in love with America, its vitality, and the generosity of the audiences. His own reviews were especially good – *Variety* declared "Chaplin will do all right for America".

In 1951, when I was with him in New York, Charlie showed me the site of the Colonial Theater, where he made his American debut, the restaurants and bookshops where he used to linger, and the Times Square area where he lodged in a tiny back room for three dollars a week. Charlie was forever exploring the past and present.

Karno's American tour lasted almost two years; Charlie scored a particular success in *A Night in an English Music Hall* – playing a drunk in a theater box, commenting on the various acts.

When the troupe returned to America later in 1912, Mack Sennett – always on the look-out for new comedians for his Keystone film company – must have caught the show. His office sent a telegram to the Philadelphia theater where the troupe was performing: "Is there a man named *Chaffin* in your company or something like that?" Yes there was – sort of. Tired of touring, Charlie signed a one-year contract to make two-reelers in Hollywood for one hundred and fifty dollars a week – three times his Karno salary. Now was the time to try something new.

But Charlie never forgot Fred Karno, his mentor. When I worked with him years later in London, he made me drive him to Taggs Island, near Hampton Court, on the Thames, where Karno had kept his house-boat and built an expensive folly, the "Karsino" pleasure palace. It had been closed and derelict since Karno's bankruptcy in 1926, but Charlie was curious and fascinated to see this ghost from the past. "What a fool poor Karno was," he said. "It's this monstrosity that made him bankrupt." Charlie never let that sort of folly happen to himself.

One of Charlie's early shorts, *A Night
in the Show* (1915), based on one of his
Karno acts.

In his first film, *Making a Living* (made in 1914), Charlie played a trickster posing as a count. But he wasn't comfortable with the character. He went into the Keystone wardrobe department and began putting on various costumes. He tried out various sizes of pants, hats, shoes, canes and mustaches. He began making faces and gestures in the mirror. Soon Charlie was transformed – dressed in baggy pants, a small bowler hat, large button-up shoes and a tiny mustache.

He started feeling the character at once: a little man struggling to survive in a hostile world, clinging onto remnants of dignity, always keeping his chin up in the face of adversity. The Tramp was born!

In his year with Sennett, Charlie made 35 two-reelers. By the end of 1914, Charlie Chaplin – the man with the funny mustache, the funnier walk, the bowler hat and the cane – had become a household name throughout the world.

Charlie liked telling me his Chicago story. He was about to sign with the Essanay film company in 1915 for $1250 a week. He met with the backers in the Alexandra Hotel lobby. But the financiers had developed cold feet; they didn't want to pay him the agreed amount of money. They told him he wasn't that popular. Without them knowing, Charlie had a messenger page him. Pandemonium erupted in the hotel lobby; everyone rushed to get a glimpse of Charlie Chaplin, the cinema's new idol. Charlie got his money. That story tickled him.

One year later he was lured away by Mutual, who offered him ten thousand dollars a week plus a fat bonus. Before settling down to work, Charlie went to New York – his first visit since his new-found success. As his train crossed the continent, telegraph operators sent messages from city to city announcing that Charlie Chaplin was aboard. When it pulled in at Albuquerque, New Mexico, mobs surrounded the platform to get a glimpse. He had to make an appearance. This happened at every stop on the trek eastwards. Through the night, people stood on the station platforms, holding candles, determined to see their idol. When the train finally arrived at New York, he had to be taken off at One Hundred and Twenty-Fifth Street to avoid the mobs at Grand Central Station.

Headlines in the New York papers screamed, "He's here!" This was the first time, Charlie said, that the huge extent of his popularity really dawned on him. He was twenty-seven years old.

OPPOSITE: THE TRAMP IS BORN.

LEFT: VISITING CHARLIE ON THE SET:
THOMAS INCE, MACK SENNETT AND
D. W. GRIFFITH.

On his return to Los Angeles, Chaplin found a letter from Fred Karno. Karno wondered if Chaplin would appear for one thousand pounds a week in a spectacular revue he was mounting with C. B. Cochran. Charlie replied in the friendliest way:

Dear Guv'nor,

The figure you mention to appear in London would have given me a heart attack once upon a time! But I am tied up now for some years and I don't see the possibility of being able to come . . . If I am able to do so one day, be sure I would let you know before anybody. Wishing you all luck, I am, Guv'nor,

Your Charlie Chaplin.

There seemed to be no stopping Charlie. For the Mutual company he made some of his funniest shorts, *One A.M.*, *The Pawnshop*, *Easy Street*, and *The Immigrant*. But his good fortune also brought resentment. British newspapers began to print articles attacking him as a shirker for not fighting with the British Army in the First World War. Charlie countered with the facts: he had raised huge sums in war bonds through personal appearances; he was registered for the draft in America, but had never been summoned. But the attacks continued; he was even sent white feathers. It hurt him deeply.

In 1918, his Mutual contract completed, Charlie moved into his own studio on the corner of Sunset Boulevard and La Brea Avenue. It was built in the style of an old English village, to get round the zoning laws and avoid complaints from neighbors who were afraid that a movie studio would lower the tone of the area. The films were now distributed through First National: classics like *A Dog's Life* and *Shoulder Arms* – a war comedy, released just a few weeks before the Armistice.

Left: Charlie prodding two cows (*Sunnyside*, 1919).

Below: Charlie was the first to make a comedy about the First World War – *Shoulder Arms* (1918). The soldiers ate it up.

Later in the year, Charlie married in secret. His bride was Mildred Harris, a young actress pushed into films while still a child by an aggressive mother. Mildred had appeared in D. W. Griffith's *Intolerance,* and *Old Folks at Home* with Sir Herbert Beerbohm Tree – one of Charlie's childhood idols. Charlie was enchanted with her, but Mildred didn't understand what living with a creative artist meant. Charlie's work came before anything else. On top of everything else, Mildred insisted her mother move in with them – a situation which wouldn't help any marriage. On July 7th, 1919, Mildred gave birth to a baby, Norman Spencer Chaplin, who lived for only three days. Some months later, the couple parted amidst much publicity. The mother announced to the press that the marriage was definitely over.

In spite of Charlie's troubles, he went on to produce his biggest hit to date: *The Kid,* a milestone in picture-making. Charlie's co-star, the child actor Jackie Coogan, became an overnight sensation as the orphan befriended and adopted by the Tramp. The film touched the heart of the world. Now, for the first time, you could cry as well as laugh in a Chaplin movie.

*LEFT: THE FILM THAT CREATED A SENSATION THROUGHOUT THE WORLD AND MADE A STAR OF LITTLE JACKIE COOGAN – THE KID (1921).
BELOW: SUNNYSIDE (1919).*

Charlie sent for his mother, and set her up in a pleasant bungalow near the sea, looked after by housekeepers and a trained nurse. Until her death in 1928 she lived contentedly, never fully aware of her son's huge popularity and wealth.

Charlie was desperately homesick for London. In 1921 he decided on a European trip. London went wild. Crowds at Waterloo station raised him up on their shoulders – a conquering hero had come home. He eagerly revisited his childhood haunts, just as he did over thirty years later with Oona and myself. He met other celebrities of the age, including H. G. Wells and Sir James Barrie. The reception was the same in Paris and Berlin; Charlie was the property of the world. Even Lenin was a fan; "Chaplin," he said, "is the only man in the world I want to meet."

PORTRAIT OF CHARLIE IN THE 1920S.

Before returning to Los Angeles, Charlie spent a day at Sing Sing prison in upstate New York with his friend Frank Harris, the writer who championed Oscar Wilde during his troubles. The prisoners were awed and elated by Charlie's visit, but kept their distance. The warden showed them over the cell blocks and the death chamber, with its crude wooden chair linked to a single electric wire. The prison doctor explained in detail how it worked as Charlie actually sat in the chair. He also caught a glimpse of one wretched man facing execution. "Did you see his face?" Charlie said to Frank Harris – "Tragic, appalling! I shall see that face until I die."

Charlie always had a morbid fascination with death. His favorite reading, I learned, was *True Detective* magazine, which always carried pictures of decapitated bodies being carried off for autopsies. For some reason, *True Detective* was also my mother's favorite reading. Every time I visited Charlie when he lived in Switzerland, I always brought stacks of my mother's gruesome copies from the States.

By now Charlie was the darling of the intellectuals. Before he came into films, highbrows from the East Coast had turned up their noses at this new bastard industry; to them, only theater counted. But Charlie had brought art into the movies. Acting lost its elaborate tricks and phony emotions. Comedy was no longer a matter of slipping on banana skins, or running pell-mell through the streets like the Keystone Cops. Chaplin's subtlety and use of the close-up was revolutionary; in his hands, the camera could read minds and thoughts.

Years later, at the Circle, he performed hilarious imitations of the Lillian Gish school of silent acting; to Charlie, the actresses always looked as though they were catching butterflies. None of that nonsense was ever in a Chaplin film: his performances were natural and totally honest. And he stuck to his guns down the decades. On stage at the Circle, and in the film studios in the 1950s and 1960s, he always hunted for the realistic approach that was psychologically right for the character. "We don't want acting. We want reality," he used to tell the Circle actors. "Make the audience feel they're looking through a keyhole."

In spite of his international fame, Charlie remained modest and shy. After I knew him, I sometimes wondered how he never became corrupted by all his wealth and fame; he could easily have decided to enjoy the idle life. But Charlie dismissed all his past efforts: only the

future mattered. He was obsessed by a burning desire to create, an insatiable need to portray beauty on the screen; it was as though he had constantly to obliterate the memories of his harsh, poverty-stricken childhood.

On the other hand Charlie always knew the value of his achievements. And he was his own best audience. In the Circle days, his son Sydney and I often went to the Silent Movie House on Fairfax Avenue. One night they were showing Chaplin shorts. We laughed, of course, but there was someone behind us laughing much harder – laughing like a maniac. We turned round, curious. There sat Charlie and Oona: Charlie was screaming with delight at himself!

In order to safeguard artistic standards, in 1919 Charlie had joined D.W. Griffith, Mary Pickford and Douglas Fairbanks in a new venture, United Artists. They were to be the first independent film-makers, financing and distributing their own product. Someone commented, "The inmates have taken over the asylum."

LEFT: CHARLIE FINDS HIMSELF IN A LION'S CAGE BY MISTAKE. THE CIRCUS (1928).

THE GOLD RUSH (1923) – ONE OF THE
LANDMARKS IN CINEMA HISTORY.
ALTHOUGH A COMEDY, THE FILM WAS BASED
ON THE TRAGEDY OF THE DONNER

EXPEDITION OF 1846, WHEN A PARTY OF
IMMIGRANTS ON A TRAIL TO CALIFORNIA,
FINDING THEMSELVES SNOWBOUND,
RESORTED TO CANNIBALISM TO SURVIVE.

Fairbanks and Charlie were close friends. They enjoyed each other's company, and both served as sounding boards for each other's films. Charlie loved telling the story of how Doug and he would walk along Hollywood Boulevard in the silent movie days, when people didn't know what their voices sounded like. Tourists would spot them and rush over. Doug and Charlie would then begin talking in high-pitched tones – to the amazement of their fans.

Charlie enjoyed being his own boss at last, and celebrated his freedom with *A Woman of Paris,* which he wrote and directed, but did not appear in. His intention was to launch his leading lady, Edna Purviance, on a new dramatic career – she was getting too old to play young ingenues. Critics piled on the superlatives, and the picture broke new ground in sophisticated film comedy. But audiences, expecting the Tramp, were disappointed, and stayed away.

Charlie quickly threw himself into another comedy, *The Gold Rush.* Searching for a new heroine, he auditioned a young girl called Lita Grey, who constantly hung around his film studios. The role eventually went to Georgia Hale, but in November 1924 Lita became the second Mrs Chaplin. *The Gold Rush* received a star-studded gala première in Hollywood several weeks after Lita gave birth to Charles Chaplin Jr. Critics and audiences hailed the film's strong story, tenderness, and drama, and the brilliant set pieces like the dance with the bread rolls.

Then Chaplin's private life erupted into the headlines. During the shooting of *The Circus,* Lita left home with Charlie Jr and their new baby, Sydney. In a 42–page complaints document she sued for divorce and issued an injunction against Charlie's new film. Shooting had to stop; Charlie hastily left for New York with cans of film, to prevent her getting hold of it. In court, Lita wept buckets and claimed she had no money for her children's milk. More headlines. The strain was too much, and Charlie had a nervous breakdown.

After a highly acrimonious court fight, a settlement was reached. The affair colored all Charlie's memories of *The Circus* – which, despite the pressures and interruptions, emerged as a charming film with a light, improvised feel. But Charlie could only remember the heartaches behind the scenes. When the film was re-released in 1970, Charlie was thrilled at how modern audiences responded, and all the bitter associations faded.

CITY LIGHTS (1931). NO SOONER HAS
CHARLIE FINISHED SWEEPING THE STREET
THAN AN ELEPHANT PASSES BY.

The cinema's most famous close-up – the final shot in *City Lights*, where the blind girl realizes it was the Tramp who paid for her eye operation.

Charlie pressed ahead with a new film, *City Lights*. This was a brave thing to do. Al Jolson had just made *The Jazz Singer*; talkies were all the rage. But Charlie had just made another silent. He knew he was the master of pantomime, and felt his public wouldn't desert him. But he was still very nervous about the film's chances; so were the exhibitors. Charlie booked it into a legitimate theater on Broadway, and took out newspaper advertisements stating: "Charles Chaplin at the Cohan Theater in *City Lights* – continuous all day at 50 cents and one dollar".

Across the street, at the New York Paramount, Maurice Chevalier was appearing in person, along with a talkie. But it was *City Lights*, a silent, that people wanted to see. Mobs gathered outside the theater from early in the morning onwards and in twelve weeks the film grossed four hundred thousand dollars, making it Charlie's most successful picture to date. The critic Alexander Woollcott, a great Chaplin fan, rhapsodized: "His like has not passed this way before. And we shall not see his like again."

I saw *City Lights* too, though not at the Cohan in Manhattan: my parents took me to the Rugby, our neighborhood movie house in Brooklyn. I must have been around eight or nine; it was a hot, humid New York summer, long before there was air conditioning. Luckily the Rugby had a roof garden, where movies were screened at night. The fresh air was blissful, though you had to contend with mosquitoes, bird droppings, passing planes and thunderstorms. I think this was the first time I ever saw Charlie on film. My mother, I remember, roared with laughter, and whenever she laughed, I laughed.

In the late 1940s, after I came to know Charlie, I saw *City Lights* again at a charity showing in Beverly Hills. After the film I couldn't sleep. It was like beholding Michelangelo's David for the first time. I walked along Hollywood Boulevard all night in a daze, feeling melancholy, exhilarated, but above all thrilled that I knew the creator of this masterpiece.

As dawn approached, I went over to Charlie's home on Summit Drive. He was having breakfast. I wanted to sit at his feet and tell him how moved I had been. Instead, we sat down and shared some sizzling hot black coffee. He told me what Harpo Marx had said as they came out of the showing: "It's easy for you, all this pantomime!" "EASY?" Charlie had replied, remembering the sweat, the hard slog, and the constant retakes.

I left Charlie's home walking on air. I was still under the spell of *City Lights* and Charlie himself. As I drove to the Circle Theatre, my mind went back to the Rugby roof garden and my childhood. I was an unknown from Brooklyn, the son of ordinary working-class immigrants, yet here I was, breakfasting in Beverly Hills with one of the world's leading artists.

Above: Me and my boat. This was a few years ago.

Right: Part of my large Brooklyn family in the 1930s. Standing, left to right: my grandmother, me, my mother and my father. On the tricycle: my little cousin Aaron, who years later became a journalist and won the Heywood Broun Award for outstanding reporting.

How did my background prepare me for this? How did it all happen? As an adolescent in Brooklyn, Hollywood was always my dream – but that's all it was. Movies had always been my great escape and passion. My dream theater was the Loew's Kings in Brooklyn: the lobby was tremendous, festooned with chandeliers. We might have been in Buckingham Palace.

Movie stars seemed unreal – I didn't believe they actually existed. I adored Carole Lombard, Cary Grant, and Marion Davies. I even loved Davies in her huge Civil War flop, *Operator 13*. Years later I found an ally . . . Oona Chaplin. Charlie used to look at Oona and me as though we were mad when we raved about this awful film (we had seen it when we were kids). To this day, Oona and I laugh about this.

I also loved the radio. My favorite show was *Bobby Benson's Adventures*: Bobby, a cowboy kid out West, became my childhood hero. One day in 1935 I read that his real name was Billy Halop, and he was playing the lead as one of the kids in a Broadway play called *Dead End*.

I wasn't quite sure what a Broadway play was, but I saved up fifty-five cents for a ticket and sat in the second balcony of the Belasco Theater, seat number D22, peering down on a stage the size of a postage stamp. It was love at first sight. I was enthralled by the New York tenement set, designed by Norman Bel Geddes; the Dead End kids would dive into the orchestra pit, as though swimming in the East River. I was totally seduced by the magic of the theater.

Charlie must have had the same experience when he was fourteen. He would sit in the gallery at His Majesty's Theatre in London and marvel at the artistry of Sir Herbert Beerbohm Tree in *Oliver Twist* and *Julius Caesar*. Beerbohm Tree made Charlie realize how dynamic modern theater could be, and the experience stayed with him throughout his life.

The thrill of *Dead End* never left me. Using a photograph of the set from the theater program, I built a miniature equivalent using balsa wood, cut-out figures and tiny light bulbs. I brought my creation to the Belasco Theater box-office in Manhattan. The staff made a huge fuss; as a result, the set was exhibited in the theater lobby with my name on a card, and for a bonus they allowed me to see the play free, every Saturday matinee.

I decided I could see every Broadway show for free by building a miniature set. In *Stage* magazine, I saw a photo of Helen Hayes in

PROGRAM FROM *DEAD END*, FROM WHICH I
BUILT MY SET.

Victoria Regina, snatching a rose. The set I built was my masterpiece. I waited patiently for Helen Hayes outside the Broadhurst stage door. But she ignored both me and my set, and swept into a taxi. I felt so crushed. That was the end of my stage-building.

My parents were unimpressed by my miniature stages, even when my *Dead End* set was written up in the *Brooklyn Eagle.* I guess I was looking for a pat on the back. But it never came.

In California, Charlie had met a young actress, Paulette Goddard. She had a certain magnetism that he liked. They became inseparable. When Charlie saw her off at an airport and kissed her goodbye, it made headlines throughout the country. Paulette announced to the press that the kiss was only friendly, and that she was to be Charlie's new leading lady in his next film.

Times were bad. My parents tried to discourage my interest in the theater; they knew the importance of education. If my grades were poor, my father Reuben rushed up to school, interrupted class, and spoke to my teachers in his thick Russian accent. I was embarrassed. He wanted so badly to give me what he never had. He kept a strict watch at home, too; when the film *Treasure Island* was playing, I was dying to see it, but he forbade me until I read the book.

My father had come to America in 1905 at the age of thirteen to escape the pogroms in Vilna, Lithuania; he worked to send back money, so the rest of the family could join him. His youthful strengths and exploits were legendary: during one street fight in Brooklyn he turned over a street trolley. He worked as a builder and carpenter, and met my mother, Ruth, in Cleveland, Ohio, where I was born as Jerome Epstein. When the Depression hit, we had to sell everything and move in with relatives in Brooklyn. I remember people coming to buy our house furnishings; my mother made me stand in front of the drapes to hide the holes.

Brooklyn felt strange after Ohio's wide open spaces. I was suddenly plunged into the slums of Williamsburg, a jungle of tenements, push-carts and peddlers. We eventually moved to the suburbs of Flatbush. My kosher cousins were not far away. Our own house was not kosher; we were considered the Gentiles of the family. I dutifully had my Bar Mitzvah, out of respect for my grandmother; but immediately after the ceremony I was at the movies, watching Eddie Cantor in *Roman Scandals.*

My Orthodox cousins were appalled when I ate bacon sandwiches in front of them ("Uggghhh!" they cried, "how can you eat it? What does it taste like?"). But I came in handy on Friday nights, when Orthodox Jews were forbidden to turn off electric lights at the start of the Sabbath. So they called me, the goy who ate bacon, to turn the lights off for them.

Friday at our house meant a lavish dinner of *gefilte* fish and brisket of beef. My mother's *gefilte* fish was mouth-watering. Years later, when my parents moved to Los Angeles, she sent her peppery *gefilte* fish up to the Chaplin house in Beverly Hills. Charlie loved it, and Oona adored my mother's home-made hot horseradish.

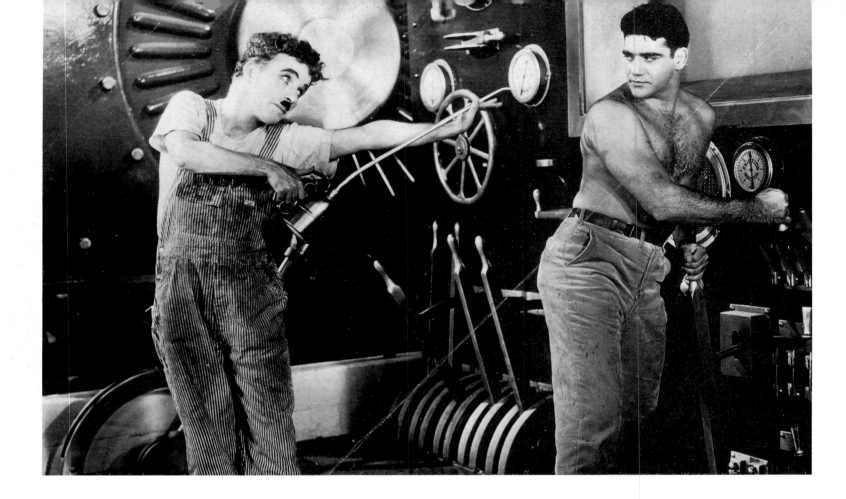

Oona and Charlie ... They became like substitute parents to me. They generously took me in, made me welcome in California and Switzerland, and gave me confidence and reassurance that I never received from my parents. Indeed, as the years went on, I began to feel so tied to Oona and Charlie that I sometimes sacrificed my own career just to be with them.

Charlie needed a sounding-board for his torrent of ideas and gags. I provided an enthusiastic audience, without ever making demands: I was happy just to be around, to share in the laughter – plus the blood, sweat and tears – of working with Charlie Chaplin. And we worked well together ...

Dead End helped spark my feelings for the underdog: I loved the way it dealt with the lives of tenement dwellers and children of the streets. And when Charlie's new film, *Modern Times* – another silent – opened at the Rivoli in 1936, I went to see it. Like *Dead End,* it spoke to me.

This was the first Chaplin film to portray the harsh reality of present-day America. Before, the Tramp had lived in a romantic, stylized world. Now he was faced with the bitter facts of life – the

Depression, hunger, unemployment, strikes, homelessness, and bread-lines. Charlie played a factory worker driven berserk by a machine, who teams up against the world with a *gamin* (played by his new discovery, Paulette Goddard). Audiences adored it, though some critics felt Charlie was getting out of his depth and should stick to straightforward comedy. But for me, I loved the film's mixture of comedy and social comment, and the way Charlie captured the despair of the times.

In spite of the Depression, New York was still exciting for me. I was always hanging around the Manhattan theaters. The Broadway bug had bitten me. I cut high school classes, and sneaked in to watch rehearsals. Then, in order to satisfy my growing passion, I found a weekend job at the St James Theater selling programs, lemonades and binoculars – anything to get inside the auditorium.

During the summer run of Maurice Evans's *Hamlet,* the weather was murderously hot and humid. Theaters still didn't have air conditioning. During the intermission I paraded down the aisles with ice cold lemonades. When the temperature really soared, my boss would go into the basement and stoke up the stoves, making the theater even hotter.

Men in the audience ripped off their jackets and ties; sweat poured

Opposite: Charlie goes berserk in *Modern Times* (1936).

Right: Charlie and his discovery Paulette Goddard in *Modern Times*.

Far right: My father visits me in camp. I was the inspiration for Alan Sherman's song "Hello Mudder, Hello Fadder".

down the poor actors' faces. Then, before the interval, my boss removed all the paper cups near the water faucets. As soon as the curtain descended, everyone dashed into the lobby for water. But there was nothing to drink from. Enter Jerry with tray, yelling "Ice-cold lemonades!" Business was sensational.

Chaplin used to roar at this story, and Oona made me tell it to their children. Perhaps Charlie sensed the similarity in construction to his own gag in *The Kid,* where Jackie Coogan goes around breaking windows and the Tramp miraculously appears, carrying plate glass and offering to fix them.

During the long run of *Hamlet,* I was almost fired for selling binoculars up and down the aisles, shouting "Have Maurice Evans in your lap for twenty-five cents!" Mr Evans was not amused.

By swapping jobs with the kids at other theaters I could get to all the shows free: *Of Mice and Men, The Man Who Came to Dinner, Life with Father, Liliom,* and most of the Group Theater productions. I also joined up with the autograph hunters hanging around the stage doors. We chased the stars all over town: Clark Gable, Sonja Henie, Joan Crawford, Judy Garland, Mickey Rooney. Sometimes I snapped them

with my little Brownie camera. Claudette Colbert, I found, couldn't be captured with a Brownie: I made her look like a little old woman.

My parents were terribly worried by my escapades. I seemed to be running wild. "I'll outgrow it," I told them. To make sure that I did, my father took my precious autographs and burned them. I don't think my parents had any moral objection to the theater; they were simply concerned that it wouldn't lead to a career and a living wage.

After the release of *Modern Times,* Charlie and Paulette Goddard took a trip to the Orient. There Charlie conceived an idea for a film about a stowaway, but on his return he abandoned this and began developing a long-cherished idea of his – to portray Napoleon in his last days at St Helena. But this too was abandoned. He was searching for a new original idea.

On graduation from Samuel J. Tilden High School, my parents insisted I go to university. I did it for their sakes, studying at night while working at the Bendix Aviation factory during the day. Before my employers discovered how maladroit I was, I worked on the lathe: I kept thinking of Chaplin getting caught up in the machinery in *Modern Times.*

LEFT: CHARLIE IN THE TITLE ROLE OF *THE GREAT DICTATOR* (1940). WHAT A PERFORMANCE!

BELOW: CHARLIE DANCES WITH THE BALLOON BEFORE IT EXPLODES.

Over in Europe, Adolf Hitler was on the warpath. Storm clouds gathered. Charlie now found the idea he was looking for. He caught the mood of the moment in his next film *The Great Dictator,* which went before the cameras just as war broke out in Europe. Hitler's resemblance to Chaplin's Tramp was remarkable; Charlie thought he had stolen his make-up! Inspired by fate, Chaplin decided to impersonate Hitler, calling him Hynkel; he also played a Jewish barber, who resembles the dictator. Once more, Paulette Goddard was his leading lady.

Charlie's gifts for pantomime were shown in two brilliant set-pieces – Hynkel's slow-motion dance with the globe (a balloon that finally explodes in his face), and the barber shaving a customer to the accompaniment of Brahms's Fifth Hungarian Rhapsody. But there was also dialogue throughout; and for the climax, Charlie delivered an impassioned six-minute speech, standing up for humanity and peace:

"We think too much and feel too little. More than machinery we need humanity. More than cleverness we need kindness and gentleness. Without these qualities, life will be violent and all will be lost . . . Let us fight to free the world – to do away with national barriers – to do away with greed, with hate and intolerance – jobs for youth – security for old age. Let us fight for a world of reason – a world of science – where progress will lead to the happiness of us all. Soldiers! In the name of democracy, let us unite!"

At the time, Charlie was criticized for sermonizing, but these final moments of the film now appear more dynamic than ever. With its fierce anti-Nazi stand, the film made history. General Eisenhower asked to have prints sent to Europe to show the soldiers. Albert Speer, Hitler's architect, found the film astonishing when he finally saw it in the 1970s: "It is impossible to satirize Hitler," he said, "but Chaplin came closer than any other artist in getting to the reality, the bone beneath the skin." He also said that Hitler, like Hynkel, had a globe-balloon in his private study. Hitler's, though, was much, much bigger!

Charlie's private life had made headlines again. Distributors were nervous about his relationship with Paulette Goddard – no one knew whether they were married or not. America was very moral in those days, and anything could affect the box-office. At the New York première in 1940, Charlie had introduced Paulette to the audience as Mrs Chaplin. Shortly afterwards they were divorced.

Over in Brooklyn, the war dawned on a cold winter's day as I walked with my cousins along Rockaway boardwalk. There was a strange rustle and bustle on the beach. Then someone shouted "Pearl Harbor's been bombed!" We were all confused. Where was Pearl Harbor? *What* was Pearl Harbor? None of us had ever heard of it before. The next day, we heard Roosevelt declare war on Japan and Germany. We didn't know what this would mean.

As the Bendix factory geared up for war production, my work and pay packet increased. My father, however, lost his current job; so did my brother-in-law. We were all living together, and my money supported the entire family. I remember asking my mother one night what we were having for supper. "Whatever you want," she replied bitterly. "You're the breadwinner now." I felt terribly guilty. It hurt me to see my father – this big, powerful man – reduced to casual work driving a taxi.

Eventually I was drafted into the Air Corps. They moved me around a great deal. Basic training in New Jersey and Miami Beach; a stint in Missouri; attachment to the medical corps at El Paso, Texas; clerical duties in Newfoundland. One night, on the base at El Paso, I saw *The Gold Rush* for the first time; Chaplin had recently reissued the film with spoken narration and a new musical accompaniment. During the screening, the projection stopped; then, over the loudspeaker, names were called out – the names of soldiers who were to be shipped off either to the European front or the Pacific. They rose and filed out in silence. We all held our breath. My name wasn't on the list yet. After a moment the film continued, but to no more laughter . . .

While the Air Corps shunted me from post to post, Charlie did his own bit for the war, speaking at various functions in support of our new Russian allies. He startled audiences at a San Francisco meeting for the Russian War Relief Fund by addressing the huge audience as "Comrades!" "On the battlefields of Russia," he declared, "democracy will live or die!" The conservative press became increasingly hostile; more storm clouds gathered.

Then, in 1943, he married the eighteen-year-old Oona O'Neill, daughter of Eugene O'Neill, the playwright. He had interviewed her to play Brigid, a young Irish girl who sees visions, in a projected film version of Paul Vincent Carroll's play *Shadow and Substance*. They fell in love. Oona turned out to be unique. Not only was she a prized Irish beauty; she also had enormous intelligence, loyalty and wit. Charlie became the center of her life. He used to tell me how lucky he was, finding someone like Oona. "I never thought it was possible to find an ideal relationship like this," he said. And their close bond continued until the end.

ME IN THE ARMY.
I WAS NEVER THAT THIN AGAIN!

OONA AND CHARLIE IMMEDIATELY AFTER
THEIR WEDDING ON JUNE 16TH, 1943 IN
SANTA BARBARA, CALIFORNIA.

Before meeting Oona, he had considered another young hopeful for the Brigid role, Joan Barry. Miss Barry was a highly emotional actress with dreams of stardom. When Charlie decided she was wrong for the role, she broke into his home carrying a gun, and claimed in the papers that he was the father of her unborn child.

Once again the conservative forces across the country mobilized against him. Apart from the paternity suit, Chaplin was called to face other charges: conspiring to deprive Barry of her civil rights, and violating the Mann Act by taking a minor over the Californian border for sexual purposes. He was fingerprinted and treated like a common criminal.

The Mann trial opened in March 1944. Charlie told me a marvelous story about it. As he looked at the faces of the jury, he became convinced that one woman juror hated him. She was the only one he was concerned about. After he was acquitted, he found out she was the one person who had held out for a Not Guilty verdict and swayed the others. In the courtroom afterwards, she came over and said to him sweetly, "We wouldn't let them do this to you, Charlie." As he related the story, Charlie's voice shook and his eyes brimmed with tears.

Oona fainted when she heard the news of his acquittal; she was by the pool, pregnant with Geraldine. But Charlie still had to face the paternity charge. He demanded a blood test, which proved conclusively that he was not the baby's father. Blood tests, however, were not yet recognized in Californian courts, and he had to pay maintenance for the child. The experience must have affected Charlie: his next film was his first bitter comedy, *Monsieur Verdoux*.

Meanwhile, I was still stuck in the Army medical corps, practicing giving shots to soldiers by injecting into an orange. I never was sent overseas. After being honorably discharged, I returned to Brooklyn, and soon realized I didn't belong. I left for Los Angeles, and applied for a science course at UCLA. I returned to my old trade – selling programs and lemonades at Earl Carroll's theater (in reality a high-class burlesque house) on Sunset Boulevard. The frightening Erich von Stroheim – even more scary in person than in films – was a regular visitor.

Then I found a job in the Twentieth Century-Fox mail-room. But I spent most of the time on the sound stages, watching the shooting, and little mail was delivered. The first film I ever saw being shot was *Laura*. There I was, on the set with Dana Andrews, Judith Anderson, Vincent Price and Clifton Webb. I was in my element. The inevitable pink slip came when I was caught watching Betty Grable rehearse a musical number.

Luckily my UCLA application was accepted. I had a GI grant from the government, but I still needed extra money, so I continued working evenings at Earl Carroll's. To please my parents, I decided to study hard and give up any notions of working in the theater. I was diligent. But I kept passing Room 170 in Royce Hall – the Drama Department. It seemed such a hive of activity. Students gathered for lectures and rehearsals; Butterfly McQueen (Prissy, the weeping maid, in *Gone With the Wind*) paraded around in green bloomers in between her modern dance classes. I was dying to join the drama students, but I had made my promise.

Then a pretty girl, Marilyn Clark, approached me. "Would you like to join our theater group?" she said. They needed young men to act in their plays. I obliged, and there was no looking back. Soon I was advising on what plays to perform. I put them off Noel Coward, and steered them towards the socially conscious dramas I had loved on Broadway: *Waiting for Lefty, Awake and Sing!, The Time of Your Life*.

Those wonderful Andrews Sisters – Maxene, Patti and LaVerne.

I also acted, but I was a bundle of nerves. I was terrified I would forget my lines, though all I had to do in our first production, Maxwell Anderson's *Night Over Taos*, was stand in the background and hold a spear. "Don't shift from foot to foot," they kept telling me, "You're distracting!" Anyway, I was more interested in getting audiences into Royce Hall to see the shows.

In my last year, UCLA lost some of its sparkle. But the excitement returned when – through one of the students, Patricia Englund – I met Maxene Andrews, a member of the famous singing Andrews Sisters. As a teenager I thought the Andrews Sisters were the cat's miaow; I collected their records and saw them at the New York Paramount. Maxene and I took an immediate shine to each other and we became fast friends. One day at her house she said, "When you graduate, Jerry, look us up. Maybe we'll have a job for you."

On graduation I contacted Maxene's husband Lou Levy, who managed the girls. He was now spreading his wings and about to produce his first play. I was hired as assistant stage manager for a West Coast tour of Ruth Gordon's *Over 21*. The play closed in Los Angeles after two weeks.

As luck would have it, the girls' road manager suddenly decided he didn't want another long tour. They needed a quick replacement for their current show, "The Andrews Sisters and Their Eight-to-the-Bar Ranch", due to play most of the western states. Lou asked me if I thought I could handle it. I didn't know what the work entailed, but I automatically said yes. I wanted that job!

I learned overnight. People were kind and guided me. I went to the theaters in advance with blueprints. I set the stage with the technical staff, worked out the various cues, and fixed the pink gel in position for "I'll be With You in Apple Blossom Time". Before the show there was a B-movie feature, a short, and coming attractions for next week's movies. Then came my big moment, when I announced over the loudspeaker: "Ladies and gentlemen, the Orpheum Theater proudly presents … T-H-E A-N-D-R-E-W-S S-I-S-T-E-R-S!" And on they marched to Vic Schoen's orchestra, dressed as cowgirls, swinging to "Rum Boogie". We played four or five shows a day – the movie, the Andrews Sisters, the movie, the Andrews Sisters – and traveled from city to city up the West Coast – San Francisco, San Diego, Vancouver, Seattle, Portland …

I had the time of my life. The girls were fun and generous, and their high spirits were infectious. How they enjoyed their work! We were a tight-knit group. Maxene was married to Lou; Patti, the vivacious lead singer, was in love with the pianist, Wally Weschler (a great wit and composer), and LaVerne fell for Lou Rogers, their trumpeter.

Maxene was always interested in the takings. When they sang, she would look straight out front, snapping her fingers in rhythm as she counted the house – her squinting eyes travelling down from the second balcony to the orchestra. The minute the curtain descended, Maxene would rush to check the box-office receipts. On weekends, if there were long lines outside, we'd lose a reel of the feature, cut out the shorts – to move the crowds in and out faster. The girls were on a percentage.

In Seattle, Mae West appeared in *Diamond Lil* at the theater across the street. Sometimes we shared the same hotel elevator. She was always dressed in her full 1890s regalia. She and Maxene were kindred spirits. "How's business?" Mae would ask in her inimitable twang. "What's the takings like?" Charlie adored Mae West; he always said she was the most relaxed person in movies.

Monsieur Verdoux, Charlie's "comedy of murders", was now in production, after tussles with the Breen Office – a Hollywood censorship body; they had even objected to Verdoux's use of the word "voluptuous". Papers were full of publicity squibs about Marilyn Nash – Charlie's new discovery, cast as the street waif whom Verdoux tries to poison. She had come to Chaplin's house with a tennis party who were borrowing the courts; and after reading several scenes from *King Lear,* she was hired. It made good copy anyway. Shooting went quickly, but Charlie must have been very anxious; this was the first film where he played a completely new character, without any trace of the Tramp. And a murderer to boot!

After the Andrews Sisters' tour, Lou gave me a job with his Leeds Music company. Songwriters kept coming in, trying to sell their songs. When one of them came in with "Mona Lisa", I said, "Lou, who's going to buy a song about a painting?" After it became a huge hit, Lou always said "Anything you don't like, Jerry, I'm publishing!"

I earned fifty dollars a week, with a nice office on Sunset Boulevard. My other UCLA chums weren't so lucky. They too had graduated, but couldn't find work as actors. Terry Kilburn – he played the schoolboy Colley in the 1939 version of *Goodbye Mr Chips* – came to the office one day, feeling very dejected. "What can we do? I can't afford to go to New York. Where do we find stage work here?" "Let's start our own theater!" I said to Terry, in the great Hollywood tradition. A cliché, perhaps, but it really happened.

I decided to give up my job with the Andrews Sisters. The girls were about to play the New York Paramount for Christmas – the year's plum booking – and I was due to travel with them. I told Maxene I was leaving to start a theater. She thought I was mad. But she was so sweet and generous. "Don't quit," she said, "We don't really need you in New York – the Paramount has its own staff, and you wouldn't have anything to do. Stay here on salary and let me know what happens." She also said we could use their rehearsal rooms on Sunset Boulevard.

Our next problem was money. Over the years my mother had put away some of my earnings – there was money in the bank from the Bendix Aviation Factory, the army, even my Bar Mitzvah. My savings now totalled one thousand dollars. I told my mother I was taking everything out to start a theater. My parents were horrified. It was supposed to be money for a rainy day. But as far as I was concerned, the money was mine, and this was my rainy day.

And this was the start of the Circle Theatre, and the adventure that brought Oona and Charlie Chaplin right into the center of my life.

CHARLIE AS MONSIEUR VERDOUX (THE
BLUEBEARD) WITH THE RAMBUNCTIOUS
MARTHA RAYE, THE ONE WIDOW HE
COULDN'T KILL.

THE 2 CIRCLE THEATRE

FROM THE CIRCLE'S MAILBAG

DEAR CIRCLE PLAYERS:

We don't know when we've ever had a more enjoyable evening in the theater than at The Doctor in Spite of Himself. *We felt we were watching a Theatre Guild production with the Lunts, Le Gallienne, Helen Hayes, and the Barrymores.*

Sincerely, HARPO MARX, MRS SAM GOLDWYN, GEORGE BURNS.
March, 1949

In the autumn of 1946, Charlie was preparing to record the score of *Monsieur Verdoux*. At this point in my life I still hadn't met him, but the fateful meeting was soon to take place . . .

For the moment I was busy launching the Circle. It was going to be a real, serious theater. I had been voraciously reading plays ever since I discovered *Dead End*. I wanted to present the playwrights I myself would go to see: O'Casey, O'Neill, Odets.

First, I needed a play to put into rehearsal. This would give us the impetus to find a theater. It had to be something exciting. I didn't want any Boy Meets Girl types, fey little comedies, or tired revivals. Those were the kind performed in Hollywood's showcase productions, where kids paid money to display their talents, hoping to be discovered for movies. Downtown at the Biltmore Theater, tired roadshows would open and close. Such was the existing theatrical life in Los Angeles.

Then at the UCLA library I came across Elmer Rice's *The Adding Machine*. I knew I had found our opener! I went sky-high with enthusiasm. This surreal modern play about the life and death of a book-keeping drudge had everything – progressive ideas, an original concept, brilliant dialogue. It was like a Shaw play that had never been discovered. There had been no production since the Theatre Guild's première in 1923, so it felt like a brand new piece.

The wheels were now set in motion.

A motley bunch turned up for auditions at the Andrews Sisters' rehearsal room. There was Naomi Riordan, a beautiful, funny girl, who had been chosen as the Pasadena Rosebowl Queen the year before. Her boyfriend, William Schallert, also came along though he had no intention of acting: he was studying music at UCLA under Arnold Schoenberg. With a large cast to find, I asked him to read, and changed his whole life: he eventually became President of the Screen Actors' Guild (Ronald Reagan's former position).

Charlie Chaplin Jr, whom I had met at UCLA, came to read, accompanied by his younger brother Sydney. (They were Charlie's sons from his second marriage.) Like Bill Schallert, Sydney was just there for the ride. I had first met him several months earlier when Charlie Jr threw a welcome home party to celebrate his brother's discharge from General Patton's Eighth Army. Syd had been in the thick of the war – he was in an ambush surrounded by Germans, and it was a miracle that he came out alive.

THE PLAYERS BUILDING THE CIRCLE
THEATRE, OUTSIDE THE GARAGE THAT
EVENTUALLY BECAME THE NEW THEATRE.
ON THE FAR LEFT ARE THE TYPICAL
HOLLYWOOD BUNGALOWS.

At the party I had rubbed shoulders with the likes of Shirley Temple and Twentieth Century-Fox's starlets. I had expected the sons of Charlie Chaplin to be conceited, uninterested in others. But they were just like my buddies in Brooklyn. And even this party, with all its young movie stars, was not much different from the basement parties we used to throw in Flatbush.

But for me, the real star of the evening had been Sydney. At that time charades were all the rage; I'll never forget Syd pantomiming the title of a movie, and then a book. He was hilarious and crazy. He seemed the funniest man I'd ever met.

At the audition I asked Sydney if he would read for the part of Lieutenant Charles, a guardian in heaven, whom I always saw as an Orson Welles type. Sydney certainly had the size – six feet two inches. He was shy and hesitant, but he finally agreed. His reading was appalling. (Even now he cannot read a cold script.) But remembering his star turn at the homecoming party, I took a chance and gave him the part. And he was marvelous! Suddenly, that lost, confused GI, uncertain of his place in peacetime, found himself. The Circle became his life.

We had a play; we had a cast. But we still had no theater. After the rehearsals, Sydney, Bill Schallert and I scoured Los Angeles for empty buildings, warehouses, shops – anything that might serve as an acting area. We didn't need a proscenium arch: Room 170 at UCLA had trained us to act with simple props within a circle of chairs – that's how the Circle had got its name. Then I received a phone call from Naomi Stevens, one of our leading actresses at UCLA, and Bob Burns, who became the Circle's lighting genius (he later supervised special effects at Disneylands all over the world).

They had stumbled upon an enormous, old-fashioned living-room, complete with balcony, in a mansion in El Centro Avenue, in the center of Hollywood. The house had once belonged to an opera singer; now it was owned by a strange, miniature woman in her mid-fifties, in need of extra money. She said we could rent the room on weekends only when her husband went fishing; we would have to remove all her furniture every Friday afternoon, place it on the lawn and convert the lounge into a theater-in-the-round. The furniture would then have to be replaced in time for the master's return on Monday morning.

Bob convinced me that the lounge was feasible, and I paid the rent. We immediately ordered small window posters advertising the play,

concluded rehearsals, and had our Grand Opening to about five people. The two spotlights were made from tin cans: Bob, hiding in the balcony awaiting his cues, would simply place two live wires together, and, presto! – the lights came on. Luckily, the fire department never paid a visit.

The play was damned good. But we were desperate for audiences. Los Angeles was gearing itself up for the holidays. A Christmas parade of garish floats, decorated on top with B-movie luminaries like Fuzzy Knight and "Gabby" Hayes, inched its way down Hollywood Boulevard. And there we were among the crowds, handing out leaflets, trying to entice them to our show. We were never successful. On one occasion, on the way back to the theater, one of our thespians turned to Sydney and asked if he thought his father would like *The Adding Machine*. Sydney just shrugged.

Our fortunes changed when I persuaded Marie Mesmer, a young critic on the *Los Angeles Daily News*, to attend our living-room production. She wrote a rave review: "In the midst of Los Angeles," she said, "something exciting is happening – real theater has come to town." She particularly noted the performances of Joe Mantell as Mr Zero, and Naomi Stevens as his wife.

Overnight, we were in business. Groucho Marx showed up. Then a distinguished-looking, gray-haired man introduced himself; it was Dudley Nichols, screenwriter of *Stagecoach*, *The Informer* and *Bringing Up Baby*. "My wife and I just came back from Russia," he told me, "and

Laying the theater floor. Left to right: Dee Tormey, Bill Schallert, Kathleen Freeman, Bob Burns and Sydney Chaplin.

this is as good as anything we saw in the Soviet Union!" They became our Number One fans. "You're going to remember these days as the most exciting time of your life," Dudley said. How right he was.

During the week Sydney and I went one night to a movie theater on Beverly Boulevard to see Jean-Louis Barrault in *Les Enfants du paradis* (French art films were just coming over to America after the war). When the lights came up, Sydney turned and saw his father sitting at the back with his wife Oona, the actress Constance Collier and a party of friends.

"Hi, Pop!" Sydney called out, waving to his father. Chaplin came rushing down the aisle. "Hello, son," he said. I was introduced to Mr Chaplin. I just nodded self-consciously. Chaplin asked Sydney what he was doing now. He told him he was in a show, *The Adding Machine*. "Call me up and tell me about it," Chaplin said.

Several days after meeting Mr Chaplin, a call came from the family butler. Mr and Mrs Chaplin wanted tickets to *The Adding Machine*. We were as nervous as kittens: Charlie Chaplin and his wife, coming to this bizarre living-room to see our play, sitting on hard little folding chairs! Actors who were not performing peeked through the window from the street to see Chaplin's reactions. He was a great audience. He roared with laughter, tears rolling down his cheeks. Afterwards he asked to meet the cast. He was enthusiasm itself. From that moment on, Oona and he supplanted Dudley Nichols and his wife as our chief boosters.

Word of mouth spread. Saturday nights were now sold out. We asked our landlady if we could use the living-room during the week. "Oh, no, no, no, no!" she said, "Only weekends when my husband's away."

Then the inevitable happened. One Sunday, as we played to a capacity audience, the husband came home earlier than expected. Fishing had been lousy. Now he found his furniture sprawled over the lawn, and his living-room crammed with total strangers, deep in the middle of a crazy play. Throwing a fit, he stopped the show and threw everyone – actors and audience – into the street. Thus ended our experience at 1141 El Centro Avenue.

We had to find a new theater quickly; we didn't want to lose momentum. Naomi and Bob scoured the town again; two weeks later, they called me to look at a discarded drugstore at 800 North El Centro, with an abandoned garage next door. I asked Bob what he thought. Bob,

who was very quiet, just nodded his head: "It'll do," he said.

I signed a lease with our new landlord and 800 North El Centro quickly became a beehive of activity. We had already announced a new show, *Ethan Frome*, and this rubbish-heap had to be converted into a theater. We begged, borrowed and stole technical equipment and material. Everyone pitched in, under Bob's supervision. Jack Kelly – later to star with James Garner in the *Maverick* TV series – had never held a saw in his hand before, but there he was sawing, hammering, painting, and plastering all through the night along with Sydney, Naomi, Kathleen Freeman and the other actors. My father – a master carpenter and a great skeptic – didn't know what the hell I was doing with my life. But he came around and looked over the premises, offering advice, if never encouragement.

800 North El Centro was in a typical, lower-middle-class Hollywood neighborhood. All around were row after row of wooden-framed bungalow houses; Rita Hayworth's family, the Cansinos, lived three doors away. RKO and Paramount Studios were around the corner. Directly across the street was the Los Angeles Orphanage, where Marilyn Monroe used to live. Zoning laws caused big problems, as the neighborhood was residential. But I took the premises before realizing we were in a restricted zone. After much convincing and conniving I got round the authorities. They warned us, though, that if any neighbor complained, our permits would be quickly revoked.

machinery from Chaplin's *Modern Times,* the bombs from *The Great Dictator,* chairs and sofas from *City Lights,* a table from the log cabin in *The Gold Rush,* lamps, rugs and assorted oddments from all his shorts. As we left the studio carrying the *Gold Rush* table and other bounty, Chaplin emerged from his editing room, stopped us and asked if we had found everything we needed. We nodded and thanked him; but he seemed to want to keep us there. He had now finished *Monsieur Verdoux,* and asked us if we would like to see it. We really had to rush back with the table, but, of course, we succumbed to temptation.

He shoved us into the big leather chairs in his modest projection room, ran the film, and sat with us. This was the first screening. Sydney and I roared with laughter and delight. It was a film with ideas as well as entertainment. European pictures, like Rossellini's *Open City* or De Sica's *Bicycle Thieves,* had that quality at the time, but not American pictures. We got every gag, and Charlie was thrilled by our reaction; he must have been convinced he had a smash hit.

Chaplin never saw *Ethan Frome* – which became a great critical success, but proved too stark to draw much business. *Monsieur Verdoux* claimed all his attention, and he soon left Los Angeles with Oona for the New York opening. The New York audience was extremely frosty. There were even some boos. Ruth Conte, who later scored a great personal success at our theater in Barrie's *What Every Woman Knows,* was there with her husband Richard Conte, the actor. Ruth told me that after the première she leaned against the theater doors, only to find someone trying to escape from the auditorium. It was Chaplin: "I should never have made this film," he said to no one in particular, "It was a terrible mistake."

Years later, when we became friends in London, the famous MGM screenwriter Donald Ogden Stewart (he won an Oscar for *The Philadelphia Story*) told me more about that night in New York. The subsequent party at the "21" Club was just as disastrous as the screening. Most of the guests ignored Chaplin, even when he performed his surefire bullfight routine. Oona left early. Stewart and the theater director Robert Lewis (who played the apothecary in *Verdoux*) then helped Charlie back to his hotel, where he sat on the bed – slightly the worse for wear after a few drinks. "That audience couldn't take it, could they?" Charlie said, mulling over his humiliation. "I really kicked them where it hurts."

Even though Hollywood was all around us, I made up my mind that *no* scout from Paramount, Fox, or wherever, would receive a free ticket at the Circle. I remembered the excitement at UCLA when studio talent scouts came to our college productions. They were sour, unappreciative little men. But the Circle was not a showcase theater, and we needed every ticket sale we could get.

During the conversion work, we kept on rehearsing *Ethan Frome,* a bleak tragedy set on a New England farm, adapted from Edith Wharton's novel. For this we needed special props. Sydney mentioned his father's large prop room at his studios; perhaps he could loan us some. "Of course," said Chaplin, when Sydney called him up. "Go down and take whatever you want."

It was like entering Aladdin's Cave. There was the factory

Worse was to come. The following day, Chaplin attended a press conference at the Gotham Hotel; the audience seemed made up of vultures, determined to attack not just the film, but also Chaplin's lifeblood and soul. "Proceed with the butchery!" Charlie said. He knew what he was in for.

They asked him to define where he stood politically. "If you step off the curb with your left foot," Charlie said, "they accuse you of being a Communist." He added: "I've never belonged to any political party in my life." He was then accused of being unpatriotic by a spokesman for the Catholic War Veterans. Charlie retorted that not only had his two sons fought in the war, but he himself had backed the war effort through donations and speeches. His opponents would not be stifled. Then James Agee, the writer and critic, stood up and shouted feverish

words about the outrage of Chaplin's treatment. In Los Angeles I read about the confrontation in the newspapers. Chaplin arrived back in California battered, but not beaten.

At the Circle, we were gathering steam. We had so much energy and vitality, building sets, cleaning the premises, rehearsing, and performing. So it was sad when we played *Ethan Frome* to only a handful of people when we could seat one hundred and fifty. Later on, whenever we had a hit, I would make up for those lean times by never turning anyone away. "Always room for two more," I used to say. The stage, as a result, became smaller and smaller. Actors used to scream at me: they were bumping into the furniture, the spectators, and each other. But business is business!

In matters of discipline I ruled the place like a martinet. Since North

WE WERE SO PROUD OF THE WAY WE'D BUILT OUR CIRCLE THEATRE — IT WAS ALL DONE WITH SPIT AND GLUE. THAT'S SYDNEY'S NEW CADILLAC.

El Centro was in a family area, and children sometimes watched rehearsals, four-letter words were strictly forbidden. (All this was to change when Shelley Winters, several years later, directed a play.) Even so it was impossible to maintain a low profile in the neighborhood all the time, as the actors made their entrances from the street, come fair weather or foul.

And the actors had such high spirits. The minute the audience left at the end of a show, those hard cushions flew off the seats and the cast began throwing them at each other. The cushion fights became a weekly event. Kathleen Freeman was the usual target: she'd run through the streets, pursued by Sydney or Bill Schallert, screaming blue murder but loving it. It was a far cry from the Actor's Lab crowd (West Coast disciples of the Method school; they would round off their shows by

Below: A rehearsal shot of The Time of Your Life. At the table on the far left: Kathleen Freeman, (?), Virginia Morton (the nurse). At the foreground table: Mary Davenport, Jack Kelly ("Maverick"), Jack Conrad. In the background, left to right: Ray Hyke, (?), (?), Sydney Chaplin (as Nick, the bartender), Manny Robinson (Edward G. Robinson's son, as the newsboy), (?), George Englund, Earle Herdan, Larry Salters and Julian Ludwig standing by the door.

going to a local restaurant to discuss their motivations). Across the street, the orphans loved our craziness, and peeked through their windows at night, watching the mayhem.

By the time Oona and Charlie arrived back from New York, we had closed *Ethan Frome* and opened *The Time of Your Life* by William Saroyan – then one of America's leading playwrights. The entire theater was converted into Nick's saloon: the audience entered through swinging doors. Some of them found the bar set so real that they asked for a drink. Sydney played Nick the bartender (one of his best-ever performances) and Charlie Jr had a small part as the Drunkard. At the time he was dating Marilyn Monroe and used to bring her to watch rehearsals. She was in awe of real, live actors, and asked me how she could join our group. I told her about our open Sunday auditions, but she was too frightened to show up.

Two weeks after we opened, Oona and Charlie saw the play and lapped it up. Charlie seemed to forget all his problems about *Monsieur Verdoux*. Unknown to me, he called up Saroyan (married at the time to Oona's childhood friend, Carol) and urged him to come down from San Francisco to see the production. He also suggested that Saroyan give us a new play to première: "You won't regret it!" Charlie said, bubbling with enthusiasm. Unfortunately, Saroyan was unable to make the trip.

Soon afterwards we opened *Love on the Dole,* an English drama set in an industrial Manchester suburb. It was the first time I had directed. The notices were beyond my wildest dreams; we were hitting one jackpot after another.

Sydney, just twenty-one, was playing the heroine's fifty-year-old father, and Oona and Charlie came to watch the performance. I think Charlie was surprised when he entered the theater and found we were playing his score from *Monsieur Verdoux*. A few weeks earlier he had given me a set of discs of the music, and it had become our signature tune. Again the cast peeked to watch their reactions. Charlie was delighted with the play, which was new to him; part of English working-class life must have come back to him. He was becoming more and more entranced with the Circle.

Then, to our utter amazement, we received in the mail William Saroyan's latest work, *Sam Ego's House.* He asked if we would consider presenting it. We were overwhelmed. Through Charlie's thoughtfulness, the Circle was suddenly on the map. We made big stories in

Variety, the *New York Times,* the *Los Angeles Times* and the international press. "Never has any group of young people been so elated and lucky!" I wrote to the author as the play moved into production. We had to install a second phone to cope with requests for tickets.

Sam Ego's House was a fascinating play. In Los Angeles, late at night, you would often see big white-framed houses being moved on wheels from one end of the city to the other. And this was the play's premise. As Sam Ego's house crosses Los Angeles towards its final destination, it stops along the way and various adventures occur around it. Some people make love in it, others rob it, children fight outside it, while the housemovers (played by Sydney Chaplin and George Englund) discuss their dreams and hopes, and the meaning of life.

The house comes to the end of its journey, where a mother is waiting for her three sons to return from the wars. They arrive, tired and wounded. "Hot bread is on the table. Won't you come in?" the mother says simply. It is the final line of the play. Slowly, the boys follow her inside. The light fades. At that point, there wasn't a dry eye in the theater.

The play had parts for some forty people, and presented us with a major technical problem: how do you move a big house up and down a tiny stage? We solved it by using a small apple crate to symbolize the house. Sydney and George carried the crate around, accompanied by beautiful music and a single spotlight. Once the crate touched the floor, the lights went up and a new scene started. The effect was electric!

Sam Ego's House became a religion to people; they read things into it that we never realized were there. I think the apple crate did the trick. Our theater-in-the round helped, too; on a proscenium stage, the play might not have been as effective. They'd have built a house.

Saroyan couldn't make it for the opening night, but he came with his beautiful wife Carol a few weeks later, and I kept him informed of events by post. "Audiences have gone wild," I wrote excitedly. "So many people are coming back again and again. After the show we can't get the audience to leave, since they're so eager to stay around and discuss it. The Chaplins were both crazy about the play. Everyone agreed, including Mrs Clifford Odets and Edward G. Robinson that the show is alive, beautiful, and exciting theater."

Fanny Brice, the great Ziegfeld comedienne (portrayed by Barbra Streisand in *Funny Girl*), was our most persistent customer. She came at least five times. "Jerry," she'd say in a sing-song New York voice, phoning at the last minute, "this is Fanny. I want six tickets tonight for my son, my daughter, and – " "I'm sorry, Miss Brice, we're all sold out." She wouldn't take no for an answer: "Not only will you get me tickets, but I want the best seats!" Sure enough, I always managed to find her a place.

On her first visit she arrived smoking, and immediately crossed swords with Sergei, a Norwegian actor who sold our cold drinks. "I'm sorry," he said officiously, "but there's no smoking allowed in the

theater!" Slipping into her funniest Yiddish accent, Fanny replied in a very loud voice for all to hear: "Not only vill I smock, but I'm smocking *marijuana!*" As Robert Mitchum had just been jailed for possessing the deadly weed, this was not the time to bandy the word about.

She was a lovely lady, completely without pretense. Charlie later told me that he wanted her for the role of the loud-mouthed wife in *Monsieur Verdoux* (eventually played by Martha Raye). But Fanny had decided she didn't want to make any more movies.

Oona and Charlie threw a first night party for the entire cast at their home at 1085 Summit Drive, in the most exclusive part of Beverly Hills. Tourists would drive by with their maps, seeking out the homes of the celebrities. The Chaplins' next-door neighbor was William Wyler, the film director. Next to the Wyler house was Fred Astaire's, and then "Pickfair", Mary Pickford and Douglas Fairbanks's mansion. Across the road lived Irene and David Selznick. The first house you saw, though, as you drove up Summit Drive, belonged to the actress Kay Francis. "How did she get on that street?" people asked.

Charlie's home, hidden from the road by a long driveway, was built in the Spanish style. Tall fir trees surrounded his vast tennis court (considered the best in Los Angeles). The party was held in his cathedral-like foyer. On your left as you entered was Charlie's organ – it looked like a roll-top desk. Above it hung a painting of Oona with her two small children, Geraldine and Michael. The drapes must

MAIN PICTURE: AT A PERFORMANCE OF *SAM EGO'S HOUSE*. LEFT TO RIGHT: MABEL ALBERTSON (THE DIRECTOR), WILLIAM SAROYAN (THE PLAYWRIGHT), CAROL SAROYAN, OONA, CHARLIE, SYDNEY (BACK TO CAMERA) AND ME. THE MIRROR WRITING ON THE WALL ISN'T A PRINTING MISTAKE – THAT IS THE ILLUSION WE WERE CREATING. INSET: CLOSE-UP OF CAROL AND OONA. I LOVE THIS PICTURE – THERE'S SUCH A CONTRAST BETWEEN THE TWO.

BELOW: THE PARTY OONA AND CHARLIE (FOREGROUND, FAR RIGHT) THREW FOR THE CIRCLE PLAYERS AT THEIR BEVERLY HILLS HOME AFTER THE OPENING OF SAM EGO'S HOUSE.

BOTTOM RIGHT: THE CIRCLE'S FIRST ANNIVERSARY PARTY. I'M SERVING OONA AND DUDLEY NICHOLS, THE ACADEMY AWARD-WINNING SCREENWRITER.

have been twenty feet high. The tables were arranged in horseshoe fashion, and, judging by the number present, the Circle cast and crew must have brought along their friends and relatives.

It was a night none of us will ever forget. After dinner, in his living-room, Charlie entertained, enacting a stirring piece of Kabuki theater. Charlie played all the parts. At first he was an old woman, alone in a house. A young man suddenly runs in – a traitor. The old woman looks around, fearful, wondering where to hide him. She spots a straw chest and quickly puts him inside. Soldiers enter and ransack the house; the woman denies all knowledge of the youth. The soldiers leave, except for one who becomes suspicious. In a flash, he plunges his sword into the chest. The woman stands frozen. There is no sound. The soldier apologizes and leaves. A second later, blood spills out from the side of the chest. The woman then emits a spine-chilling scream … This was Charlie, the supreme actor, pantomimist and dramatist, at his best.

The Circle was now one year old, and we decided to celebrate with our own party. The theater was packed with Hollywood friends and celebrities, and anyone else who'd helped make the Circle a success. Charlie, Oona and Constance Collier were there; Dudley Nichols came with the cast of his film *Mourning Becomes Electra* – Michael Redgrave, Leo Genn, and Katina Paxinou. Joseph Schildkraut lent his presence, as did most of the critics in town.

The climax to the evening came when Charlie performed two hilarious pantomime routines. One was a French farce, in which he played all three parts: the cuckolded husband, the unfaithful wife, and the lover discovered in the act of a passionate embrace. Everything was timed to perfection – the romance, the guilty looks, the screams of horror when the husband returns, and the flight of the lover through an imaginary window.

The other routine was his bullfight speciality (which he'd performed after the *Verdoux* première). The matador swirls his cape towards the helpless bull, maneuvering and hypnotizing him into a prone position. As he acknowledges the cheers of the crowd and stoops to pick up a rose, the bull scores a bull's-eye on the matador's bottom.

After Charlie's firework performance, the guests gave testimonials to the Circle. Charlie's guest, the veteran English actress Constance Collier, grandly proclaimed that I was the theater's new bright light, while others spoke flatteringly about the Circle's future. The actor Joseph Schildkraut, a terrible ham, rose to declare, "My father Rudolph once said that there are only two things to respect in life – God and

Charlie Chaplin." Everyone squirmed. Charlie was embarrassed. Sydney turned to me and said, loudly, "How did God get top billing?"

That restored normality, and everyone went nuts, cheering and pounding their feet, asking Charlie for an encore. Suddenly two policemen entered with complaints from the neighbors about the noise. My heart sank. Our zoning permit! But when they discovered the cause of the laughter, they happily sat down and joined the festivities.

I soon became a regular visitor to 1085 Summit Drive. Some weeks after the anniversary party, I was invited to my first Christmas at the Chaplins' house. I'd never spent Christmas at anyone's home before, and Charlie's Christmas seemed like something out of a fairytale. In the hallway stood the largest tree I'd ever seen. And there was a multitude of gifts under the tree for everyone.

ABOVE: CHARLIE ADDRESSING THE CIRCLE ACTORS.

LEFT: OUR FIRST ANNIVERSARY PARTY. LEFT TO RIGHT: CHARLIE, LORRAINE AND JOHN CRAWFORD, SYDNEY, GEORGE STERN (FOREGROUND), BILL SCHALLERT, ME, JOSEPH SCHILDKRAUT AND DEE TORMEY CUTTING THE CAKE. AFTER EVERYONE HAD LEFT, SYDNEY AND I POLISHED OFF THE CAKE!

Left: Charlie playing with Geraldine.

Top right: Constance Collier as Cleopatra opposite Beerbohm Tree's Antony in the early 1900s.

Bottom right: Constance as I knew her in the late 1940s and 1950s.

For the next five years I spent Christmas Day with Oona and Charlie. The guests were usually the same: Charlie's older brother Sydney, with his lovely wife Gypsy; his half-brother Wheeler Dryden and his son; his cousins, Betty and Ted Tetrick; Amy Reeves, the widow of his studio manager; Constance Collier and Phyllis Wilbourne, her young English companion; Sydney Jr and myself, and the children.

As Geraldine and Michael opened their gifts, Charlie's mind went back to his own childhood. "All I ever got for Christmas was an orange," he'd say. The orange story became an annual ritual. One Christmas, Sydney Jr was tempted to give Charlie an orange as his present, but I persuaded him not to.

This particular Christmas, Charlie seemed more interested in the Circle than anything else. "How many people did you play to on Christmas Eve? How did the audiences respond?" His curiosity was boundless. Even though it was Christmas, we still performed *Sam Ego's House* in the evening, and Sydney and I had to get back.

I was supervising our next show, John Galsworthy's *The Skin Game* – an old-fashioned play in some ways, though with great dramatic power. As we said goodbye, I asked Charlie if he'd like to watch rehearsals.

Charlie arrived the following night with Oona and Constance Collier. Constance was an extraordinary woman. At the turn of the century in London, Charlie had watched her from the gallery at His Majesty's Theatre when she played star parts in Beerbohm Tree's lavish productions. She was Cleopatra to his Antony, the original Nancy in *Oliver Twist,* Portia in *Julius Caesar.* Charlie had first met Constance in 1916, when she befriended him in Hollywood. Now she lived in chaotic splendor with a disgusting parrot, various other pets, and her devoted companion Phyllis from the suburbs of London.

Although she was in her seventies, and found employment scarce, Constance had a great capacity for friendship and bringing people together. Everybody loved her. At the time she was coaching Linda Darnell, a half-Mexican actress cast as an English courtesan in *Forever Amber*. After a particularly hard day's slog with her, she told us, "That girl should be home, over a hot stove, cooking tamales."

Charlie, Oona and Constance sat while we ran through the second act of *The Skin Game*. At first Charlie watched. Then he turned to me, and said the magic line, the "Open Sesame" to a marvelous theatrical adventure: "Do you mind if I suggest something to the actors?" Before I knew it, he had left his seat and was on the job.

"Wouldn't it be better if you phrased the lines like this?" He knew by instinct exactly what he wanted and relayed his feelings by acting out all the parts. A few words of text from the actors, and he was up and down like a yo-yo: "Wait a minute, wait a minute, I don't like this . . ." He'd move the players to another position, then start again. Just as the actor got one word out, there was another interruption. Up and down, back and forth. Nothing escaped his eagle eye: he hunted for dramatic possibilities in every speech and line.

This first rehearsal demonstrated something uncanny about Chaplin's theatrical sense. He never took time to prepare himself by reading the text of the plays, yet he had an unerring sense of the next line. And he stressed the importance of making effective entrances and exits. He was very emphatic about this. "You see, I'm essentially an entrance and exit man," he'd tell us. And he'd explain: "It's very important to establish your character with something compelling the first moment you enter; that way, you have the audience in the palm of your hand. The same with your exit – you must make it memorable." We absorbed every word he said.

Early on in our *Skin Game* rehearsals, we had made cuts in Galsworthy's text. Charlie instinctively spotted them. "Wait a minute, wait a minute," he'd say, "You can't exit with that line of dialogue. Something's missing!" And he'd restore the very line that we had eliminated, without even knowing what the line was.

Charlie helped enormously in sharpening up *The Skin Game*. The actors found him stimulating and magnetic. At his first session he kept them busy until the early hours, and then announced that he'd return the next evening to rehearse Act Three. We left feeling wilted, elated and nervous: the play was about to open in a few days' time, and panic was setting in.

The next night, Charlie arrived as before with Oona and Constance. But he was not allowed to make a quiet entrance. Before rehearsals began, Constance decided to address the company. "You should all get down on your *knees*," she declaimed in her deep, *grande dame* voice. "Lunt and Fontanne would give their right arms to work with Charles Chaplin . . ." As Constance warmed to her theme, we began to feel increasingly small and self-conscious, until the balloon was punctured by Charlie himself. "Modesty forbids!" he murmured, in a soft, quiet voice. That broke the tension, and we all burst out laughing.

"OK, let's get going! Set up for the first scene, and don't lay any eggs!" Then the fun started again. "Keep it light, keep it clean!" Charlie was a stickler for simple choreography, and the minimum of gestures: "I naturally use my hands a lot. Luckily I have the luxury of seeing myself on the screen the next day, and I cut down all unnecessary gestures. Only use your hands when you want to make a point – that's when it becomes effective."

During a break in rehearsals he illustrated the vices of fussy stage behavior with a hilarious demonstration of what he called "chair acting". He walked over to a chair and stood behind it, talking gibberish; still talking, he leaned against it, folded his arms on it, moved it in a circle, and did everything but dance. The Italians, he said, were especially good at the dubious art. He also told us about seeing the great Eleonora Duse perform in his youth in London. There, on stage, were two "chair actors" hamming it up. Duse slowly entered and unobtrusively, silently, walked to a fireplace and just rubbed her hands. The audience, he said, was riveted. The other two actors pulled every trick in the trade with their chairs, but you couldn't take your eyes off the great Duse.

When directing the actors, some of the things Charlie illustrated came naturally to him, but proved difficult for the other actors. Earle Herdan, cast as the auctioneer selling off a property in *The Skin Game*, had a particularly hard time trying to emulate the high-speed gabble that Charlie made so riotously funny. Following in Charlie's footsteps was a daunting task.

As Charlie directed, Constance – who had a great knowledge of theater – watched with an eagle eye. A conflict began to develop between the two. Seated behind him, Constance became increasingly irritated, and kept shaking her head in utter disagreement. Finally she could contain herself no longer, and muttered loudly, "No! no! no! Charlie! You haven't read the script! That's not the way it should be played!" Suddenly, these two old friends were at war with each other over interpretation, and the Circle actors were caught in the middle. They didn't know who to follow.

Charlie turned, gave her dirty looks, then whispered to me to get rid of her. "I won't have her behind me, making those comments!" But Constance couldn't be silenced; and I found it too difficult to ask her to leave. "You haven't read the play, Charlie, you don't know what you're talking about!" These feuds amused us all, but for them they were deadly serious. Yet even Constance had to admit, after she saw the end result, that Charlie gave new life to an old-fashioned play. He worked so hard. I learned through the years that whatever Charlie tackled, he threw himself into it wholeheartedly: directing at the Circle, making films, playing tennis, choosing furniture – he always gave his all.

The cast included Bill Schallert, Sydney, and a well-known radio actress, Barbara Fuller. As Chloe, the nouveau-riche wife with a guilty secret, she had several highly dramatic scenes, and her performance impressed Charlie sufficiently for him to consider her briefly for the heroine in his new film project. He was working on a screenplay with a London theatrical background called *Footlights;* during the next few years, the title became *Limelight,* and the search for a girl to play Terry, the highly-strung young dancer, continued. When we were doing *Major Barbara,* Charlie became enchanted with Diana Douglas (then the wife of Kirk Douglas, and the mother of Michael), who played the title role; he thought she, too, could play Terry. Any Circle actress with youth and fire was liable to be given a mental screen test.

After *The Skin Game* Charlie contributed to seven more shows, always in the same inspired, but ad hoc fashion. In many ways, he rehearsed the plays as though he were back in his film studio. Sometimes he'd expect instant performances; he'd create a piece of business through endless improvisation, and painstakingly polish short scenes. He didn't worry so much about the overall continuity or building a character over three acts. In films he was always able to retake a scene the next day if a new idea occurred to him. He applied the same method at the Circle: every rehearsal was another retake, as fresh ideas poured in to wipe out whatever he'd staged the previous day. This process went on practically until opening night. Charlie could never

accept that in the theater the performance must at some point be frozen, so the actors know what they're doing. But the productions still emerged perfect, exquisite, with characterizations stripped of the obvious.

By two o'clock in the morning, Charlie had generally exhausted the cast, but his own stamina was endless. Oona would telephone to summon him home. "The old lady's on the phone!" he'd say, "I'd better be going." She was in fact thirty-five years younger than he. But Charlie couldn't leave until he perfected what he was doing. Sometimes Oona had to come down herself, to drag Charlie away from his new toy. "Charlie!" she'd plead, "these poor kids need their sleep!"

Despite Oona's phone calls, Charlie usually stayed until daybreak, enthralling us with theatrical stories and his ideas for interpreting the classics. As the sun rose, he would take the survivors to Hollywood Boulevard for wheat pancakes and maple syrup. We'd shuffle along with him, bleary-eyed; Charlie, however, strode out eagerly, just as sprightly as he had been hours before when rehearsals started. He loved the color of the dawn sky; "Drunkards' blue," he called it, after the drunks who staggered through the early morning streets.

"My fee for directing," he used to say to me once we reached the pancake parlor, "is thirty-five cents and a cup of black coffee!" He gave so much to our young actors – his time, his energy, his love and affection, the fruits of his experience learned over decades of painstaking work on stage and film. All for thirty-five cents and a cup of black coffee. This was the bargain to end all bargains!

On other occasions, the meals were more formal. Once he and Oona invited the entire Circle – actors, technicians and various helpers – for dinner at Lucy's, an exclusive restaurant across the street from Paramount Studios. As we entered, Charlie said, "Now order their spaghetti! They're noted for it. It's delicious!" Oona interrupted: "Oh Charlie, let them order steaks!" That broke the ice. We all dug into big juicy steaks – with spaghetti on the side.

The Circle soon became part of Charlie's daily routine. When he had nothing to do in the afternoon, or wanted a break from his *Limelight* script, he'd drive down to the theater in his Ford and sit with me in the box-office. While he was there one day, the income tax man arrived. Charlie became very nervous and tried not to be noticed.

We hadn't paid our admission taxes, the man said. I looked him straight in the eye: "We can hardly pay our actors, and you're asking for admission taxes! If you want that extra money, we'd have to close! I'm not going to pay you!" Charlie slumped further and further into his chair.

"Here's a couple of seats for our show; bring your wife. Then we'll discuss things," I told him. I placed him at the top of our guest list for every opening night. After that, the Los Angeles tax man became one of our biggest fans. Admission taxes were forgotten until he was shifted to a new area; then we had to pay up.

Charlie was always amused by my confrontations with officialdom. He loved it when I told him about Actors' Equity, who were hounding us for not paying our casts the full union salary – which we simply couldn't afford. "Look," I told them, "none of us are getting rich – I'm walking round with holes in my shoes!" I took off my shoes and displayed them on the table. Equity didn't bother us for quite a while after that.

I think Charlie enjoyed my enthusiasm for theater, and the way I managed the Circle. Although he was a world figure, I never played up to him, made no demands, and asked no questions. I think he appreciated that. He was just a new-found friend, although an important one; I felt completely myself and at ease with him. As Constance commented to Oona once, "Isn't it amazing how that young boy knows how to handle Charlie?"

But the main attraction for Charlie was naturally his son Sydney. Before the Circle, I don't think they knew each other very well, especially since Sydney grew up. But now Charlie spotted a star in the making and wanted to help him along with his budding career. Sydney was handsome, charming, over six feet tall, and able to play all the romantic parts that Charlie must have felt he hadn't the height for himself. He began writing a part for Sydney in his *Limelight* script. Charlie always enjoyed launching people: he tried to do this with Edna Purviance in *A Woman of Paris,* when she could no longer be his own leading lady, and years later, I saw the same process at work with his young daughter Victoria. He would look at her hard and say, "That child has *genius!*" Then he began creating a movie, *The Freak,* to launch her career.

Charlie's contributions to Circle productions went uncredited in our programs. He didn't want any publicity, and I respected his feelings.

But it was difficult to keep the secret, as so many actors and friends saw him at rehearsals. When a paragraph appeared in *Time* magazine mentioning his work at the Circle, I was very embarrassed, and went up to his house to apologize. I expected him to be angry, but he brushed the matter off, and read me a new scene he had just finished for *Limelight.*

In retrospect, the Circle must have been a small haven for Charlie, a place where he could temporarily forget his problems. We took him to our hearts, and were sympathetic about the damaging publicity he was suffering from the FBI and the Un-American Activities Committee. This Committee – which laid the groundwork for the McCarthy witch-hunts – was now terrorizing the Hollywood community, trying to find evidence of Communist infiltration in the film industry. They would victimize and pillory innocent people, who would often be left without a livelihood. Charlie never mentioned his problems, and we never probed. We were simply grateful that he was so generous with his time and talent. And if he found something in return, we were happy.

In the meantime, pressure on Charlie was building. Two days before we opened with a revival of *The Adding Machine,* he was visited at Summit Drive by the FBI and the Immigration Service. Earlier, Charlie had applied to the Service for a re-entry permit: he was planning a trip to London, to show Oona his roots. They had come, the FBI man said, to take evidence, under oath.

For four hours, Charlie frankly and courageously answered hostile questions about his personal life and beliefs. He was asked about his racial origins, even about his sexual activities. "What kind of reply is a healthy man who has lived in this country for over thirty-five years supposed to make?" Charlie said.

The investigators raked through the speeches he'd made at pro-Soviet rallies, the occasional dinners at the Soviet Consulate, the telegram he'd sent to a Moscow festival of Chaplin films – anything that might link him to the Communists. He denied all connection with the Party. "I have thirty million dollars' worth of business – what am I talking about Communism for?" When they asked if he thought the Communist way of life was better than America's, his answer was firm: "No. Of course, if I did, I'd possibly go there and live. At the same time, I am not antagonistic. But if they were to invade America, I'd take up arms."

Joe Mantell as Mr Zero and Strother Martin as Shrdlu in Elmer Rice's *The Adding Machine*. Strother was a lifeguard in Santa Monica when he auditioned for me. He later became a great success in Sam Peckinpah films.

"Why didn't you ever become an American citizen?" "Since I was nineteen," Charlie replied, "I have always had a sense of internationalism. I feel as much a citizen of America as anyone, and my great love has always been here in this country. But I don't feel allied to any one particular country. I feel I am a citizen of the world."

This was not the kind of answer the FBI wanted. In any event Charlie called off his trip, and the problem of his re-entry permit lay dormant, for the time being . . .

The liberals in Hollywood all looked up to Charlie, and everyone knew the stand he took with the Un-American Activities Committee. He almost wanted them to invite him to testify. But, realizing his enormous fame and the bad publicity they might receive overseas if he was victimized, the Committee never sent for him. There was one Hollywood writer who admired the strong stand Charlie took with the Committee, and told him that he was going to behave in the same manner as him. Charlie admonished him: "Be careful. I'm a wealthy man. They can't do anything to hurt me." He was concerned that this person, by following in his footsteps, could lose his livelihood.

Life at Summit Drive continued as normal: Charlie had a wonderful capacity for putting his personal problems to one side. "I'm like a weed," he used to say, quoting a line from *Limelight,* "the more you cut me down, the more I grow."

He maintained his resilience and good spirits by keeping busy and fit. Charlie was a firm believer in physical exercise. "The bloodstream is like a river," he was always telling me. "When it isn't in motion, it becomes stagnant and diseased." In his youth he smoked, but now he scorned the habit. "How's your cancer coming?" he'd say to Constance as she sucked and puffed incessantly on the dregs of a cigarette. This was years before the dangers of smoking became confirmed. Later, when he lived in Switzerland, he'd sometimes make his guests freeze by opening the windows to let the fumes escape.

For relaxation, his big passion was tennis. Sometimes his butler called up the Circle and asked Sydney to come over; Greta Garbo was due for a game, and they needed a fourth for doubles. Hearing this, I rushed along to watch.

Garbo was magnificent. I saw her on several occasions – once at one of those marvelous Sunday teas in the Chaplin tennis house, where cucumber sandwiches were served. I remember Charlie telling Garbo,

"You should go back to movies and film the life of Eleonora Duse. What a love story there'd be between Duse and the poet-warrior Count D'Annunzio!"

"I'd only do it if you directed me!" she replied. Now in her mid-forties, Garbo asked if she could use Charlie's studios for a secret screen test: she was anxious to see how she photographed. Her favorite cameraman William Daniels, who worked on most of her MGM films, was summoned to shoot the footage. According to legend, after staring hard at herself on the screen in Chaplin's projection room, she turned to Daniels and said, "Billy, you're getting old."

Bill Tilden, the great Wimbledon international tennis star, currently gave lessons on Charlie's court; Bill had recently served a prison term for a sex offence, and Charlie was generously helping him back on his feet. I duly took lessons.

Bill had the great knack of interpreting tennis from the point of view of your profession – in my case, the theater. When two actors stand on stage, he told me, they listen hard to each other, in order to return their line correctly. Tennis is the same: you cannot properly return the ball unless you concentrate on your partner's play. This was brilliant advice, but I remained the worst athlete in the world.

Bill was trying to become a playwright. He submitted his masterpiece to me for consideration. Late one night Bill Schallert, Sydney and I read the play out loud in the Circle box-office; we ended up on the floor, laughing hysterically. His dialogue was just like my tennis game. It's a terrible thing when you know someone, and have to turn down their work, their precious baby. But somehow Bill understood.

Apart from tennis, one of Charlie's favorite relaxations was movie-going. Charlie, Oona and I went to the latest movies all over town and behaved like kids at a Saturday matinee, stocking up with goodies at the kiosk. Charlie's favorite candies were Almond Joys (chocolate bars with coconut filling) and Bon-Bons (chocolate covered balls of vanilla ice-cream). We munched through *Carrie, The African Queen,* and *A Place in the Sun,* which he adored. When Charlie hated a film, he used to moan, mutter and grunt. "I'm not going to sit with you," Oona would warn him, "if you make all that noise!" One day, I read an open letter in the *Los Angeles Daily News.* A woman complained about a man who killed her enjoyment of a film by talking and moaning throughout; she turned round, and it was Charlie Chaplin!

If Oona didn't feel like a movie, Charlie and I might sneak off to Hollywood Boulevard and the newsreel theaters. Charlie loved to watch travelogues and news items from all over the world – these were the days before TV. He was especially fascinated by shots of Queen Elizabeth of England (then Princess Elizabeth), bobbing up and down on horseback.

At other times, Charlie and I went on walks in the evening through Skid Row in downtown Los Angeles. Charlie always found great poetry in slums – although today I don't think he'd chance it.

Some nights we'd motor down to Malibu, have dinner at the Holiday Inn and drive along the coast. Going out with Oona and Charlie to restaurants was always an event, because Charlie made every meal an occasion. We ate hot pastrami sandwiches with pickles, walking along Venice Beach, and big juicy hamburgers at Dolores' Drive-In on Sunset Boulevard. Later, in London, curries and kosher meals at Blooms were the order of the day. Oona loved spicy foods. Give her a hot Mexican taco, and she was in seventh heaven.

Oona was a fantastic cook herself, and Charlie was her most appreciative fan. One night she cooked a delicious roast lamb for Charlie, Constance and myself. Over dinner we discussed possible plays for the Circle. Charlie suddenly came up with *Othello*. As a rule he found Shakespeare uphill work, but this play intrigued him and he wanted to direct it. The Circle players had never had any training in Shakespeare, but I was willing to take the gamble if he was. I took a risk with everything else. Charlie thought Sydney – with his height and fine, deep voice – could play Othello, and he contacted a Shakespearean scholar living in California, Reginald Pole, to train him in diction, movement, and Elizabethan verse. Sydney worked hard.

Over dinner, Charlie excitedly explained his conception of *Othello*. He felt the play was essentially about sex, and he wanted to convey the sexual attraction that bound Desdemona to the Moor. Without sex as its theme, the play didn't make sense, he said. Desdemona should be portrayed as outwardly virginal, pale and pure, but inwardly a girl on fire. Othello's jealous rage, he thought, would then make more sense.

Constance was outraged. "Charlie, *read* the play!" she said. "Look at what Emilia says: 'The sweetest innocent that e'er did lift up eye!' 'Moor, she was chaste – ' She's *innocent,* Charlie, not some harem harlot!"

"I don't care what the lines say," Charlie replied testily. "This is a play about rampant sex. We'll give the play a new, modern conception." Oona and I kept very quiet, hiding our laughter and giving each other sidelong looks as their feuding raged on.

But who was to play our passionate Desdemona? At the time Sydney was dating the actress Evelyn Keyes, who had just divorced John Huston. Sydney brought her to Summit Drive. Charlie took one look and detected a certain sexual hunger in her eyes. He had found his Desdemona! Evelyn was completely confused, but willing to have a go. She came from the deep South; she had played Scarlett O'Hara's sister, Sue Ellen, in *Gone With the Wind,* and was now a Columbia star. I was just about to ask Constance to coach her, when Columbia yanked her away for another film. So Charlie's provocative *Othello* never materialized. I would love to have seen his conception in action – not to mention those rehearsals, with Constance and Charlie at each other's throats.

Although Charlie kept insisting he didn't like Shakespeare, the Bard popped up again and again in his thoughts. He had his own conception about playing *Hamlet*. "You can't make the Prince a wilting poet, a sensitive little flower. That's so boring. The only way to make the role effective is to play Hamlet mad! This makes all his entrances, exits and soliloquies exciting – it keeps the audience on edge!" (Years later, he slipped a little of this conception into his film *A King in New York*.) Another time, Charlie, spoke excitedly about filming *Antony and Cleopatra*. He loved this play, and was thinking of Hedy Lamarr as the heroine; she had the beauty, at least.

Ironically, when the Circle finally made its Shakespearean debut in December 1950, Constance was the director. She chose *Twelfth Night;* in her possession she had Beerbohm Tree's original annotated script from his famous production of 1904, and she followed his staging. She directed the piece magnificently. There was no declaiming, no nonsense; even the comedy sequences were played naturally. Ricki Soma, John Huston's new wife (and the mother of Anjelica), was the most beautiful Olivia imaginable; Marjorie Steele, an inexperienced newcomer, played Viola. On the opening night, the poor thing tripped on her first entrance, but she recovered and received ovations. Constance coached her well. Sir Andrew Aguecheek was played by the veteran comedian Gus Schilling; his wife Betty Rowland, the queen of American burlesque, known throughout the country as the Ball of Fire, watched rehearsals between her own strip-shows. Constance looked at her bright red frizzy hair and thought her marvelous. "One day, my dear," she said in her grand manner, "you *must* play Mistress Quickly!"

None of Charlie's Shakespearean ventures materialized, but another of his Circle suggestions – *Rain* – became one of our biggest successes in October 1948. To me this dramatized version of Somerset Maugham's story didn't seem the right type of Circle play – I liked choosing less familiar properties. But Charlie's enthusiasm won me over. "It's a marvelous, theatrical piece," he said, "but it's never been done correctly!"

Jeanne Eagels, he thought, stank in the original Broadway production – she played Sadie Thompson like a cliché backstreet whore, swinging her handbag as she picked up men. The psychology of Rev. Davidson was also wrong, he insisted; they never looked into the dark recesses of this repressed religious fanatic. Here was another play about hidden sexual urges! He couldn't get his conception into *Othello*, so he was now putting it into *Rain*. Charlie got me very excited. "Direct it, and I'll do the play!" He agreed.

The hardest part was casting Sadie Thompson. So many actresses read for us, but it was difficult to find the right one. As fate would have

RICKI SOMA AS OLIVIA, JOHN ABBOTT AS MALVOLIO AND MARJORIE STEELE AS VIOLA, TAKING THEIR CURTAIN CALLS IN CONSTANCE'S PRODUCTION OF *TWELFTH NIGHT*.

it, among our Circle audiences were June Havoc and her husband, the radio producer William Spier. June was well-known as the vaudeville child star Baby June, and the younger sister of Gypsy Rose Lee (the musical *Gypsy* was based on their lives). June, then establishing herself in films, asked if she could audition. I hesitated: we had never had a movie personality in our shows before. Charlie left the casting to me. June was chosen.

Before Charlie began rehearsing, Constance arrived early to address the cast and to put in her pennyworth. "Acting," she said, with that marvelous twinkle in her blue eyes, "is like building a house. First you lay the foundations. Next you construct a skeleton, then s-l-o-w-l-y you position your bricks, brick by brick. The building's finished. Then you put in the furniture and fittings – filling the role with details. Finally, everything is completed and you turn on the lights – and that's your *inspiration!*" Over the years she told us this several times, and I never tired of hearing it. I was like Lenny in *Of Mice and Men,* asking her to repeat the same story again and again.

Charlie arrived and work began. This time Constance kept quiet; she wanted to see what he was up to. Charlie spent hours devising a stunningly effective first entrance for Bill Schallert (playing Rev. Davidson); Bill came in almost at a gallop, very preoccupied by some weighty matter, throwing away his first line. Bob Burns converted the

CHARLIE DIRECTING THE FIRST REHEARSAL OF *RAIN.* LEFT TO RIGHT: CHARLIE, LEAH WAGGNER, AN UNKNOWN ACTOR, KATHLEEN FREEMAN, SYDNEY CHAPLIN, JOHN PERI. BACK TO CAMERA: JUNE HAVOC.

entire theater into Joe Horn's trading post in the South Seas. The audience sat under a specially constructed tin roof; water was hosed over it to simulate tropical rain. And June was superb – Charlie ironed out all her mannerisms and made her simple, lovely and vulnerable. It was a beautiful, poetic production.

The cast also included a monkey – a hateful creature called Jocko, obtained from the Wilshire Pet Center. He lived in a cage in the tiny flat I shared with Sydney at the back of the theater, and caused us endless trouble. Like a miniature King Kong, he would grab the bars and shake his cage until he knocked it over and escaped, tearing our clothes and scattering them through the room. Then he'd take off for pastures new, jumping across the back fences of Hollywood. Rita Hayworth's brother generally returned him, held by the scruff of the neck.

DURING A PERFORMANCE OF *RAIN.* ABOVE THE ROOF WE HAD RAIN FALLING. LEFT TO RIGHT: LEAH WAGGNER, ALICE WELLMAN, JOHN AUSTIN, JUNE HAVOC. BACK TO CAMERA: BILL SCHALLERT AS REV. DAVIDSON.

AFTER A PERFORMANCE OF *RAIN*. THE
GREAT FANNY BRICE WITH OUR LEAH
WAGGNER, CONSTANCE AND JULIAN
LUDWIG.

He was no better behaved in captivity. When one of our actors, Al Supowitz (later to win Oscars as the writer Alvin Sargent), was given a radio part by June's husband, he proudly brandished his first pay check, holding it high for everyone to see. In a split second, Jocko had shot his arm through the bars and ripped the check to shreds. And the noise he kicked up was horrendous: "Beep, beep, beep, beep!" all day long, rocking back and forth in his cage. Bill Schallert discovered that the only way to quieten him was to spit in his face. He would stop his beep-beeps, wipe the saliva off, and look at it intrigued. Then he'd return to normal.

One evening, the nightmare arrived. During a tense scene when a Marine tries to stop Sadie crying and tells her, "Look, even Jocko wants you to stop!", Jocko, the brute, yanked June's hair, slipped out of his lead, and jumped into the audience. Ladies screamed. The actors continued as though nothing had happened, groping all the time for the little monster, who leaped from one member of the audience to another before landing on top of the exit sign. As he swooped down onto the set, grabbing and drinking a Coke, a boy in the audience casually went onstage, snatched the creature, and handed him back to the actors. The play resumed.

Luckily this never happened when the critics came. The reviews were tremendous, and all of Hollywood started to descend: Lucille Ball, Jeanette MacDonald, Benny Goodman, Roddy McDowall, Howard Keel, Artie Shaw.

Sydney would always invite Paulette Goddard, his former step-mother and Charlie's third wife, to the shows. Whenever she came, her infectious laugh set off the audience, and made many of our shows a hit. For the *Rain* première, she arrived every inch the movie queen, with a long evening gown and tiara, and sat on the front row. She found Oona and Charlie sitting on one side, and Charlie's second wife, Lita Grey, on the other. Never before had three of Charlie's wives been in one room together. Charlie took it all in his stride.

Before the show began one evening, sirens blasted outside the theater. Two large limousines pulled up, and security men came in to check the theater. We thought it was the FBI! But it was only Earl Warren, the Governor of California, coming to the show with his family. Warren had just been through an arduous election campaign, running for Vice-President of the United States. (Later, as Chief Justice of the Supreme Court, he headed the committee investigating John F. Kennedy's assassination.) When June made her first entrance, everyone applauded and, in a reflex action, Warren waved to the audience, thinking he was still campaigning!

Constance loved our production of *Rain*. Besides coming one night with our fan Fanny Brice, she saw it again with Dorothy Parker – though I wondered how Parker could have seen the show with her hat half-covering her face.

Constance was everyone's friend. Oona adored her company. When she and Charlie were first married, Constance rang inviting her for lunch. Oona, only eighteen at the time, was shy at the prospect of dining alone with someone she hardly knew. But Charlie insisted they meet. "You'll like her," he said. He was right; Oona took to her immediately – she had such zest, humor, and took an interest in everything.

One day, after Oona and Constance had lunched at Romanoffs, a swanky Beverly Hills restaurant, a group of autograph-hunters surrounded Constance. As she grandly signed their books, Oona walked several feet away. Constance then whispered to the fans, loud enough for Oona to hear, "And you know who's standing over there? That's Mrs Charles Chaplin! Why not ask for her autograph, too?" This was the last thing in the world Oona wanted; she was always so self-effacing. But Constance thought she was doing her a favor.

These were hectic times at the Circle. There were so many actors,

TOP RIGHT: SHELLEY WINTERS TALKING TO CONSTANCE COLLIER. SEATED ON HER LEFT IS DOROTHY PARKER – ONE HALF OF THE SHOW SHE COULDN'T HAVE SEEN, WITH THAT HAT! AND ON DOROTHY'S LEFT, DARLING MARIE WILSON.
BOTTOM RIGHT: DURING A PERFORMANCE OF *THE DOCTOR IN SPITE OF HIMSELF*, KATHLEEN FREEMAN IS ADDRESSING THE AUDIENCE. SPOTTED IN THE BACK ROW ARE RHONDA FLEMING, JEANNE CAGNEY AND FLORENCE MARLEY. MIDDLE ROW, LEFT TO RIGHT: LEO PENN (FATHER OF SEAN), OLIVE DEERING, ME, CHARLIE, GENE TIERNEY, OONA, CONSTANCE. VISIBLE IN THE FRONT ROW ARE HENRY WILCOXON, KATHERINE DE MILLE, BARBARA BRITTON, RODDY MCDOWALL AND ELIZABETH TAYLOR.

and I knew the best way to maintain a happy company was to keep them busy. We decided to convert the garage next door into another auditorium. This became our New Theatre. The actors had a free rein to experiment and present practically anything they wanted; they could also do plays I felt were unsuitable for the Circle itself.

Antigone was one – directed by a young drama graduate from Yale, who hardly fitted in with the Circle crowd. I didn't care much for his production, but Charlie loved it. He was obviously right about the director's talent: the man from Yale was Alan Pakula, the future director of the films *All the President's Men* and *Klute*. The New Theatre also held evenings of improvisations, where the audience suggested situations and characters, and discussed the results with the actors afterwards.

After the huge success of *Rain,* I became hungry for more shows. I expanded further, and took over the Coronet Theater on La Cienega Boulevard, where Charles Laughton had recently appeared, with little success, in Brecht's *Galileo*. In my lunacy, I then took over another theater, the Las Palmas, off Hollywood Boulevard. Success was sweet, and I was now running four different theaters.

But sometimes you can keep actors too busy. Some of them appeared in several plays all in the same night: Naomi Stevens, or Strother Martin, would often start off in a play at the Circle, dart into a waiting car and change costumes en route, arriving at the Coronet just in time for their second act entrance. The car would then speed them back for the third act at the Circle. Some nights the actors walked into the wrong play: it was easy to make the mistake at the Circle, with the New Theatre adjoining. The only thing the actors could complain of now was exhaustion and overwork, not a lack of parts.

Clearly, we were heading for disaster, and it arrived in the shape of *Caligula*. A Circle fan kept hounding me night after night about Albert Camus's play. He had seen the Paris production with Gérard Philippe, and found it the greatest theatrical experience of his life. "Get the rights to this play!" he insisted.

I read the text, and couldn't make head or tail of it, though I sensed it had dramatic possibilities and might suit the experimental theater next door. I managed to reach Camus by phone in Algeria; over a crackling line he agreed to give me the rights. Albert Band, who later made horror films, began rehearsals and received the official credit. James Anderson, from the Actor's Lab, was cast as Caligula.

During rehearsals at the New Theatre, our deal at the Coronet came through sooner than we thought, and we needed an opening production. *Caligula* was far from ready, and I felt unable to whip it into shape myself: it was not my kind of play. So I decided to put the problem before Charlie and took off for Summit Drive.

As I approached his driveway, I noticed an emissary from a foreign country, dressed in distinguished clothes, waiting fruitlessly for an audience. I roared past in my tin lizzie, T-shirt and slacks, leaped out, and stormed into the Chaplin living-room. Charlie greeted me profusely, even though I was interrupting his work on *Limelight*. I pleaded with him to take the show over. He was the only one, I said, who could make sense of Camus and straighten out the mess I had witnessed on stage. He agreed to help, since Oona was in hospital, awaiting the birth of her new baby.

At the Coronet, the cast awaited Chaplin's arrival with bated breath. He rolled up his sleeves, ready for work. The actors began with the first scene. Usually Charlie was so sharp, but this time he was as confused as everyone else. "What does *this* mean?" he kept asking.

Charlie always enjoyed figuring out the psychology behind every line, but Camus floored him completely. What to do?

He decided the play needed gags – anything to hold the audience. He made Earle Herdan, playing an old Patrician, walk with a funny little hop. He spent much time choreographing a scene where Caligula commands the Roman senators to lick their writing tablets with their tongues. Charlie had a field day: he made the actors lick, shake and writhe at the same time. Then Caligula snapped his fingers, and they'd stop; he'd snap his fingers again, and they'd start licking again. It may not have been what Camus had in mind, but we did get laughs. James Anderson, at least, took his part as the mad emperor seriously. A Method actor, he prepared for his performance every night by knocking his head against the brick wall backstage. Chaplin watched aghast.

Rehearsals were squeezed in at the Coronet between Cole Porter's preparations for the Los Angeles opening of *Kiss Me Kate*. The theater was huge, with a proscenium stage. But Charlie behaved just as he did at the Circle – leaping up from his seat every few seconds to interrupt the action. The distance from the orchestra to the stage was about three feet, but Charlie managed it in one go – something quite beyond the younger players. We needed a lavish set. Again, Chaplin's studios came to the rescue. Stout pillars, originally used in the ballroom set in *The Great Dictator*, were now employed in Caligula's palace.

While Charlie racked his brains over the play, Oona gave birth to Josephine, their second daughter, on March 28th, 1949. *Caligula* opened, after various postponements, on April Fool's Day. The notices were diabolical. "A monumental error of judgment ... woefully lacking in polish," said the *Daily Variety*. Frank Eng from the *Los Angeles Daily News* was particularly harsh: "It failed to scratch the surface of the Camus work ... the cast lacks the authority and presence required ... the staging looked wooden ..." The list of his complaints went on and on; I think he knew Charlie had had a hand in the production. Sydney – who didn't understand a word of his own dialogue – received the only complimentary notice from one of the most eminent critics: "Sydney Chaplin, as Helicon, seems to be the only cast member who knows what the play is about."

The day after the opening, I stood in the Coronet box-office. "Are you sure you want to see this play?" I said when a customer came to the window – I hated taking money for a dud. "If Jerry Epstein's name is on the program," he replied, "I know it's good!" My heart sank to my boots. During the second performance I found Charlie fuming in the lobby. He had seen the reviews too, and was itching to write to the *Daily News*, attacking Frank Eng. "What does he mean about us not scratching the surface? *He's* the one who doesn't understand the meaning of the play!"

I told Charlie to forget it. With all his problems over the Un-American Activities Committee, the Immigration Service and the FBI, the last thing he needed was a pointless controversy defending a play that none of us understood. *Caligula* was a big flop, and we just had to live with it.

Directing *Caligula*, Charlie shows the actors how to shake their tablets. Watching with amusement are Naomi Stevens and Earle Herdan. The pillar is from *The Great Dictator*.

THE CIRCLE: 3 THE STORY CONTINUES

The Coronet seemed jinxed. Nothing seemed to work. The theater was turning into a white elephant. *Caligula* quickly closed, and as a stop-gap venture, I mounted an evening of one-act plays. Naomi Stevens was superb as Bertha in Tennessee Williams's *Hello from Bertha;* she then quickly switched to brazen Lilly Pepper in Noel Coward's *Red Peppers.* All good productions, but where were the audiences? Panic set in. Determined to make the Coronet work, I secured the rights to Philip Yordan's smash hit *Anna Lucasta* – performed on Broadway by an all-black cast. We were to present the play as Yordan originally wrote it, with Polish-American characters. But, due to a leading lady with a drinking problem, we had a flop.

Then I gave the West Coast première of *The Respectful Prostitute* by Jean-Paul Sartre. Hurd Hatfield was excellent as the Senator's son, but we had more leading lady trouble. Our star was replaced a week before opening; she then picketed the theater, shouting to our customers about her unfair dismissal. We closed. I finally decided to abandon the Coronet and concentrate on the Circle Theatre. After all, this was where we had established our identity and first found success.

During this period Oona and Charlie never lost faith in the Circle. I was always guaranteed a sympathetic ear.

I was still feeling low. My mother and father came to the Circle and took me for a drive. From the back of the car, I told them I was giving everything up. I couldn't take it anymore. I was exhausted, I said, and tired of the whole business. My father, who had always been against my involvement in the theater, abruptly turned round: 'I'll never have any respect for you if you give up now." His words moved me deeply. Of course, I stuck it out.

With Bernard Shaw's *Major Barbara* at the Circle, our fortunes and reputation started to soar once more. I auditioned many actresses for the title role. After Diana Douglas read for me, I eagerly contacted Terry Kilburn, the play's director. "I've found our Major Barbara!" I said. Our run of bad luck with leading ladies was over. Diana was wonderful, with just the right spirit, and a radiant smile. Her husband Kirk, newly elevated to stardom in the film *Champion,* watched rehearsals coldly. He never seemed to react, or give encouragement; he appeared to disapprove of his wife acting.

Once again, the Chaplin studio came to the rescue with props: for the munitions factory scene, we used the large bombs from *The Great Dictator.* Gladys Cooper, the distinguished British stage actress now working in Hollywood, also helped, after attending a rehearsal with her son-in-law, Robert Morley. "The furniture's all wrong for an English household!" she cried. The next day she came with suitable replacements from her own home. Katharine Hepburn arrived with her director George Cukor and signed up some of our actors for their film *Adam's Rib.* It was their start.

The Circle was bursting with romance and marriages. Bob Burns married Naomi Stevens; having no money, they lived in the dungeon-like basement of the Circle; Bill Schallert tied the knot with Leah Waggner, another wonderful actress. I, too, fell in love with one of our players, but although we were very close, she was in love with someone else. Ah me, unrequited love!

But the Circle romance with the most intrigue was between Sydney and a lovely young girl, Marjorie Steele, the future Viola of Constance's *Twelfth Night.* Charlie was to play a major role in this romance.

When Syd first met her she was selling cigarettes from a tray in Ciro's nightclub on Sunset Boulevard. She was a poor girl from San Francisco who lived with her large family in a small apartment and worked to support them. (Charlie was especially touched by that.)

Simultaneously, one of the richest men in America, Huntington Hartford, the A & P heir, spotted her and fell in love. Marjorie now had two suitors – both of them handsome, attractive and eligible – and she loved them both. What was she to do? First, she would go out with Hunt for the evening. Outside her flat in Laurel Canyon, Sydney waited for him to say goodnight. As soon as Hartford left, Marjorie would bounce into Sydney's car and go out with him. Once, on the Chaplin tennis courts, Sydney and Hunt played a hard game – and whoever won the match took Marjie out. It was crazy; it was Hollywood.

Desperately in love, Sydney went to his father and told him Marjorie and he wanted to marry. He was about twenty-three at the time. "Do you love her, really love her?" Charlie asked. "Yes, Pa," Sydney replied. "Do you see yourself spending the rest of your life with her?" Sydney pondered. "No, Pa," he replied, "I guess I'll be like you and marry several times!"

Charlie went into a white-hot rage. "Listen," he said, "I never went into any of my marriages with that in mind. You don't get married with the thought that you're going to have other wives! Now listen to me – if this poor girl has the chance to marry one of the richest men in America, you keep out of the way. You've got plenty of time. You're a young actor – concentrate on your career." Marjorie married Huntington Hartford; for a while, Sydney was heartbroken.

Charlie spent long days getting *Limelight* right, fleshing out the story by ransacking his memories of the London music-hall and the world he knew as a child. He even wrote a one hundred thousand word novel to work himself into the characters.

Charlie kept to a strict daily routine. By ten o'clock, after a breakfast of crisp bacon and eggs with toast, English marmalade and hot coffee, he was ready to work with a secretary. Then he wrote or dictated part of the *Limelight* script. He would stop for lunch, but never a heavy meal – something light – perhaps one chop, or cottage cheese, or a hard-boiled egg. He wanted nothing that could dull his senses. After lunch he'd go back to the script until four o'clock. Then it was tennis. He played as though it was a matter of life and death. After an intense game, he'd

RON RANDELL and Diana Douglas have leading roles in George B. Shaw's "Major Barbara," Circle Players' production at the Circle Theater. Kathleen Freeman and Strother Martin are group members.
PACIFIC COAST LEAGUE

RON RANDELL AS ADOLPHUS CUSINS AND DIANA DOUGLAS (MOTHER OF MICHAEL) AS BARBARA IN SHAW'S *MAJOR BARBARA*. THIS PRODUCTION RESTORED OUR PRESTIGE AND FORTUNES AFTER OUR DISASTROUS PERIOD AT THE CORONET.

walk back to the house with his head covered in towels, ready for a steam bath. Then he'd emerge fresh as a daisy, looking forward to the evening: one drink and a great dinner, and afterwards perhaps a visit to the Circle.

While Charlie was busy working on *Limelight*, Constance enlisted Oona to join her in exercise classes. The class was run by Walter Saxer, a German Swiss imported by David O. Selznick to help groom his new wife, Jennifer Jones. Constance would appear in her leotards, and go through all his modern dance techniques. His male clients included Gary Cooper and Humphrey Bogart. Saxer also taught etiquette and comportment, and showed young actresses how to cultivate the aura of a star. Those were the days!

Constance felt I needed grooming too, and insisted I join the men's class. I enjoyed my lessons. Overnight, I became a new person. Saxer was now giving me the star treatment – teaching me to hold in my chest, keep my head at the correct angle, and sit with my back erect. He was so impressed with my progress that he asked me to demonstrate my new look for Oona and Constance. I dangled my hands between my legs like Gary Cooper, and walked with my head held high, overlooking the heads of everyone present. After I had proved my mettle, to the applause of Oona and Constance, I slowly slipped back to my former self.

One evening, when Constance, Phyllis and I were invited by the Chaplins for dinner at their home, Charlie insisted that I read the *Limelight* script aloud. As I read, Constance, seated on the couch, would murmur in her low, resonant voice, "Marvelous, Charlie, marvelous! It'll be the best thing you've ever done!" The next thing I knew, she was snoring. One night Charlie told me, "When *Limelight* goes, I want you to work with me." I was flattered, pleased, but I didn't know whether he was serious or not.

Thinking it would please Charlie, for our next production I presented William Gillette's *Sherlock Holmes*. He would often entrance the Circle actors by reciting complete scenes verbatim; this would have been at least forty years after he had played Billy the pageboy in the show. The play opened, but Charlie never came. Revisiting the past can be painful, and he probably wanted to stay with his memories.

The Circle's fortunes were still not completely restored; we needed a thumping smash hit. To help boost the actors' confidence, I presented a revue, *Meet the Circle*. The first half consisted of scenes from past

LEFT: OONA'S MOTHER, AGNES BOULTON, WITH GERALDINE.

CENTER: ME AFTER BEING GROOMED BY WALTER SAXER.

BOTTOM: OONA IN BEVERLY HILLS.

LEFT: SYDNEY CHAPLIN, PAUL LEVITT AND AN UNKNOWN ACTOR IN A SONG-AND-DANCE ROUTINE IN OUR MEET THE CIRCLE REVUE.

BELOW: CHARLIE ON THE SET OF CHARLEY'S AUNT, WITH HIS BROTHER SYDNEY AS CHARLEY'S AUNT.

productions; the second was a variety show. Among other highlights, Bill Schallert performed a comic piano routine; Sydney provided impersonations of the great French star Raimu speaking gibberish while hunting for a collar button; Kathleen Freeman did a look-alike imitation of Charles Laughton in *Mutiny on the Bounty.*

Charlie's older brother Sydney, who had starred in the first film version of *Charley's Aunt,* came to the revue with his wife Gypsy, and told me about an old music-hall skit he knew. I roared with laughter, and quickly put it into the show.

The routine starts with a tap-dance number performed by two brothers. As one of them retreats backstage, the other brother (played by Sydney Jr), addresses the audience: "Ladies and gentlemen, my brother and I have decided to give up tap-dancing. My brother has developed a strong-man act, which he's been rehearsing for years." The brother now enters in leotards, and invites the audience to feel his biceps.

Then Sydney announces, "For the first time tonight, my brother will perform the *impossible*. We would like five members of the audience to stand on this table, while he lifts the table up WITH HIS TEETH!" There's a slight titter from the audience, as Sydney helps the five volunteers onto the small table. They stand squashed together, feeling embarrassed. The brother now surveys his task and flexes his muscles. To the sound of a drum-roll, he crouches and bites the edge of the table, struggling to lift it. As he grunts and groans, he spits out slivers of wood (we had balsa wood hidden there). Alas, he can't do it.

The strong-man ponders, stares at the table, then consults his brother. He's ready again. Another drum-roll. He crouches on his knees, bites the table – and again can't lift it. Finally, Sydney walks forward and announces, "Ladies and gentlemen, my brother and I have decided to go back to tap-dancing." Blackout.

Our audiences loved this ridiculous sketch, especially when the lights came on again, and the five volunteers were still standing sheepishly on the table. There was so much laughter, we couldn't go on with the show.

One night Sydney Sr volunteered to stand on the table. Then, to our astonishment he suddenly performed a flip-flop, thinking he'd get us an extra laugh. But as he twirled, he hit his head against the edge of the table and fell to the floor. Gypsy and the audience gasped; it was dreadful seeing this elderly man lying prostrate. Luckily he rose unharmed, smiled, and the act continued. But we lost our laughs for the rest of the night. Charlie was shocked and shook his head when he heard about the accident: "Leave it to Sydney!" he said, "He'll do absolutely anything for a laugh!"

Little did I know that, despite the success of our revue, a group of Circle actors were plotting a mutiny behind the scenes. Some leading players felt they were not getting the parts they deserved. But it was the infiltration of two newcomers that spread the seeds of dissent. They began a whispering campaign to ruin the theater and me.

It's very hard in an organization to satisfy everyone. Theater groups are like miniature governments, and actors become very competitive for the big parts. And small egos grow into big ones. At the Circle, many actors suggested plays, and I produced any that I thought had merit. Luckily I wasn't an actor, so they couldn't accuse me of choosing plays for myself.

But their grievances, I learned later, went beyond plays and parts. Most actors are conservative, and these were troublesome times. The Un-American Activities Committee was in full swing; blacklisting and Senator Joe McCarthy's witch-hunts were around the corner. The breakaway group apparently felt I was too political. I had allowed petitioners campaigning to ban the bomb to stand outside the theater gathering signatures. Like Charlie, I was sympathetic to the plight of the Hollywood Ten, who'd been thrown in jail for refusing to answer the famous question "Are you now, or have you ever been, a member of the

Communist Party?"; the writer Waldo Salt, blacklisted after his testimony before the Committee in 1950, spoke one night at the Circle. The mutineers thought my politics would come to reflect on themselves.

Some even felt that Chaplin's connection with the theater would also reflect on them. After all, the press were smearing him daily as an outright Red or a fellow traveler. At the Circle one afternoon, one of the actors approached Charlie with a copy of *Life* magazine, and showed him an article where he was called a pinko, along with Albert Einstein and Thomas Mann. Charlie jokingly replied, "Well, I'm in very good company!"

Years later, I was shown the FBI report on Chaplin. Hidden away in the voluminous pages was a reference to the Circle and myself; the FBI had even found out that I had worked with Charlie in Europe.

Other investigations in this frightening period involved my own family. When the Un-American Activities Committee began checking on the medical profession in Los Angeles, my mother's brother Milton London was among the doctors they were looking for. He was a dedicated socialist, and regularly tended to the Circle actors without charging them. My mother – who was completely apolitical, and didn't know what was going on – hid my uncle in her apartment. Several years later, she gave dinner to his friends Karen Morley, a film star in the 1930s, and her boy friend Lloyd Gough; they too were dodging the Committee.

I remember telling my mother about the nightmarish things that were happening. She looked at me, her face full of fear, her mind returning to the pogroms of Vilna, where both my parents' families came from. "You mustn't speak like that. As a Jew you must be careful. You'll get in trouble!" She didn't realize she too might have gotten into trouble for hiding and feeding her brother and his friends.

Los Angeles was a nervous town, and the atmosphere affected almost everyone. With the papers taking pot-shots at Charlie, he feared that he could become the victim of some fanatic. One evening at his house, after Oona had gone to bed, he was reading me a new scene from *Limelight,* where Calvero (the part Charlie was to play) tells Terry about the new romance that will come into her life: "And in the elegant melancholy of twilight, as the candles flutter and make your eyes dance, he will tell you that he loves you. And you will tell him you have always loved him . . ."

Afterwards, Charlie went to the piano and played the *Limelight* theme. Although he wasn't a trained musician, no one ever performed it with such feeling. It was just after midnight. I was about to say goodnight when we heard what sounded like someone walking across the lawn. From Charlie's glassed-in verandah, he thought he could see a figure moving. He was convinced that someone was out there, determined to get him.

He rushed towards a chest of drawers, picked up an enormous samurai sword, with a long, glistening, curved blade, and stood there frozen, waiting for the intruder. I gulped. We waited and waited for the villain to arrive. There was no one. We eventually decided the noise was caused by his favorite Siamese cat, Monkey, overturning something in the grounds. To this day, all Charlie's children have respect for that samurai sword.

The flashpoint for the Circle mutiny was a new play, *Mulligan's Snug*, by Robert McEnroe, author of the Broadway success *The Silver Whistle*. This was to follow our revue. The action took place in a Third Avenue bar across the street from Bellevue Hospital; the clientele were crazy young interns, who carried the tools of their trade with them – from stethoscopes to kidney specimens in jars. It was like a medical version of the TV comedy series *Cheers:* funny and wild, with great parts for all our actors. McEnroe – a strange Irishman whom we tried hard to please – came to the first reading. But he seemed to take a dislike to us, and suddenly pulled his play away. We were all shaken.

Once *Mulligan's Snug* was called off, the disgruntled actors asked to see me. They announced they were leaving, there and then, if I did not give in to all their demands for more involvement in the choice of plays and casting. But I was too angry at the way they held secret meetings, and refused to be blackmailed. The breakaway hurt me deeply – among them were the nucleus of actors who had approached me to start the theater. But I resolved to carry on, helped by stalwarts like Sydney, Bill Schallert, Naomi Stevens and Bob Burns. I felt Charlie approved of my attitude; he, too, would never succumb to blackmail.

Oona and Charlie invited me for dinner. I was happy to get away from the problems at the theater. When I arrived, Charlie was on the lawn with his barbecue red-hot, about to grill charcoal broiled steaks. No one charcoaled steaks better than he. They were perfect: burnt on the outside, medium rare inside. Even now my mouth waters at the thought of them. The butler came over with a tray of drinks, including a bottle of Pernod – that's what Oona and Charlie were drinking. I had never heard of it before; I very seldom drank – one drop of wine would make me tipsy. But Oona and Charlie insisted I taste it. I thought it was time to live dangerously.

I took one sip of the green liquid and turned to Oona and Charlie. "It tastes just like licorice!" I said; "What's the good of drinking if it doesn't have any effect?" Then I let out a cry. "My legs are numb! I can't feel a thing!" I touched my tongue: "It feels as though I've had novocaine!" I was completely and utterly plastered! Charlie and Oona roared with laughter.

The splinter group announced they would be opening their own theater-in-the-round shortly. I set my heart on making the next year, 1950, the Circle's greatest. The race for our smash hit was on!

Our publicist, George Boroff, introduced me to Aben Kandel, a Hollywood screenwriter and novelist, author of *City for Conquest* (filmed with James Cagney). He had written a play called *Kitty Doone* about a movie star fashioned after the likes of Joan Crawford and Ginger Rogers, who clawed her way up the ladder, achieved success, and fought to stay there. The title character was a fading star dying to play the virginal young heroine in a big costume picture; she felt it would revive her flagging career. I loved Aben's wit: he told me many tales of Hollywood, how Twentieth Century-Fox went berserk the minute Shirley Temple hit puberty, and how the studios groomed doubles to replace ageing or troublesome actresses. This was the stuff of *Kitty Doone*. The play was both funny and hard-hitting. I quickly put it into production: we desperately needed a new play, not another revival.

Our Kitty was Eleanor Reeves (wife of George Reeves, the TV Superman); she had all the necessary allure and toughness. And as the handsome country bumpkin with whom Kitty falls in love, we cast Allan Nixon, married to the actress Marie Wilson.

I remember the opening night vividly. The preview the night before had been great, but now it just wasn't taking off; the tempo collapsed, the actors had lead in their tongues. I was dying in my seat – we needed a success so badly. Nerves had completely taken over. I felt myself becoming ill. I wanted to leave; I tried to rise, but my legs wouldn't let me. I turned to Charlie, sitting next to me, and whispered semi-

TOP: OONA CONGRATULATING SYDNEY –
AND CHARLIE BEAMING PROUDLY – AFTER A
PERFORMANCE AT THE CIRCLE.

CENTER: ME OUTSIDE THE CIRCLE IN FRONT
OF A SMALL MARQUEE ANNOUNCING THE
WORLD PREMIÈRE OF SAROYAN'S THE SON.

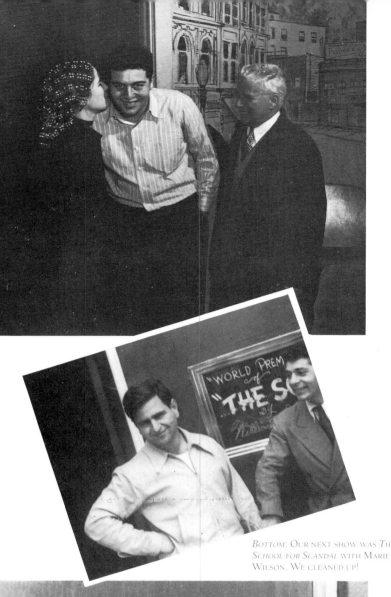

hysterically, "My legs are paralyzed! I can't feel my legs!" "Calm down,"
he whispered back, "you'll be alright." Sure enough, as soon as the play
began to take off, everything was fine. But for that brief period, I was
suffering from nervous paralysis. I always felt that moment in *Limelight*,
when Terry the ballet dancer cries to Calvero, "My legs!.. I have no
feeling in them! They're paralyzed!", was inspired by that incident at
the Circle.

Charlie's antennae were always up, responding to life around him.
Working with him in later years, I saw how much inspiration he drew
from his surroundings. Indeed, I always felt the Circle helped stimulate
him to make a film about the romance of the theater. Being around
actors must have rekindled his love for the stage. I recall his advice
when Robert Parrish (a child actor in *City Lights*) offered me a job on
his first directional assignment, *Cry Danger*. "Stay with the theater for
the moment," Charlie told me. "That's the trouble with movies –
directors don't know their theater. Everything comes from the stage.
Learn your theater first, and then you'll be more effective on the
screen."

Charlie found the premise of *Kitty Doone* fascinating. For a while he
dabbled with the idea of acquiring the film rights for Paulette Goddard.
They had been divorced since 1942, but I heard that as part of his
settlement, he had agreed to direct her in one more film. *Kitty Doone,* he
thought, would make an ideal vehicle.

While I was searching for the Circle's next hit, Charlie continued
his search for an actress with a special sparkle to play the heroine in
Limelight. Early in 1950, on a trip to New York with Oona, he passed
Radio City Music Hall and was riveted by a photo of one of the
Rockettes. "That's the girl!" he said excitedly. Arthur Kelly, vice-
president of United Artists, found out who she was and arranged for
Charlie to meet her. Charlie's face dropped when she introduced herself
– a terrible Brooklyn accent emerged. All her ascetic beauty seemed to
vanish into thin air.

Charlie and Oona went with Constance to see Katharine Hepburn
on Broadway in *As You Like It*. In the cast was a young actress, Cloris
Leachman. Charlie was impressed by her, and thought she could play
the girl in *Limelight*. But it was still early days. Backstage, Oona and
Charlie were introduced to Hepburn's mother – well-known as an
outspoken advocate of birth control. Pointing to Oona, Constance

BOTTOM: OUR NEXT SHOW WAS THE
SCHOOL FOR SCANDAL WITH MARIE
WILSON. WE CLEANED UP!

proudly declared, "Isn't it wonderful? This young girl is the mother of three children!" Mrs Hepburn quickly replied, "Nothing wonderful about that. The wonderful thing would be *not* having them!"

We followed *Kitty Doone* with a new William Saroyan play, *The Son of a Bitch*. Only Saroyan in those days would have given a play that title. The newspapers wouldn't advertise it, so we changed the title to *The S.O.B.* They still wouldn't take the ads, so we ended up performing *The Son*. This was second-rate Saroyan, yet we staged it with flair, and business was good.

During rehearsals, Saroyan's cousin Ross Bagdasarian sang a song he'd written with Saroyan, "Come-on-a-my House". Entranced, I worked both Ross and his song into the show. When Charlie heard the song, he too fell for it and sang it incessantly around his house, though he could never remember more than the first line: "Come-on-a my house, I'm gonna buy you candy ...". I arranged for Al Youngman, a music publisher friend of mine, to hear the song, hoping he'd do something with it. "Jerry," he said, "it's not good, but because of you, I'll publish it, and give the Circle fifty per cent of any profits." It was published, but nothing happened. I kept asking Al what he was doing about the song. "No one wants it," he said. "It's just lying on the shelves."

A year later, "Come-on-a-my House" became the Number One hit in America. I called up Al: "Al," I said, "they're playing our song! 'Come-on-a-my House' is a big hit!" "Do you know," he replied, "we're losing money on that song?" I said to him, "If you lose money on a hit, how do you make money?" Of course, we never saw a cent. A year later he had the chutzpah to ask if I could get him the rights to Charlie's *Limelight* music. "Al," I asked, "are you still losing money on 'Come-on-a-my House?'" That ended that.

"Come-on-a-my House" catapulted Rosemary Clooney to fame. At least we had the satisfaction of seeing on all the discs: "From the Circle Players' Production, *The Son*."

The breakaway group's theater had just opened. We were now in direct competition. Where was our smash hit?

It turned out to be just around the corner. During our production of *Kitty Doone*, Marie Wilson, one of Hollywood's original dumb blondes, begged me to let her appear in a show. Marie was a Warner Brothers contract player who had made her mark starring opposite James Cagney and Pat O'Brien in *Boy Meets Girl,* and rose to greater fame as the scatterbrained Irma in *My Friend Irma.* The type of vehicle she was known for was not the type of play we did at the Circle. But Marie was persistent. She would wait for me outside the theater, sitting on the curb. She looked like a waif, in a white angora hat that completely covered her blond tresses.

I succumbed. I told Marie I would do a play when I found the right vehicle for her. I went to the downtown Los Angeles library (always my favorite reading place) and pored over their theater books, searching for something suitable. I hit on Richard Brinsley Sheridan's Restoration comedy *The School for Scandal*. When I read the part of Lady Teazle, the little country bumpkin who comes to town and captivates London society, I knew I had found the right one!

The critics said it was the casting sensation of the year. Robert Balzer in his Bulletin observed, "The ghost of Garrick bows to Jerry Epstein of the Circle Theatre for casting Miss Wilson as Lady Teazle. No less a thespian than Charles Coburn was heard by our ears to offer his gratification that at long last an actress had been cast who could bring to the role a fresh and youthful naivety always absent in performances by ladies with more ponderous reputations." *Life* magazine ran a story on Marie and the Circle. We could have filled a thousand seats a night; tickets were impossible to get.

During the run, Marie came to the theater at about four in the afternoon. The first thing she did was get down on her hands and knees to scrub all our toilets. Then she applied her make-up. I loved going into her dressing-room and watching her at work. She arrived looking like Little Orphan Annie, unrecognizable as a glamour girl. Then the most amazing transformation took place – better than any Spielberg special effect. First she powdered her face, shoulders and bosom. Then she rouged everything; then the white powder again, until they blended together into a peaches and cream complexion.

Now came her magnificent bosom, which she made up with equal zeal. By the time she had put on her blonde wig and squeezed into her costume – especially designed to emphasize her assets – she seemed the most tantalizing beauty on earth. When Marie made her first entrance, the audience gasped; they did the same whenever she leaned forward, which was often.

Charlie came to watch rehearsals and was equally captivated by

OPPOSITE: THIS PICTURE OF MARIE WILSON IN *THE SCHOOL FOR SCANDAL* APPEARED IN *LIFE* MAGAZINE IN JUNE 1950. I'D ALWAYS THOUGHT THE AUDIENCE CAME TO SEE SHERIDAN, BUT I WAS TOLD I WAS MISTAKEN!

RIGHT: ANNA NEAGLE AFTER A PERFORMANCE OF *THE TIME OF YOUR LIFE*, DISCUSSING THE PLAY WITH ME. ON HER LEFT IS HER HUSBAND, FILM PRODUCER HERBERT WILCOX AND, ON HIS LEFT, ELSA SCHALLERT (MOTHER OF BILL).

Marie. He told her he had wanted her in *Monsieur Verdoux,* as the girl who sells Verdoux a flower, but thought she'd consider the role too small. Marie sounded so disappointed: "Oh, I would have done it!" she cried.

Then Charlie watched the scene where Marie, as Lady Teazle, plays cards with Lady Sneerwell and others. Standing behind Lady Teazle observing the card game, was Crabtree, played by Charlie's half-brother, Wheeler Dryden. Wheeler, the son of Charlie's mother and a well-known music hall artist, Leo Dryden, had turned up on Charlie's doorstep one day, announcing "You may not know it, but I'm your brother." Charlie, who placed a high value on family loyalty, put him to work.

While rehearsing, Charlie saw a place for a new piece of business with Marie. He made Wheeler look over Marie's shoulder; seeing him, Marie quickly hid her cards close to her bosom. Updating Sheridan, Charlie improvised a line for his brother: "Madame, I was *not* looking at your cards!" The laughter shook the theater.

After rehearsals, Charlie showed the cast a book about the Delsarte theory of acting. François Delsarte, a nineteenth-century French philosopher, argued that the physical stances an actor adopted – the way he stood, slumped, sat, etc. – indicated character and inner feeling. From that point on an actor built his characterization. In his book, *The System of Dramatic Expression,* every position and attitude was illustrated. "You'll be amazed how helpful it can be," Charlie said. Our actors eagerly rushed out to find copies.

Marie found it hard to learn lines. Especially Restoration lines. She was used to films, where she memorized about three minutes of dialogue per day. The Circle's theater-in-the-round allowed for no prompters: there was simply nowhere to hide them. One night, during the famous screen scene where Lady Teazle is discovered by her husband in another man's house, Marie launched into her long speech asking for his forgiveness. "Hear me, Sir Peter!" she began. An expectant silence. "Hear me, Sir Peter . . . Oh Jerry," she cried, spotting me in the audience. "I've forgotten my lines! Will you ever forgive me?" She then turned to the audience and begged *their* forgiveness. The audience took her straight to their hearts and applauded – she could get away with anything. Bill Schallert, as her husband, gave her the line, and the play continued.

British actors came in droves to see *The School for Scandal.* Charles Laughton, a regular visitor, sometimes took the actors to the Gotham restaurant on Hollywood Boulevard. Sitting at the head of the table, he'd say, "Come, you whores, eat up!" Then he'd perform monologues from Shakespeare. Anna Neagle came after a day's shooting, and saw *The Time of Your Life* with her husband Herbert Wilcox. "I arrived exhausted," she told us afterwards, "and now I'm completely refreshed!"

David Niven and Robert Coote were frequent visitors. Niven was always intrigued as to how we managed to stage plays in such a tiny environment and not be worried by the proximity of the audience. The situation never bothered Alfred Hitchcock, who came with Sidney Bernstein (now Lord Bernstein, creator of Granada Television), sat in the front row and watched the play with his eyes closed. Later, I told Sidney it was rather embarrassing having Hitchcock asleep, especially when everyone recognized him. Sidney relayed the message; Hitchcock told Sidney to tell me, "I wasn't asleep. I see through my eyelids!" I never swallowed that one!

While *The School for Scandal* was playing, Brooks Atkinson of the *New York Times*, the dean of American critics, asked me if he could possibly meet Chaplin. I called the house; Charlie said to bring him over for a drink the following evening. Charlie always mixed up names, and all night long he called Brooks Atkinson "Dean" and discussed politics.

To this day I believe he thought he was entertaining Dean Acheson, the American Secretary of State.

While *The School for Scandal* went its merry way, Shelley Winters begged me to let her direct a play. I put her into the New Theatre, next door. She was a Method actress, and the noise that came through the walls was phenomenal. Four-letter words finally came to the Circle!

The School for Scandal could have run for ever. But we had to close because of our subscriptions. I had to top this somehow: there could be no letdown, now that we were gathering momentum. But new plays were hard to find. I thought of mounting Barrie's *The Admirable Crichton*, but Constance steered me away – "It's not Barrie's best" – and suggested *What Every Woman Knows*. I read it and shared Constance's enthusiasm. This was the drama of an impoverished Scots scholar who becomes an MP thanks to the support of his plain but spunky wife. Charlie agreed to help with directing.

Opposite: The card-playing scene from The School for Scandal. Standing behind Marie Wilson is Wheeler Dryden, Charlie's half-brother, to whom Charlie gave the line that became a show-stopper – "Madam, I was not looking at your cards." Seated on the left is Naomi Stevens as Lady Sneerwell, and opposite her is Janet Brandt as Mrs Candour.

Right: In the street during an intermission, seemingly unperturbed by my crazy tie, David Niven and Robert Coote discussing the Circle Theatre with Terry Kilburn and me.

Sydney was a natural choice to play the young Scotsman, John Shand. Charlie was still determined to help his son's career – when MGM offered Syd a contract after seeing him at the Circle, his father urged him to hold off until he had worked with him in *Limelight*.

Finding Maggie, our heroine, was a problem. No one at the Circle fitted the bill. Then Oona suggested Ruth Conte, Richard Conte's wife. She was petite, oozing with charm. I asked if she was an actress; yes, she said, from the New York stage. She read for me; we had found our Maggie.

Bill Schallert was the nominal director and blocked out the play. Then Charlie came in to watch rehearsals, squatting on his haunches on top of his seat. On this project he excelled himself. Charlie's trick was to allow no sentiment or self-pity to creep in to the playing. Barrie always had a tendency to sugary writing, and Charlie knew that you must play against it. Once the lines were delivered hard and factually, the piece took on another dimension. He also toned down the heavy Scots accents our actors were attempting. "Suggestion is all you need. People have to understand what you're saying, and here they're all California-born and bred!"

As Charlie buckled down to work in the main auditorium, Shelley Winters entered her third month rehearsing Robert Ardrey's *Thunder Rock* next door. By now Anthony Quinn had come in to advise. The profanities shook the building. We shut the doors firmly, and went back to our work on gentle Barrie.

Among those observing our rehearsals was Lillian Ross, the writer and journalist. She was as fascinated as the rest of us with Charlie's direction, and wrote down her impressions, published in *The New Yorker* in 1978:

Let's get away from acting . . . Give the audience the feeling that they're looking through the keyhole . . .

Chaplin slouched down in his seat, biting his thumbnail, and watched quietly . . . until Sydney Chaplin came onstage, in the role of the ambitious young man who breaks into the family's home to study their books . . . Chaplin leaped to his feet, and, elbowing his son out of the chair, demonstrated how an interloper makes himself comfortable in someone else's house . . . "Get the drama in this, Sydney," Chaplin said, returning to his seat. "It's a situation. Make it clean."

BELOW CENTER: PAUL HENREID AT THE PIANO AFTER A PERFORMANCE AT THE CIRCLE, ENTERTAINING ME, KATHLEEN AND SYDNEY. HENREID STILL HAS HIS *NOW VOYAGER* CIGARETTE. I MUST HAVE REALLY LIKED THAT TIE!

Again, he hunched down in his seat. A moment later, he was back on his feet. "Sydney, for Christ's sake . . . Just say the thing. You're not cheeky . . . You're indignant. They think you're a burglar, and, goddammit, you're not. You're a student."

Shortly afterward, he burst out laughing with what seemed to be pure pleasure. "Great humor!" he said as Sydney spoke with indignation . . . "Charming," he went on. "Lovely humor. Lovely." He gave a little sigh of satisfaction.

Once again Constance was there, letting the world know she totally disagreed with Charlie's approach. He whispered to me, annoyed, "I don't want her here." This time Constance removed herself. But from the foyer she bellowed: "Charlie, you *haven't read the play!*"

Their battle came to a head over the performance of Ruth Conte. According to Ruth, Charlie took her aside and told her, "If Constance tries giving you direction, don't listen!" Shortly afterwards, Ruth received a phone call from Phyllis, suggesting tea and a talk with Constance. Ruth accepted, hoping for an innocent chat. But Constance insisted on discussing how she should play the part. Charlie was furious when he heard about it and told Ruth to forget everything Constance had told her.

In our final production, James Barrie's *What Every Woman Knows*, Charlie surpassed himself; it was our best production ever. To this day I meet people who talk about it.

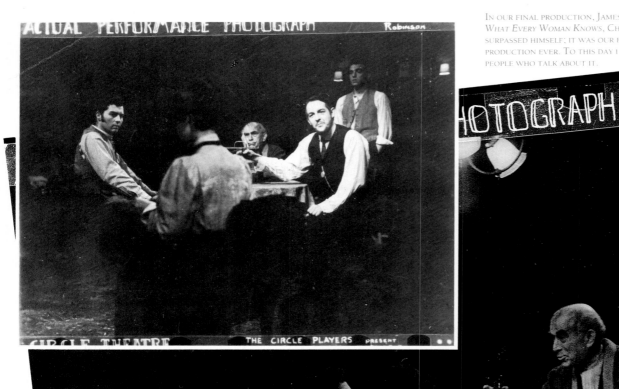

ACTUAL PERFORMANCE PHOTOGRAPH Robinson

CIRCLE THEATRE THE CIRCLE PLAYERS PRESENT

PHOTOGRAPH Jerome Robinson

THE CIRCLE PLAYERS PRESENT
"WHAT EVERY WOMAN KNOWS"
PRODUCED BY JERRY
CIRCLE THEATRE DIRECTED BY WILLIAM SCHALLERT
HOLLYWOOD CALIFORNIA

Main picture: In the foreground, Ruth Conte as Maggie; behind her, Sydney Chaplin as John Shand; and to the right, Bill Schallert as her elder brother.

Inset: Bill Schallert and Bob Sherman on the point of making a deal with Sydney Chaplin regarding their sister Maggie.

Bob Sherman, cast as one of the family's young brothers, has fond memories of the production: "Charlie's whole body would impart to you what he wanted you to do. It was osmosis. When he gave line readings, he didn't worry about the exact words, he'd say, 'And so and so and so and so', concentrating on the choreography and the emotion. But Charlie's 'so and sos' were worth an hour of detailed instructions from any other director."

Ruth responded beautifully to Charlie's style, and he grew more and more excited with her performance. He couldn't wait to return to the theater the next day and start rehearsals with her all over again. "He'd never verbalize what he wanted," Ruth told me recently. "He'd only articulate technical things, about gestures and moves. You had to put yourself in his place and feel intuitively what he wanted."

As on previous plays, Sydney found working with his father trying but exhilarating: "He'd expect me to fall into the performance immediately. With the other people, he'd give them more time. But he did give me a sense of tempo and realism; he was a great theater director – better than any of the Broadway directors I eventually worked with. My father said he learned about the theater when he was directed as a kid by some old Scotsman with a strange tic. He used to scratch his leg when he was excited and say 'Yes, that's good!' Then he'd whip off his hat and scratch his leg again. Everything about the theater, my father claimed, he learned from this Scotsman with the tic!"

For me, that production was our greatest triumph. It showed Charlie and the Circle at their best. Charlie was delighted: everything worked out just as he wanted. All of Hollywood came: Gene Kelly, Betsy Blair, John Garfield, Eleanor Powell, Rhonda Fleming, Jane Russell, Otto Preminger, Glenn Ford. The audience loved it, and even the critics appreciated Charlie's approach to the play. "Characters behave like hard-headed human beings," wrote Patterson Greene in the *Examiner*. "There is salt in the dialogue as well as sugar, and the Barrie tenderness is not allowed to befog the Barrie craftsmanship."

On the opening night, the producer Sam Spiegel threw a big party for the cast (his wife, Lynn Baggett, was playing the Countess). The Circle folk moved among the celebrities, standing tall, feeling proud at bringing off a successful show. After Zero Mostel had performed his coffee percolator imitation, Bob Sherman found himself sitting next to Humphrey Bogart at the Spiegel bar. Bogart was snarling beady-eyed at the Circle actors: "Who are all these creeps?" he said. We were completely deflated.

Later I found Constance and Charlie sitting on a sofa, both complaining about needing sleeping pills at night. They were overheard by an Oscar-winning female star, who must remain nameless. She piped up: "Oh, I never take a sleeping pill! I just place my head on the pillow and fall right to sleep!" Constance looked at her and murmured in a low voice, "That's because you *are* a sleeping pill, my dear."

The powerful columnist Hedda Hopper showed up one night, which took us all by surprise. Several weeks earlier, she had dug her knife into Charlie over a benefit showing of *The Circus*: "While our boys die in Korea," Hopper wrote in her column, "Chaplin's picture is making money for the Commie opposition!" All of which was a bundle of lies. Years later, I discovered that Hopper regularly fed slanders and slurs about Charlie's alleged Red activities straight to the FBI, and wrote to Richard Nixon for his help. Nixon wrote back agreeing that something must definitely be done about this man.

After the performance, Hopper gave me a grilling: "Is it true Charlie Chaplin had a finger in this?" she asked, her voice drenched in vitriol. It was like being before the Spanish Inquisition. As with all such questions, I just laughed the matter off.

When Charlie came to see the play some weeks later, he was appalled that the things he had worked so hard to keep out – the self-pity, the superfluous gestures – had now crept in. But the audiences still loved it.

The ending remains one of the most moving moments I have ever seen in the theater. Just before the final curtain, Maggie Shand turns to her husband: "Oh, John, if only you could laugh at me. Laugh, John, laugh …" And John, now realizing that Maggie is the reason for his success, comes to her and slowly tries to laugh. We accompanied the moment with beautiful music by Grieg.

Oona, who is not sentimental, was misty-eyed.

Oh, yes: Shelley Winters's *Thunder Rock* finally opened, and closed.

I always used to say I didn't want to die in Los Angeles. I was still in my twenties, and I wanted to see the world. After the breakaway, for all the successes of 1950, something had been lost. Especially when I discovered that the breakaway group were trying to close down the

AFTER THE OPENING OF *WHAT EVERY WOMAN KNOWS* SAM SPIEGEL THREW A PARTY AT HIS HOME. LOTS OF STARS WERE PRESENT – OONA AND CHARLIE, HUMPHREY BOGART, LAUREN BACALL, JOHN GARFIELD.

MAIN PICTURE: SPIEGEL WITH HIS WIFE, LYNN BAGETT, AND ZERO MOSTEL.

INSET: THERE I AM AT THE PARTY, STILL DISCUSSING THE THEATER WITH CONSTANCE! AFTER MY SELF-IMPROVEMENT CLASSES, I'M NOW WEARING BROOKS BROTHERS SUITS AND BLACK TIES!

Circle. They had filed complaints with Actors' Equity against the Circle management – Sydney, Bill and me; Equity declared we had to increase our actors' salaries. It was now impossible to do Saroyanesque plays with forty people. We had always been totally honest, giving our actors whatever we could from the box-office receipts. But how much money could you take in? The top price was three dollars, we only sat one hundred and fifty, and there were all the bills for rent, electricity, props, costumes and royalties. Once Equity stepped in, it was clear we had to rethink.

The heart was taken out of me and I wanted to leave Los Angeles. Although Charlie still talked about finding a job for me on *Limelight,* the script was not yet finished. I didn't know when production would start, or if he really wanted me. It was all very vague. Besides, I was tired. It was very difficult putting on plays at the Circle, the New Theatre, the Coronet, Christmas pantomimes for children . . .

After a rest, I decided to go to New York, and start a new Circle, the city's first theater-in-the-round. I was walking away from all my achievements in Los Angeles, but I knew it was necessary; I felt stifled. Before I left, Constance called me. "You can't go to New York with the clothes you have – you'll freeze! You must get a good winter coat. I'm speaking to Huntington Hartford, and I'm coming with you to buy one."

She did. Bless her. Constance, Phyllis and I went to Magnum's on Wilshire Boulevard, and they picked out the most beautiful black cashmere coat, costing a hundred dollars – a big sum in those days. Constance grandly sent Hunt the bill. I was so moved by her sweetness and kindness. I still am to this day.

I don't know how Charlie really felt about my departure for New York. He was wrapped up in *Limelight,* and nothing else seemed to concern him. But he wished me luck, bade me farewell, and before I left I received a message from his studio: he was giving me a gift of a thousand dollars, via Sydney.

In retrospect, I see that if I'd had more foresight, I would have held onto the Circle. I could have leased the building, returned when I wanted, and mounted many more plays. I still regret not doing Chekhov, my favorite dramatist. But I'm proud of the fact that we were always self-supporting and I've had the great pleasure of seeing many young people launch their careers in our makeshift theater at North El Centro. I've watched the Circle's influence spread throughout Los Angeles to the Mark Taper Theater and Ted Mann's Circle-in-the-Square in New York, and many other theaters-in-the-round. I know the Circle meant a lot to Charlie and Oona. And now I was giving it all up – everything I had accomplished – to try my luck in New York.

LIME 4 LIGHT

New York was freezing when I arrived. I moved into a cold 2 × 2 room with one electric bulb. The apartment house was filled with layabouts, drunks and screaming children, and the room had no heating. I slept at night with my new cashmere coat wrapped around me. What a contrast from Los Angeles.

Nearby lived Marilyn Clark, the girl who had first enticed me into the theater at UCLA. She was now married to a theatrical agent, Danny Hollywood (yes, that was his real name), who eventually hit the jackpot with his client George Axelrod and *The Seven Year Itch*. They lived in a large one-room apartment on West Seventy-Fourth Street, which became my home away from home. When it was too cold in my room, I slept on their sofa. Their apartment also became a meeting place for old and new faces: Naomi Riordan, from the Circle, Cloris Leachman and her future husband George Englund (later to direct Brando in *The Ugly American*). We kept sane by playing Monopoly every night.

Marilyn and Danny were kind. They listened to my dreams for a theater-in-the-round in Greenwich Village. I decided to stage a performance of *The Adding Machine* to entice backers, and we rehearsed at night in Marilyn's apartment. With Danny's help I rented a ballroom for one night at the Hotel Pennsylvania. We rounded up chairs and a platform and began struggling to find an audience. It seemed to be my destiny.

Joe Mantell repeated his role of Mr Zero. Marilyn Clark was our best Daisy yet, and Sheldon Harnick, later to win fame as the lyricist of *Fiddler On The Roof*, appeared in the company scene. People were astonished by what we accomplished. But one performance was not enough to raise the necessary money. Although they were intrigued by

the idea of theater-in-the-round, no one thought it would work in New York. Besides, Easterners had an in-bred disdain for anything emanating from the West Coast.

Money was running short. How long can you live on Nedick's hot dogs?

Sydney was entrusted to give me the thousand dollars from his father. I kept calling him at the Beverly Hills Tennis Club, asking him to send the money. Unfortunately, Sydney was short of cash at the time – so the money was a very long time coming. I had to get a job: I found one as a night receptionist in a slinky hotel on Eighth Avenue, full of pimps and prostitutes. Weekends were spent with relatives in Brooklyn. What a salvation! Aunt Rose, Uncle Harry and my two cousins Irving and Lennie took me in and gave me enough food to last a week. There is nothing like family.

The Andrews Sisters opened at the Roxy Theater. They always gave me a lift, and for the next two weeks I found another home away from home. Patti had now married Wally Weschler, and LaVerne married their trumpeter. Maxene divorced Lou Levy.

Constance and Phyllis were also in town. They had a small but lovely apartment on Fifty-Seventh Street, across from Carnegie Hall. Every time I visited, Constance would say, "You *just* missed Garbo by five minutes!" I was always missing Greta Garbo by five minutes. Even when I arrived five minutes early, I always missed her by five minutes.

Katharine Hepburn was due to meet John Huston and the *African Queen* film crew in London. Constance and Phyllis were accompanying her, and I went to see them off on a tramp steamer. Before Hepburn arrived, Constance was dreading the trip. "That woman has so much *energy*," she sighed, "I'll have to race with her every morning around the deck!" Then Hepburn stormed onto the boat. Constance threw her arms around her, bubbling over with excitement: "Oh Kate, won't it be *marvelous!* Every morning the two of us will run around the deck! We'll get *so* much exercise!" I caught Phyllis's mournful expression. I could tell she was not looking forward to it.

Before Constance left she called Lawrence Langner, of the Theatre Guild, on my behalf. He had visited the Circle two years before. In his office I told him my plans about starting a Circle Theatre in New York. Langner, who was very shrewd, became very excited. He introduced me to his son Philip, and suggested the two of us look for a site; he himself would help with the financing. I was overjoyed. The breakthrough had come. But Philip didn't seem keen to follow in his father's footsteps. They were formidable steps to follow: the Theatre Guild, at the time, was the most prestigious theater organization in America. Philip was more interested in films.

In California, Charlie was putting the finishing touches to the *Limelight* script and composing the music-hall numbers he'd perform as Calvero, the ageing comedian. But he was still preoccupied with finding a leading lady. He interviewed every ingenue in Los Angeles, including Marilyn Monroe. But no luck.

Arthur Kelly of United Artists contacted me. Charlie asked if I would audition actresses in New York. So I too began interviewing ingenues, including an unknown Anne Bancroft (then known as Anne Marno). I recorded the best of them on disc, doing the "I'm walking" scene, where Terry discovers she has regained the use of her legs. Oona and Charlie told me later they had the biggest laugh listening to these actresses with New York accents, trying to be English. "Calvero, look!" they'd all say, "I'm *warking!* I'm *warking!* … I'M WARKING, CALVERO!!"

Charlie realized he'd need an English actress for the part, although he always said he preferred working with American actresses – they were so relaxed. Arthur Laurents, the playwright, had seen Claire Bloom on the London stage in Christopher Fry's *Ring Around the Moon*, and suggested her to Charlie. She was supposed to send photographs, but didn't; she couldn't believe Chaplin was seriously interested. But they were quickly sent off after she received a telegram from him.

Claire always felt Charlie was interested in her because of her

Léo Kouper's painting "Charles Chaplin dans *Limelight*".

resemblance to Oona. But, though they were both young and dark-haired, Charlie would never pick an actress for that reason. He wanted the best person for the part. He adored ingenues like Deanna Durbin and Priscilla Lane; they had a special warmth and sparkle in their eyes that he loved. He always insisted that personality was the most important ingredient for the screen. But for the role of Terry, as he would say, he needed a young Duse.

Claire Bloom was flying to New York for a screen test and Charlie asked if I'd help him. He arrived anxious and excited, the script held tightly in his hand. *Limelight,* his newest baby, was about to be born!

He immediately took me on one of those blister-inducing walks through Manhattan – down Fifth Avenue, Broadway, Fourteenth Street, the Village, the East Side, the Battery – always reliving the past. It was Sunday in New York. Charlie was tireless, and he never seemed hungry. I was starving. He talked about the great meal we'd have at night, and that's all I looked forward to as we trudged through the city. Night came; Charlie still wasn't hungry. Finally, he realized the color had drained from my face. "You need some hot soup!" Charlie cried. We went to Luchow's, on Fourteenth Street, for boiled beef. He raved about it. But the great meal was an anti-climax. Charlie had never tasted my mother's boiled beef.

As we walked through the streets Charlie went completely unrecognized – so unlike his first visit to New York after his Hollywood success, when he stopped traffic on Broadway. In the evening, we strolled through Times Square. Charlie loved mingling with the crowds and watching them meander (later he tried to capture that feeling in *A King In New York*). Walking towards Forty-Seventh Street, we passed Ava Gardner and Frank Sinatra (currently appearing at the New York Paramount). No one seemed to recognize them either.

The next night Charlie took me to Le Pavillion, the most exclusive French restaurant in New York. Joan Crawford sat at the best table eyeing everyone who came in. I was living it up, working with Charlie during the day, enjoying the comforts of fabulous restaurants at night. But afterwards I returned to my cold, 2 × 2 room with one electric bulb, no rugs, and no heating. Charlie used to tell me how the *Ziegfeld Follies* depressed him: he knew that when the show was over, those glamorous girls dressed to kill in feathers and sequins all went home to miserable cold water apartments. That's the way I felt.

Claire – only nineteen at the time – arrived the next day with her mother. Charlie knew the correct thing to do and met them at the airport. Riding back to his hotel, the Sherry Netherlands, he told them the story of *Limelight* and the atmosphere he was trying to capture, and listened fascinated to Claire's stories of what his London now looked like.

He gave Claire a script, and marked two scenes for her to learn. The script had to be returned to me every evening. Charlie wouldn't allow it to go out of our hands. He was always afraid of people stealing his ideas.

The next day, rehearsals began in Charlie's suite. It was the scene when Calvero comes home after being booed at the Middlesex Theater. "It's no use. I'm finished; I'm through," he sobs. The "I'm walking" scene then followed. Charlie gave Claire every look, inflection and gesture. And, just as when he directed at the Circle, he would change his mind as soon as he discovered something better.

Claire was quite remarkable. She had a perfect ear, and followed Charlie's instructions to the letter. Charlie thought her performance wonderful, but wouldn't commit himself until he saw how she looked on film. I directed the test with Charlie at Twentieth Century-Fox's New York studios. I loved Charlie for that. He just threw me into the cold water and made me swim.

Later, in his hotel suite, Charlie suddenly panicked. "She's to play a ballet dancer," he cried, "and we haven't seen her legs!" Both of us were too shy to ask Claire to lift her skirt. Charlie eventually came up with the answer: "We must ask her, very casually, to get into a ballet costume and dance around." That way, we'd be able to tell. Claire states in her autobiography that she was wise to our ruse. Thank God her legs were good!

Claire and her mother were desperate to know what Charlie thought before they returned to London. I tried to be encouraging, and told her Charlie liked her very much. But I knew enough not to overdo it, since it would be such a disappointment if Charlie decided not to use her. I learned very early on, working with Charlie, that he was liable to change his mind. And this decision had to be his alone. Claire waited months before she knew the result. I wouldn't like to have been in her shoes.

What a let-down after Charlie left for Los Angeles! I went back to the business of looking for money for an off-Broadway theater, and trying to support myself. Arthur Kelly, realizing I was broke, loaned me ten dollars for dinner one night.

I had no news from Charlie. I was dying to know about Claire's test and his future plans. Did he still want me to work with him? "Out of sight, out of mind," I was beginning to think. Then I received a telegram from Oona and Charlie announcing the birth, on May 19th, of their third daughter, Victoria Agnes.

A letter finally arrived from Charlie. Oona must have made him write, because he was a terrible correspondent. He said he was still undecided about Claire, but had shown the test to many Hollywood friends, including Salka Viertel, Garbo's screenwriter and great friend. She thought Claire was wonderful and could play the role of Terry; but Charlie still could not make up his mind.

Charlie always agonized over decisions – so afraid he'd make the wrong one. Even if his revered Duse had auditioned, he would suddenly have had doubts. But now, with the script finished and the music composed, he was anxious to start production. I still didn't know if he wanted me; there was no word in the letter. But shortly after, I heard that Claire Bloom had been selected.

Winter arrived. Although I had just directed a play at the Theatre Guild's Westport summer theater, I was becoming desperate. That room was getting me down. And then I received a call from Arthur Kelly. Charlie wanted me to come to Los Angeles to work on *Limelight*. He offered me a hundred dollars a week.

I met Arthur at his office. I had gone through such a tough time with money in New York that in my own mind I thought it would be nice to clear a hundred dollars a week, *after* taxes. Arthur suggested I ask Charlie for a hundred and twenty-five dollars (I knew twenty five dollars would be deducted), and assured me it would be alright. When Charlie heard that, he apparently hit the ceiling, and I was quickly notified that he was employing someone else.

At the time I was shaken. But in retrospect I realize I behaved stupidly. He had offered me a unique opportunity and I should have grabbed it – money shouldn't have been my consideration. Charlie could be very generous when it came to much larger sums. I also know that when I eventually produced films, with a tight budget, I watched the pennies just like Charlie.

I called up Sydney in California. I didn't know how to survive the winter. I had never been able to borrow money from people. To my parents, borrowing was a deadly sin. If you didn't have, you did without. Nothing on credit, and bills had to be paid the day they arrived. I had the wrong upbringing for the movie business!

Luckily, Judith Kandel, Aben Kandel's wife, invited me to stay at their lovely farm in Bucks County, Pennsylvania. We were snowbound, but dear Judith inspired me to keep fighting and gave me contacts to help get my dream theater started. I found a theater I was crazy about in the Village, the Irving Street Theater. I was feeling optimistic, triggered up. I would show them.

Sydney called. The man Charlie had hired for my job was leaving for a better position. If I was willing to accept the hundred dollars, I should leave for Los Angeles immediately. I felt Oona's hand in this.

In my own mind the filming would only take a few months. I would earn some money, enabling me to get back to New York with cash in hand to continue my quest.

Now I was returning to Los Angeles to work with Charlie. What was his attitude towards me going to be?

After settling in with my sister and brother-in-law in Cheviot Hills, Los Angeles, I went to Charlie's for dinner. Oona and he greeted me effusively. I was happy to see them, but that money business had destroyed some of my confidence. For the first time, I felt ill-at-ease with them. I was hired to assist him, yet didn't know what my job was. I don't think Charlie knew either. And I was nervous: I had never worked on a film before. We were both playing it by ear. But now that I was his employee, I decided to be the best person he ever hired.

Claire and her mother had arrived a few days later, and moved into a charming Spanish-style apartment, not far from Schwab's drugstore off Sunset Boulevard. Claire's mother was very discreet, and never once appeared on the set. The first night at dinner, Charlie told Claire she had to diet; the screen put weight on, he said, and he too was dieting. The butler then came in with an enormous feast, but Charlie served himself the tiniest lamb chop I ever saw. Even a mouse would have gone hungry. I felt sorry for Charlie. Living in his grand house, he was eating like a pensioner. But while he starved, I gorged myself.

Charlie was a great disciplinarian. He wouldn't touch alcohol when he was filming. He claimed the slightest drop could affect his

CHARLIE ON THE *LIMELIGHT* SET DIRECTING
THE BALLET SEQUENCE, WATCHED BY
CAMERAMAN KARL STRUSS (THE TALL MAN
IN THE CENTER) AND BUSTER KEATON (I'M
STANDING BEHIND HIM). STANDING BEHIND
CHARLIE IS ROBERT ALDRICH, THE
ASSISTANT DIRECTOR.

performance, and he wanted to be in complete control of his faculties.

The following day we began rehearsals on his lawn, working from 11 a.m. to 4 p.m. Each scene was rehearsed over and over. Once again Charlie gave Claire every nuance and line reading. Occasionally Claire delivered her dialogue as though she was still acting at Stratford-on-Avon. Charlie quickly corrected her. "You're working for Charlie Chaplin now," he'd say. "No Shakespeare, please!"

Nowadays actors hate being told how to read a line; they feel that is their domain. But sometimes it's the quickest way to make them understand what you mean. Luckily, Claire was smart enough not to ask about her motivation. Charlie's answer would probably have been the same as George Abbott's, when Abbott told an actor to make a move and the actor asked: "What's my motivation?" Abbott, veteran of a hundred Broadway shows, replied: "Your job."

Charlie rehearsed his own lines again and again. He had to be letter-perfect. The same went for the movements in a scene, the number of steps he took, where he turned and on what line; he had to know his choreography without thinking. Then he'd be able to exercise his inspiration. This method, he said, was essential for comedy. It gave you your timing; with that fixed, you could place your laughs where you wanted.

Many of Charlie's short films were improvised. But his classic set pieces – like the dance with the globe in *The Great Dictator* or the prize-fight in *City Lights* – were rehearsed and choreographed step by step, gesture by gesture, until he could perform them like clockwork. In a way, Charlie's methods illustrated Constance's story of constructing a building, brick by brick, until you finally turned on the light of inspiration.

Rehearsals finally moved to the sound stage at the Chaplin studio, where the main set, Calvero's apartment, was erected. For two weeks we blocked, interpreted and honed each performance.

I made up my mind to concentrate on my new job so completely that nothing would distract me. I knew nothing about motion pictures, but was determined to learn, absorb and contribute. I made a note of every piece of business Charlie improvised. I was able to tell him how he varied his performance from take to take, and remind him which was the best. At night I went home and drew master diagrams of every camera set-up, and memorized them. Charlie loved the fact that

someone was watching him so carefully. And he was the easiest person to give notes to. You'd think someone like Chaplin would resent being told things by an underling. But he was always eager to hear any suggestions that could possibly improve his performance.

I soon mastered how the camera worked. More importantly, I knew what Charlie wanted. We were both anxious to bring this picture in on time and on budget. After all, it was his own money, and the best of movies are a gamble. He was brave. He had financed *Monsieur Verdoux* out of his own pocket, and the film had barely been released. Yet here he was, gambling again.

To help save time and money, we planned every camera set-up and lighting change in advance. All the long shots in Calvero's apartment were filmed together, even though the scenes were out of continuity. We didn't move the camera: once one shot was finished, Charlie would simply change outfits, and we'd film the long shots for another scene. After weeks of intensive rehearsals, Charlie and Claire knew their scenes inside out, so nothing threw them if we boldly stepped out of continuity. With the long shots completed, we moved our camera into a new position for the medium shots and close-ups.

Filming began on November 19th, 1951. We sailed through all of Claire and Charlie's scenes in Calvero's apartment, and within two weeks, the heart of the film was in the can. This was the way we were going to bring in a multi-million dollar motion picture on a 36-day schedule. And we kept to the schedule, until Charlie came down with flu; then we had to close down for a week.

Robert Aldrich – who later directed films like *The Dirty Dozen* and *What Ever Happened to Baby Jane?* – was appointed assistant director. I felt disappointed. Charlie had originally wanted me, and I felt I could do the job – especially with Charlie behind me. I was hoping to get into the union; then if things went badly I'd have something to fall back on. But the production manager talked Charlie out of it.

Bob was a big whale of a man, with a strange, laid-back personality; he was part of the Aldrich banking family. I felt slightly superior to him at the time, since he had to listen to me for instructions on all the camera set-ups. Every evening he'd consult me to find out what had to be shot the next day.

Bob thought Charlie was very old-fashioned. Bob wanted lots of different camera set-ups: endless travelling shots, shots through the

fireplace, shots through the window with rain pouring against the panes, shots with the camera virtually up the actors' crotches. Everything Charlie loathed in film-making.

Charlie believed in simple set-ups. He insisted the audience must never be confused by the geography of a scene, especially in comedy: they must always know the lay-out of the room, the position of the props and characters. Close-ups were only to be used for emphasis; over-use destroyed their impact. And script girls were the bane of Charlie's existence. He couldn't bear them fussing over little details of

CLAIRE BLOOM AND CHARLIE IN THE FAMOUS "I'M WALKING!" SCENE. I CAN'T REMEMBER HOW MANY TIMES WE DID THIS SCENE, BUT WE SHOT ENOUGH FILM TO MAKE ANOTHER COMPLETE MOVIE.

continuity. Sometimes, just to frustrate the script girl and Bob, he'd change the background of a scene in the same set-up.

"It doesn't *match!*" they would scream. "If that's what they're watching during this scene," Charlie always replied, "then I'd better give up – I have no film." Look at Claire's "I'm walking" scene in *Limelight,* and you'll notice how Charlie intercuts between three camera angles. Each time the pictures on the walls are different. He didn't care. Charlie's concern was for the best of Claire in each take, not the goddamn pictures.

The "I'm walking!" scene must have been shot more than forty times. Whenever we finished a major sequence on another set, Charlie would grab hold of Claire and say, "Come on, we're doing your big scene again. It could be better." Poor dear – she never complained. Charlie demonstrated how to do it over and over. Charlie was so brilliant, that no one could ever match him. He really was asking for the impossible. But Claire proved her mettle.

Bob was funny. After I gave him the camera set-ups and showed him exactly the lines Charlie would say and where he'd walk, Bob

Above: Charlie directing Claire Bloom and Sydney in their love scene.
Opposite: Charlie brings home street musicians. Left to right: Charlie (bowing the violin with his left hand), Julian Ludwig from the Circle and two well-known silent screen comics, Loyal Underwood and Snub Pollard.

would relay the same instructions to the camera crew (I wasn't allowed to – I was non-union). But instead of giving them the dialogue, he'd say: "Calvero – talk talk talk talk talk talk talk talk. Moves to the right. More talk talk talk talk talk talk talk. Then cut." After the years Charlie had spent creating and polishing his dialogue, it all spewed out of Bob's mouth as "talk talk talk". Charlie laughed when he found out. After all, it was equivalent to his "so and so and so and so" at the Circle.

Sydney played Neville, the romantic lead. This was to be his launching pad. Charlie had made him diet so much that he was hardly recognizable as the Sydney we all knew. He became a shadow of his former self. He seemed to have lost his chin, his backside, and, most important, his charm. But I think what took off most of his weight was the feeling of insecurity. Throughout filming he was scared, in a panic, a nervous wreck.

This was his first film. He was anxious to please his father, and his father was equally anxious that Sydney make an impact. Charlie worked so hard with him, trying to make him relax; but the harder he worked with him, the stiffer Sydney became. Charlie told me, "Well, it took years before Cary Grant broke through. He was like a board too when he first started. Then he made one film, and suddenly it all happened – he learned the secret behind acting."

Whenever Cary Grant's name came up, Charlie would always say "You know, Cary Grant is ten years older than I am." Oona and I would laugh and say it was impossible. But Charlie insisted that he knew him when he was Archie Leach and walked on stilts on the Brighton promenade. If it was true, Cary would have been one hundred and seven when he died in 1986!

There was one sequence I never tired of – the scene where Terry is lying in bed, and Calvero talks about the pain of being a comic, and the thrill when the audience laughs. Terry is surprised: "I had the impression you were in fear of an audience, but you really love them!" "Maybe I love them," Calvero replies, "but I don't admire them. As individuals – yes, there's greatness in everyone. But as a crowd ... they're like a monster without a head. You never know which way it's going to turn."

Charlie didn't appear to be acting. It was absolutely real; more importantly, the words he was saying seemed to reflect his recent troubles with the American public. Actors should look at the scene for

its lack of artifice. There are none of the slurrings of words and hair-fiddlings that you sometimes observe in Method performances, where the actors work so hard at being real that they become phony. As Charlie said to the actors at the Circle, "You should make the audience feel they're looking through a keyhole." That's what I felt in this scene. Chaplin's performance is totally honest and, as a result, magnetic.

Charlie had the knack of assuming any character he wanted. Whether it was the Tramp, a floor-walker, a painter, a house-builder, an immigrant, or Hitler, Charlie *became* these people. I remember him telling me once, "If you have to play a great dancer like Nijinsky, *think* Nijinsky, *become* Nijinsky." Then in front of my eyes he bedazzled me, transforming himself into the mad, tortured dancer. I saw him do this many times: study a person and then become him. Charlie worked from the outside in; in his own way, he was a complete advocate of the Delsarte school of acting. By looking at the way people walked, dressed, moved their hands, cleared their throats, or made nervous gestures, he was able to get straight to the heart of a character.

In front of the camera Charlie was completely uninhibited, relaxed and shameless. He would take possession of it, look straight into it and defy the audience not to be gripped by what he was doing. The camera was his toy to play with. He was its master, the camera his slave.

There is a scene near the end, after Terry enjoys her big success, where Calvero, feeling left out, goes to a bar with his old music-hall cronies (played by extras and bit players). On the screen you can hear him directing them – "Keep it going, keep it going, don't drop it!" – telling them to keep the dialogue going and not to drop the tempo. Fortunately, Calvero is supposed to be drunk. Only Charlie would be bold enough to act and direct simultaneously!

Charlie got a great kick out of directing the scene where Calvero brings three buskers back to his apartment and joins them in a tipsy music session. His fellow musicians were two silent comedians – Snub Pollard and Loyal Underwood – and one of our Circle actors, Julian Ludwig. As Charlie directed, he instructed them to play *con amore*. Charlie liked so many things to be played or spoken *con amore* – it was

JUST BEFORE MAKING HER DÉBUT, TERRY
(CLAIRE BLOOM) CLAIMS, OUT OF
HYSTERIA, THAT HER LEGS ARE PARALYZED
AGAIN. CALVERO (CHARLIE) FORCES HER
ON STAGE.

one of his favorite expressions. When the buskers' music became a little rowdy, he used another favorite word; "Not too *outré*, please!" The actors didn't understand what he meant.

But our publicity man Harry Crocker, an old friend of Charlie's (he played a leading role in *The Circus*), knew all about *outré*. After the day's work was over he told me a funny story about Charlie's love of new words – *outré* included. During the making of *The Circus*, Harry said, Charlie's assistant director Chuck Riesner had suggested a gag. Charlie replied, "No, Chuck, it's a bit too *outré*, and with my Tramp character we simply can't have him *outré!*"

Riesner was completely confused, but tried to cover his tracks. "If you don't want him *outré*," he said, "who am I to argue with you?" He then asked Crocker what the word meant; Crocker led him to the dictionary in Charlie's office. "Extravagant, bizarre," it said. Riesner then asked Crocker to give him a word that Charlie wouldn't understand. Crocker dipped at random into the dictionary: "How about *quidnunc?* – 'One who seeks to know all the latest news, a gossip, a busybody.' " Riesner liked it, so he scribbled a little note, slipped it between the dictionary pages, and returned to the set.

Charlie had now thought of a new gag, and asked Riesner what he thought. "It doesn't work," said Riesner, "It makes you too much of a *quidnunc*." Charlie was taken aback. The criticism sounded logical, but what did it mean? But Charlie replied, "Oh, I don't think so . . ." and returned to the work in hand.

Charlie couldn't concentrate. He mulled the word over: "*What* did you say it made me seem like?" he asked Chuck. Riesner told him again, with extra relish: *"Quidnunc!"* "Chuck," Charlie said, "there's no such word."

"Charlie!" Chuck protested. "You're too *outré* in your accusation!" The cast and crew burst out laughing. So Charlie called a halt to the shooting and slipped out to his office. Chuck followed and watched him as he thumbed through his huge dictionary until he reached the letter Q. There Charlie found Chuck Riesner's note – "I knew I'd send you to the dictionary," it said. Charlie let out a terrific roar of laughter.

In the original *Limelight* script, Calvero was presented as an atheist. All references to this were removed during shooting – why, I don't know. Then, when we were running slightly behind schedule, Charlie decided to save time by cutting the scene where Calvero goes behind a stage flat and prays for Terry's success after pushing her on stage to dance her first solo. A stage hand sees him, and Calvero, embarrassed, pretends he's looking for a button.

I was appalled when Charlie proposed cutting it. "When I used to tell the story to friends," I cried, "that was the scene that always got them!" Charlie listened impatiently, then to satisfy me filmed it, without rehearsal or preparation, in ten minutes. Today that small, simple scene is a real crowd pleaser.

Immediately after, we were scheduled to shoot overhead shots of the scenery being changed backstage at the theater. Aldrich and the production manager convinced Charlie that the scene should go, since it did nothing to advance the storyline, and would take too long to film. Once again I sulked; I just didn't like him fiddling around with the finished script. Charlie seemed slightly annoyed at me, but decided to do the scene.

The camera was hastily put on a grid. Charlie yelled instructions to the actors down below, and before you could say Jack Robinson the scene was filmed. Charlie always worked very fast when he was annoyed. No one at the time, including myself, realized the impact that scene would have until we saw the rushes the following day. In that one quick shot, Charlie captured all the magic and mystery of the theater.

Wheeler Dryden, Charlie's half-brother, assisted him on the film. He had a maddening way of interrupting Charlie in the middle of a creative thought – only to remind him to straighten his tie, or comb his hair. He was like a little gnat, darting round the set, inspecting every scene from every angle, and casting a critical eye on "Charles" (as he always called him). It would drive Charlie crazy. Wheeler always tried not to be noticed by hiding behind one stage flat or another. But his efforts at being unobtrusive only made him more noticeable. "You're settled in?" Charlie would ask as he finally came to rest. "Good. Now we can start shooting!"

One day Charlie and I drove up to the studio in his small Ford. We spotted Aldrich driving ahead of us in his brand-new black Cadillac. Charlie grumbled: "Look at him driving a Cadillac while I'm driving a small Ford!" "You can afford a Cadillac," I said, "Why don't you buy one?" "But I don't like big cars, I like small ones." "Well Bob likes big cars, so leave him alone!" I said.

After shooting for one week, Charlie woke me up at my sister's

TERRY (CLAIRE BLOOM) WISHES CALVERO (CHARLIE) GOOD LUCK BEFORE HIS BENEFIT PERFORMANCE.

house and asked me what I thought of Rollie Totheroh's camerawork. Rollie had been Charlie's cameraman since the silent days. He was a small spry man, in his early sixties, like Charlie. He hardly ever worked on other people's films. Yet Charlie still kept him on salary during his long periods of idleness.

But what did I know about film photography? I only owned a little Brownie. "It looked good to me," I said. Charlie was nervous. He wanted *Limelight* to have a beautifully textured black-and-white look. He knew he was being called old-fashioned, and he didn't want the picture criticized for not being lit and photographed well. I was not able to help much; it was my first film and I was still learning.

The following day, in a meeting with the production manager, Charlie decided to replace Rollie and hire Karl Struss, who had previously worked on *The Great Dictator,* Murnau's *Sunrise,* the original *Ben Hur,* and many films for Paramount. Rollie was to be his assistant.

Although he didn't sulk on the set, Rollie kept himself hidden behind the camera, but he never stopped observing the action. Sometimes he'd walk over to Charlie and tell him nicely, "Keep your head up, sweetheart. Too many chins showing!"

At the end of shooting, we ran everything we had filmed. Charlie looked at some of Claire's close-ups and said, "Oh, these are beautiful. They're the best in the whole picture." These were the work of Rollie before he was taken off! But when you're filming, especially when you're using your own money, so many doubts arise. And who knows whether or not Rollie could have delivered the whole film. It must have been a very difficult decision for Charlie to make.

When Charlie was forced into exile and sold the studio, he generously looked after his entire studio staff, and Rollie received twenty-five thousand dollars in severance pay. No major studio, with all their vast sums, would consider taking care of their staff as generously as Charlie did. Rollie accepted the money and afterwards wrote a vitriolic article attacking him. Things I'll never understand.

Sometimes Charlie worried about the film being sent to the laboratory overnight for developing. The following day you might get a report that the negative was scratched, or the film stock was no good, and the entire scene would have to be reshot. This depressed Charlie no end, especially when he felt the scene was perfect. He was convinced it was sabotage.

Charlie grew particularly suspicious of our camera loader. He took me aside one day and whispered, "Check the ring on that man's finger! I know he's a member of the American Legion and he's out to destroy the negative!" The American Legion was very anti-Chaplin; they had picketed cinemas showing *Monsieur Verdoux*. I dutifully circled around the camera loader, trying to appear nonchalant while I checked out his fingers. I reported to Charlie that it was a perfectly ordinary college ring.

Another day, after filming a sequence many times, Charlie and I became very excited about a particular take. "Make a note of it," he said. "Take Three is the best one." We both agreed. But when we looked at the rushes, Take Three didn't seem to come off. "Are you sure that was the take we liked?" Charlie asked. I showed him my notes. It was Take Three. But something was missing – the scene's feeling had vanished. The same thing happened again with other takes. We had the emotion on the set, but the camera didn't capture it.

Charlie came up with a theory. He felt that every time the shutter came down, in that brief fraction of a second emotion was being eliminated from the film. He would have loved video today. No shutters!

But once he became excited about the rushes again, the shutter theory was thrown out of the window. And *Limelight* excited him enormously. Although Charlie always used to say you worked solely on nerves when making a film, he was euphoric during the shooting of this film. Each scene seemed to invigorate him more. He was dancing on air, and Oona added to his happiness. At lunchtime, she would arrive on the set with a carton of cottage cheese and pineapple, or hard-boiled eggs.

They would sit in his little portable dressing-room, nibbling away contentedly until Aldrich called, "O.K.! Ready for the next shot!"

I was enjoying *Limelight* too, but at times I felt like a fish out of water. I missed the Circle, though I tried not to think of it. At the back of my mind, I still had plans to return to New York when the film was completed and try again, though the struggle ahead did not appeal to me.

The Circle had been my private domain. Here I seemed a small cog in a vast machinery of men and women. The first day on the floor had been terrifying. I felt so out of place and alone, with all those technicians up on the rafters looking down on me. Charlie's advice was: "Ignore them. You know more than they do. Remember that." I did, and it worked.

BELOW LEFT: CHARLIE IN HIS DRESSING-
ROOM TRYING OUT MAKE-UP FOR HIS
COMEDY ROUTINE WITH BUSTER KEATON.
RIGHT: CHARLIE LIMBERING UP BEFORE HIS
MUSIC-HALL ACT.

Once the major scenes of *Limelight* were shot, Charlie pressed on
with exteriors. We rented the backlot at Paramount for three days,
filming the outside of Calvero's house and an establishing shot of
Edwardian London. The only trouble was that for our London we used
the Washington Square set from William Wyler's *The Heiress*. When
Roy Boulting, the English director, was shown the film, he told Charlie
those were New York brownstones in the establishing shot. Charlie
looked him straight in the face: "I can show you where houses in
London look *exactly* like that!" As far as Charlie was concerned a house
is a house is a house.

Being at someone else's studio was like having a few days off school.
At the Paramount canteen, Charlie and I sat next to Bing Crosby, the
kingpin on the Paramount lot. He stared at us hard, as though we were
intruders in his territory.

We were now ready to film the music-hall and ballet scenes. We
rented the Selznick studios, where *Gone with the Wind* had been filmed.
It had just what we needed: a composite theater set consisting of a large
stage, auditorium, backstage area, corridors and dressing-rooms – all
ready to be used. We wouldn't have to build anything. What a saving!

First we shot the ballet sequence. Charlie was in his element when
André Eglevsky and Melissa Hayden – two stars from the New York City

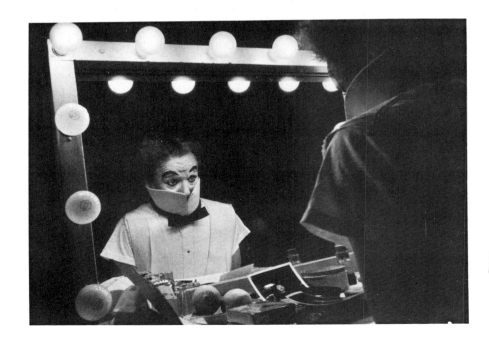

Ballet – arrived to dance the special ballet he had conceived and written. Charlie showed them exactly what he wanted done, and then took a back seat. He was overwhelmed by their artistry, and watched elated as they danced to his music.

Charlie was now ready to shoot his big pantomime number for two comic actors; this was going to be the climax to the film. He was nervous about it. Charlie would play the violin, his partner the piano. I have read in various books how Charlie discovered the character of the Tramp. I was always a bit skeptical. And yet I saw the same process at work when he developed the mad, obsessed violin player for the music-hall sequence. He went into the wardrobe room, tried on different outfits and mustaches, adopted various attitudes in front of the mirror, and slowly I saw a loony violinist emerge before my eyes.

LEFT: CHARLIE, AS THE VIOLINIST, TUNES UP BEFORE HIS LEGS BEGIN TO SHRINK.

ABOVE: IN THE MIDDLE OF THEIR ROUTINE, CHARLIE, AS THE SLIGHTLY MAD VIOLINIST, DROPS HIS VIOLIN – AND KEATON, AS THE NEAR-SIGHTED PIANIST, STEPS INTO IT!

Charlie had only prepared a few gags and bits of business for the sequence. He knew he was going to shrink in size (wearing a trick pair of huge trousers); extract the piano's insides, like a doctor taking the guts from a patient; step onto his violin, and cause the pianist's music sheets to cascade to the floor. The rest of the scene he would improvise.

But Charlie still hadn't found his partner. At one point he thought Sydney's stand-in, who had a long lugubrious face, could play the pianist. But he was undecided. Then just before shooting, someone told him that Buster Keaton was available – that he was also broke, and needed money. That did it. Charlie hired Keaton.

Buster arrived on the set wearing his old Buster outfit with the small pancake hat. Charlie took him aside and said gently, "We're not playing our old characters now. I'm not playing the Tramp; you're not playing Buster." Keaton, like an obedient pupil, replied, "Yes, Charlie, of course," and removed his hat and went to wardrobe for a costume change.

Before our picture began, all the technicians had been excited about working with Charlie Chaplin. He hadn't made a film for years and of course he was a legend. You could feel the buzz in the air. But after a few weeks of shooting, Charlie Chaplin became just another actor. Now their affection switched to Keaton. He was the new boy in town. But if Ben Turpin had showed up two weeks later, I'm sure Keaton would have been dropped like a hot potato. Charlie must have been aware of the technicians' attitude, but chose to ignore it. He just wanted to get on with the business ahead.

For the next week, Chaplin and Keaton improvised what became one of the most hilarious comedy sequences ever put on film. Charlie, as the crazed violinist, worked himself up into a feverish pitch, he dripped with perspiration. His clothes and undershirts were absolutely soaked – though none of this is visible on the screen. From early morning until evening, he improvised the pantomime routine over and over, and was never satisfied. I now understood why Charlie always said that silents were much more difficult to make than talking films. "Talkies are a cinch," he'd say. "You just film dialogue, but filming thoughts, communicating without words, is much harder." After one week of gruelling shooting, Charlie collapsed with flu.

Keaton was a silent, sad, isolated man. He sat on the set with his wife, hardly talking to anyone. He seemed anxious to prove to Charlie

Opposite: Charlie going nuts on the violin.

Above: Rendezvous in the dressing-room. Charlie and Buster Keaton before their big number.

RIGHT: CHARLIE EDITING *LIMELIGHT*, WHILE I WATCH LIKE A HAWK — LEARNING AND ABSORBING.

OPPOSITE: CHARLIE AS THE ANIMAL TRAINER WITH HIS PERFORMING FLEAS. BEFORE LONG, "PHYLLIS" WAS TO ESCAPE AND CAUSE HIM BODILY HARM.

that he hadn't made a mistake in casting him. There was a rapport between the pair, but it was all on a business level. Neither reminisced about the "good old days" – Charlie, in any case, never liked gossip. There was work to be done, and they both attacked their parts like the pros they were.

Keaton scored a great success with the music-hall scene when the film was released. And rightly so. But stories began circulating that Keaton had been even funnier on the set, but Charlie had cut out the best of him. I know this wasn't so.

I was with Charlie during the entire editing of the film; I never left his side. On that sequence, we must have had enough footage to release at least five complete pictures. The problem was weeding out and making sense of the best things in both their performances. Of course, Charlie cut some of Keaton's gags. If he hadn't, the picture would have run for ever. But he cut just as many of his own best laughs. Out went a hilarious gag when he shrank into his trick trousers only to shoot up like a giant. I pleaded with him to keep it in. But he said, "You've got to

keep the narrative going. You can't stop the picture for this one scene." Then I remembered the time he showed me two brilliant sequences he had cut from *City Lights* and *Modern Times*. "How could you cut them?" I had asked, "They're marvelous!" And he replied, "If it slows down your story, no matter how funny it is, out it goes."

And much of Buster's performance was devised by Charlie in the cutting room. The shots of the music sheets slipping off Buster's piano were all filmed in a single take: it was Charlie who decided to make it into a running gag. Every time you cut to Buster, he was still battling with the tumbling music sheets. The cutting built the sequence, and made Keaton's routine outstanding.

During dubbing, Charlie refused to put in any audience reaction to the Chaplin–Keaton scene. I couldn't understand why. He said the real audience watching the film would supply the laughter. "What if the film's showing at a matinée to a half-empty house?" I said. "Won't it sound strange, playing the scene in complete silence?" He looked at me peeved. But that was Charlie. He was a law unto himself. He made the

rules, and he enjoyed breaking them.

Harry Crocker, our publicity man, was a long-time associate of the newspaper tycoon William Randolph Hearst. He came from a famous banking family in San Francisco; he knew everyone, and was well-liked. During the shooting of the Keaton sequence, he told Charlie he wanted to bring Louella Parsons onto the set. Charlie was apprehensive. During the 1920s Charlie had been very friendly with Hearst and Marion Davies, and had known Louella, Hearst's old Hollywood gossip columnist, for years. But now the Hearst press had turned against Charlie and were attacking him viciously.

Harry convinced Charlie that Louella was on his side, and would write nice things in her column. Like her rival Hedda Hopper, Louella had tremendous influence. The columns were syndicated daily throughout most of the major American papers, and their poison pens broke many a star's career.

Louella arrived on the set, looking like the queen bee herself. Someone rushed off to fetch a canvas chair. She watched expressionless as Charlie and Keaton performed. I felt *she* was wearing the American Legion ring. Charlie spotted her, but he kept on filming. Possibly she resented this: everything usually stopped when Queen Louella arrived.

During a break in the shooting, Charlie went over and chided her impishly, "Now don't you say anything nasty about me." He couldn't have said it in a gentler, more charming way. But her hackles were up and the next day in her column, this innocent remark was made to sound like heresy. "The nerve of this man to say that to me! Why would I say anything nasty about him unless there was something nasty to say?" The diatribe went on and on. Harry was most apologetic, but Charlie, now accustomed to a bad press, dismissed it.

Gentle Nigel Bruce, the well-known English actor (Watson to Basil Rathbone's Holmes), joined the cast for a few days' work. He played Mr Postand, the impresario of the Empire Theater, where Calvero gives his final performance – a very small part. One day I overheard Bruce telling reporters the plot of *Limelight*: "It's about this impresario, Mr Postand, who runs the Empire Theater," he explained in his bumbling manner, "and one day he hears that this great comedian, Calvero, is down on his

NIGEL BRUCE AS MR POSTAND, MANAGER
OF THE EMPIRE THEATER, TRYING TO
ENCOURAGE CALVERO (CHARLIE) BEFORE
THE GALA BENEFIT.

Opposite: Claire comforts Charlie. As the climax to his violin routine, he has somersaulted into the orchestra pit, fallen into a drum and hurt himself.

Left: The filming completed, Charlie relaxes at home with Oona and their four young children, Geraldine, Victoria, Josephine and Michael.

luck. So he throws a benefit for him, but little does he know that Calvero . . ." Everything was told from Postand's viewpoint. Chaplin had suddenly become a supporting player! Charlie roared when he heard this – it was a typical actor's story, and Nigel endeared himself to us all the more.

Limelight was nearing completion. In two weeks, Claire would be returning to London. She felt sad. London was drab, still suffering the effects of war, and here she was in the land of plenty. The Chaplins had become almost a second family to her. She and Sydney had grown very fond of each other; he promised he'd come over to see her and be at the London opening.

Charlie and I worked in the cutting room for a little over six months. Charlie never allowed anyone but himself to edit his films. The cutter's job was merely to assemble every sequence into long shot, medium shot and close-up, and splice the film together after Charlie had decided where he wanted the cuts.

It could have been clear sailing, but we had a bungler as our editor. Cutting rooms are usually well-ordered; all the film takes are labelled and easily located. Ours was in total chaos; our editor couldn't find anything. The minute Charlie asked for a take, he began shaking and opening every tin in sight. Rolls of film tumbled onto the floor. It was like a W.C. Fields film. I thought Charlie would have a stroke. His precious *Limelight!* Luckily I knew each take by heart, and was always able to locate what Charlie wanted. The editor, meanwhile, would be muttering, "But that was never filmed; there's no such take!"

Now that shooting on *Limelight* was finished, Charlie couldn't stop singing my praises. He was so pleased with my work, that he raised my salary to two hundred dollars a week.

During lunch breaks, Charlie and I went to Farmer's Market, off Fairfax Avenue, where we'd sit at the little tables under an umbrella, and enjoy cottage cheese and pineapple with black coffee. Oona often joined us. Charlie was never recognized until she arrived; people were able to spot them as a couple. Charlie – ever curious – loved walking through the stalls, buying pâtés, or enjoying the outsize fruits on display. Friends spotted him at once. Sally Eilers and Antonio Moreno (Clara Bow's leading man in *It*) greeted him warmly; even my Maxene Andrews was there one day. Other times we went to the Gotham or Musso Frank's restaurant on Hollywood Boulevard. Charlie didn't enjoy being served by waiters; he preferred waitresses. There was something sad, he thought, about young men working as waiters.

In July we were in the middle of mixing the sound, music and dialogue of *Limelight* onto one track. We had finished the first two reels; the following day, July 22nd, we were due to start Reel Three. That evening, as I was in my bedroom, I thought the walls were caving in around me. It was an earthquake! I watched the phenomenon with awe.

The next morning, the streets of Los Angeles felt eerie. Everyone looked at each other strangely; it was as though we had all experienced the end of the world.

Oona and Charlie had also felt the earthquake. In the mixing room, Charlie and the staff all related their experiences quietly, with awe. There was still the possibility of an aftershock. But there was work to do. We put on Reel Three. Charlie came onto the screen as Calvero, smiling broadly to Terry: "The sun's shining, the kettle's singing, and we've paid the rent. There'll be an earthquake – I know it. I know it, I know it!" It broke the ice; we all burst out laughing, and continued with our mixing.

Claire was now back in England, preparing to play Juliet at the Old Vic. But *Limelight* was still on her mind. She wrote to me from Stratford:

Sometimes, when I think of working with Mr Chaplin, it seems like a wonderful dream and I cannot believe it was true; if the film doesn't hurry and come, I will soon not believe it either. Does Mr Chaplin still mean to open it in London? I have a feeling he won't. He would get the most wonderful welcome if he does come.

While editing the film, Charlie wanted to sell his share in United Artists. The company was losing money fast. Mary Pickford and he were offered a vast sum. But at the last minute Mary refused to go ahead with the deal. Charlie was furious. To make matters worse, Mary's cat ambled down Summit Drive every morning during the negotiations and spent the day in the Chaplin kitchen, where she was well fed. Mary used to call up, furious, and insisted Charlie send her cat back. She was practically accusing Charlie of cat-napping. I always felt that cat was partially to blame for the collapse of the United Artists deal.

During this time, the Royal Ballet made their first visit to Los Angeles. Margot Fonteyn and Beryl Grey were the prima ballerinas. Oona and Charlie invited Fonteyn and others for dinner. At the table, Charlie and Fonteyn got into a heated political discussion. She was very

right wing. The talk turned to peace. This was the big issue of the time: the Cold War was hotting up, and people were taking sides. Fonteyn asked Charlie, "Would you take peace at any price?" Charlie, thoroughly tired of *all* wars, said, "Yes, at *any* price." But Fonteyn wouldn't let the matter drop. Just to be provocative, Charlie added, "And I'd rather be Red than dead!!" Anyway, he preferred Beryl Grey as a dancer.

Limelight was now ready to be previewed. We booked the largest movie theater on the Paramount lot and invited the top directors, actors, actresses and agents in Hollywood. Sidney Skolsky, the Hollywood columnist and producer of *The Jolson Story,* a good friend of mine, was the only journalist invited. Charlie did this for me – Sidney had always been very kind to the Circle. Here are Sidney Skolsky's impressions of the first screening of *Limelight:*

The guest list ranged from such celebrities as Humphrey Bogart to Doris Duke to several old ladies and men who had worked with Chaplin since *The Gold Rush* back in 1924. Charlie was as nervous and excited as a newcomer. He didn't behave like a man who had been making movies for forty years, who has already become a legend.

Chaplin and his assistant Jerry Epstein ran the picture at two in the afternoon, because Chaplin wanted to check the print personally. Chaplin, who wrote, produced, directed and starred in the picture, had to do everything personally. He even ushered at this preview showing. Then when the lights in the projection room went off and the picture started, this little gray-haired man sat at the dial-controls in the rear of the room and regulated the sound for the picture. It was the most exciting night I ever had spent in a projection room.

There was drama and history in the room. There was comedy and drama on the screen, and there was a backdrop of drama running along with the picture *Limelight* itself ... After all these years and years of picture making you'd think Chaplin would be the same without anything new to offer. But this is a different Chaplin with many new tricks, yet a Chaplin who is enough of the same ...

The projection room lights went on. The entire audience from Ronald Colman to David Selznick to Judge Fecora to Sylvia Gable stood up and applauded and shouted "Bravo". It was as if all Hollywood was paying tribute to Charlie Chaplin. Then the little gray-haired fellow

CHARLIE AND OONA IN LONDON FOR THE *LIMELIGHT* PREMIÈRE. YOU'D NEVER KNOW FROM CHARLIE'S GALLANT GESTURE THAT HE'D JUST BEEN REFUSED RE-ENTRY TO THE STATES.

walked up to the platform. He said; "Thank you. I was very scared. You are the first people in the world to have seen my picture. It runs two hours and thirty minutes. I don't want to keep you longer. I do want to say 'Thank you-—'" and that's as far as Chaplin got. A woman in the audience shouted, "No! No! Thank you!". And then others in the audience took these words and shouted them at Chaplin.

Somehow I think this is the key to *Limelight*. It doesn't matter whether some people think it is good and some people think it is great. The degree doesn't matter. This is no ordinary picture made by an ordinary man. This is a great hunk of celluloid history and emotion, and I think everyone who is genuinely interested in the movies will say "Thank you".

Skolsky's article appeared in the *New York Post* and was syndicated throughout the States.

Charlie couldn't have been happier. Afterwards, there was an enormous tent party on his lawn. Charlie was talking to John Gielgud (in Hollywood for *Julius Caesar*), when a female guest interrupted. "Oh Charlie," she gushed, "why didn't you play the Tramp in the music-hall sequences? I was *so* disappointed!" Gielgud interjected: "Because he has too much taste." Charlie liked that.

All during the shooting Bob Aldrich was skeptical about the film. He never believed in it. It was old-fashioned (that word again), and, more important for him, Chaplin's camera was static. Aldrich was an action man, and above all a technician; Charlie broke all his rules about how pictures should be made. But after the preview, Bob came to Charlie, shattered, with tears in his eyes. "I take it all back," he said. "You know exactly what you're doing. The picture was marvelous!" We were all touched, coming from this skeptic. But the greatest compliment Bob paid to Charlie was in his own film *Autumn Leaves,* where he borrowed some of Charlie's own camera set-ups and lighting effects.

The picture was now ready for release. Charlie and Oona prepared for their fateful trip to New York and the première in London. Everything was being wound up. Charlie excitedly took me aside, and told me he was going to give me a bonus once *Limelight* had opened. On September 6th, 1952, Oona and Charlie left Los Angeles and headed east with their children, and the nanny, Kay-Kay. Just before leaving, Charlie persuaded Oona to put her signature on a joint bank account. I

saw them off at Union Station. Charlie later told me he sensed, from the look in my eyes, that he would never return. The picture was previewed in New York, and I was instructed by Charlie to cut two more sequences. On September 17th, the family sailed on the *Queen Elizabeth*. Two days later, it all happened.

In mid-Atlantic, Charlie received a telegram from James McGranery, the Attorney General under Harry Truman's administration, revoking his re-entry permit to the United States. Charlie could only return if he re-applied for admission under the immigration laws. McGranery quoted a ruling which barred aliens for reasons of morals or Communist associations. What Charlie had planned as a short holiday to show Oona London suddenly turned into a nightmare.

Los Angeles now seemed terribly empty. No Oona. No Charlie. No Circle. Carol Saroyan was in Los Angeles, so I had someone to commiserate with. Although I was seeing a lot of Maxene Andrews, I had to get out. The Andrews Sisters were leaving for New York to appear on Perry Como's television show. I flew east with them.

CHARLIE AND OONA, ACCOMPANIED BY
MERLE OBERON, ENTERING THE COMÉDIE
FRANÇAISE IN PARIS, WHERE A GALA
PERFORMANCE WAS HELD IN CHARLIE'S
HONOR.

Limelight opened at the Astor and Translux theaters in Manhattan. It seemed strange, seeing the film with an audience. After all those months in the cutting room, watching the footage with Chaplin, the film had become so personal to me; now it was everyone's. I no longer seemed to be part of it; *Limelight* belonged to the public.

But I devoured the audience's reactions. I was amazed at how distributors allowed the prints to become scratchy and dirty within a week. We had spent so much time making sure the film looked beautiful. Suddenly it looked like an old movie brought out for revival. I sent Charlie a letter in London, and he contacted United Artists. They changed the print immediately.

I was shocked to hear that many theaters in the United States were cancelling showings. The American Legion was at work again. Charlie refused to suffer this humiliation and promptly took the film out of distribution. *Limelight* still hasn't been seen in many theaters in the United States.

My cousin, Michael Tolan, was appearing on Broadway in *A Majority of One* with Gertrude Berg, so between Michael, Philip Langner and Marilyn, I had friends to see. Constance, too, was back in New York. She had seen *Limelight,* and was annoyed that one of the fleas in the animal-trainer sequence was called Phyllis. "You don't name a flea after someone you know!" she remonstrated. I told her I didn't think Charlie had consciously named the flea after her devoted companion.

On November 14th I received a telegram from Oona in London: she was arriving in New York, and asked if I could meet her at the Sherry Netherlands Hotel. She was on a secret mission, to settle Charlie's affairs in Los Angeles. Thank God she had signed that joint bank account! Charlie was terrified the Government would try to attach everything he possessed. But Oona moved faster than they did, and she was able to get everything out of the country before anyone was the wiser. She got into Charlie's vaults, and stuffed everything – money, stocks, papers – into a valise. She was so quick, the Bank of America didn't know what was happening. She then closed up 1085 Summit Drive, paid off the staff, and flew back to New York. It was real cloak and dagger stuff.

Charlie called from London. Oona reported "mission accomplished". That night, Oona and I had dinner at Manny Wolf's Steak House on Third Avenue. Someone behind us spotted her and began

making insulting remarks. "Commie Red" was one of them. I was outraged, but Oona just laughed it off.

After Oona returned to Europe, I began thinking up ideas for films. Making movies had opened up a new world, and I forgot about starting another Circle. Although I loved theater the most, I didn't want to lose any impetus by switching horses in mid-stream. And I was still reeling from the impact of Charlie's deportation.

With my credit on *Limelight,* I was convinced I would get employment. But to my amazement, I found that people in the film world were wary of my Chaplin connection. Charlie Chaplin had suddenly become a dirty word, and I was advised by a United Artists executive that it would be better if I kept quiet about my association. My credit was now meaningless. But I was proud of *Limelight* and my work with Chaplin. I couldn't have cared less about the nervous people in the film industry.

The papers, radio and television were full of the Ethel and Julius Rosenberg case. They had been imprisoned for stealing atomic secrets and giving them to the Russians; now, such was the hysteria of the times that they were to be electrocuted, after two years in the death cells. Eisenhower, who had just become President, would not rescind the order.

Mass protests were held throughout the world. Never before in American history had a husband and wife been given the death sentence. The sentence was especially abhorrent because their treason had been committed in peacetime, when treason was not a capital offence. New York streets buzzed with tension and rallies. I was glad I was there instead of Los Angeles.

From out of the blue, Arthur Kelly phoned me. He had just received a call from Chaplin. Charlie was now living in Switzerland; he had found a large house overlooking Lake Geneva, and invited me to visit him for two weeks.

I was elated. I wanted to get away; the last nine months had been so full of stress and anxiety, and it was always my dream to visit Europe. I left New York on June 18th, one day before the Rosenbergs were due to be electrocuted. The White House was bombarded with appeals to save them. I had no idea of their fate as I boarded the plane to Switzerland.

I was off on a new adventure. But the Rosenbergs were foremost on my mind. Would they be given a stay of execution?

A KING 5 IN NEW YORK

TOP: CHARLIE POSING AS PAN ON THE LAWN OF THE MANOIR.

CENTER: CHARLIE TOOK THIS PHOTO OF ME — AFTER MAKING ME POSE FOR ABOUT TWENTY MINUTES! THE MANOIR IS IN THE BACKGROUND.

BOTTOM: OONA AND CHARLIE SITTING ON THEIR LAWN DURING THE HOT SUMMER OF 1953.

"What happened to the Rosenbergs?" I asked Charlie as he greeted me at Geneva airport. "They were executed a few hours ago," he replied bleakly. For the moment, the excitement of seeing Charlie and being in Switzerland evaporated. We drove towards his house in Vevey in silence; on the way he pointed out newspaper placards reading "ROSENBERGS SONT MORTS". The news of the Rosenbergs' fate was to color my first days in Switzerland.

My first impression of Switzerland was of thousands of cyclists in the street. I had expected to see medieval castles out of a Disney film, but instead Geneva was a bustling, modern city – except for the cyclists.

Oona and Charlie were now ensconced in what to me resembled the White House. The Manoir de Ban was on a forty-acre estate. It had large white pillars, and a well-manicured lawn overlooking Lake Geneva. Charlie had been indecisive about taking the house. But Oona, now pregnant with her fourth child, had grown tired of living at the Hotel Beau Rivage in Lausanne and put her foot down. The Manoir de Ban was the house she wanted.

A wise decision. When I arrived Oona and he seemed to be well settled in, although there were still large crates in the hallway stacked with books, and they needed more furniture. It was difficult starting a new life in a foreign country, checking out schools for the children, finding staff, and generally adjusting to a new environment. Oona spoke French, which made things easier, but Charlie was always to have trouble with the language. Oona seemed happy to see me, and did everything to make me comfortable.

I helped Charlie unload his leather-bound books and arrange them in his new library. The Manoir de Ban was enormous. As the family

expanded, they needed even more room. The children slept on the top floor, along with the staff. I was given a large room on the main floor.

Although Charlie had left America only nine months ago, it must have seemed like an eternity. He was eager to hear what was happening with the McCarthy witch-hunts, the blacklist, and the Rosenberg protests; eager for news of friends and the latest films. I could tell he was itching to start work.

Before leaving New York, I had seen a demonstration of Cinema-Scope. With the advent of television, movie receipts had plummeted and the studios were desperate for new ways to exhibit their films. Cinerama, which used three projectors, was cumbersome. So Fox had developed CinemaScope, which could operate with only one projector. At the Roxy Theater they showed clips from *The Robe* with Richard Burton, and *How to Marry A Millionaire,* with Lauren Bacall and Marilyn Monroe. Cinema-Scope was going to save the industry, "they" said.

Charlie listened fascinated as I described this new mail-slot approach to the size of the movie frame. He laughed when I told him how actors in *The Robe* were positioned on the extreme opposite sides of the screen – you had to keep turning your head from side to side to watch the next person talking.

But it was the Rosenbergs who dominated our conversation. He had heard about the letter Mrs Rosenberg sent President Eisenhower just before their execution. "Take counsel with the mother of your only son," Ethel Rosenberg had written; "Her heart which understands my grief so well and my longing to see my sons grow to manhood like her own – her heart must plead my cause with grace and with felicity! Respectfully yours, Mrs Ethel Rosenberg." But both the Eisenhowers were apparently unmoved.

Charlie wept when he talked about it. Then he would explode. "Those bastards, how could they murder those people?" Whether the Rosenbergs were guilty or not did not enter into the argument. It was the humanity of the thing.

Strangely enough, several years later a woman representative of President Eisenhower telephoned Charlie at the Savoy Hotel in London asking to see him. It was all hush-hush. Charlie, sensing something was up, asked me to meet her. It turned out that Eisenhower wanted to roll out the red carpet and welcome Charlie back to America. But first they were making soundings.

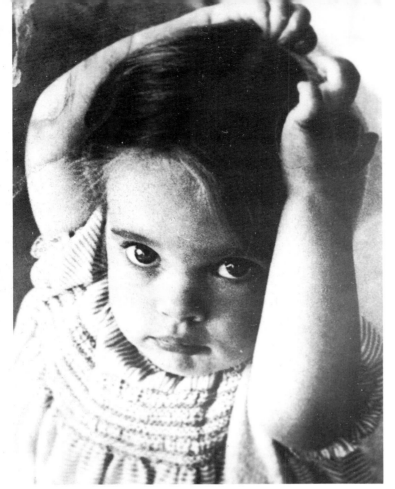

Left: Charlie loved this photo of Vicky. It was always in his bedroom.
Below: Charlie and Josephine.

Above: Charlie and Geraldine.
Right: Charlie did several versions of this picture, which he called "Hiding from McCarthy".

Top: Charlie and me sunning ourselves on the lawn.
Bottom: Charlie called this picture "Yearning for Hollywood".

When I started to convey the message to Charlie, he stopped me in my tracks; we left the Savoy, took a red double-decker bus, sat upstairs, and drove around London. I whispered the message into his ear. "Repeat it once more," he said. It was like something out of a Graham Greene thriller. Charlie then told me to tell the representative that he was declining the invitation.

When I arrived in Switzerland, he was still angry about the way America had treated him, but was nervous about saying too much to the press. He still owned part of United Artists; neither his studio nor the house in Beverly Hills were sold yet, and he knew Uncle Sam could attach his holdings. So he had to remain silent.

I remember in California, while he was being attacked by the American press, late one evening he read me part of a statement he wanted to issue to the newspapers. It was fiery ... he said he wasn't going to be blackmailed by fascist gangs, or bend down on his knees to anyone when he'd done nothing wrong. I felt he was still anxious to issue some statement, but he had to keep his feelings bottled up.

Michael Chaplin, seven years old at the time, was very homesick for California. When the family first arrived in London, he thought they were just having a short holiday. As their stay at the Savoy Hotel became prolonged, Michael kept asking his mother, "When are we going home? I want to go back to California."

One day Charlie and I were sitting in the living-room at Vevey. Once more Charlie was getting worked up about what was going on in America. As he let off steam, little Michael walked in, and suddenly began singing, loudly and defiantly, Irving Berlin's "God Bless America, Land that I Love" right into Charlie's face. Charlie, yelled, "Oona, get that boy out of here! I'm trying to work!"

Several days later, a letter arrived for Charlie from America. It was from Mickey Cohen, a West Coast member of the underworld, who was now in prison. He told Charlie how hurt he was by the way the American Government had treated him, and added that if there was anything he could do to help, Charlie just had to say the word. The implication was clear. I guess he still had plenty of power, even behind bars.

That summer of 1953 was one of the hottest on record in Switzerland. How Charlie loved the heat; he even relished the most humid days in New York. We would sit on reclining chairs on his lawn, basking in the sun, and he'd start kicking around ideas for a new film.

RIGHT: CHARLIE KIDDING AROUND, DOING
HOLLYWOOD CHEESECAKE POSES.
BELOW: WHENEVER CHARLIE SAW A GOOD
LOCATION FOR A PICTURE, HE LIKED TO
POSE IN DIFFERENT ATTITUDES.

He thought he'd like to re-release three of his silent shorts, *Shoulder Arms*, *The Pilgrim* and *A Dog's Life* in a single feature, under the title *The Chaplin Revue*. As a linking device, he had the notion of parodying Somerset Maugham, who'd recently introduced filmed selections from his short stories in a film called *Quartet*. The camera had always caught Maugham in an off-moment, as though he was taken by surprise and had no idea he had to introduce his stories.

Charlie's idea for his first introductory spot in *The Chaplin Revue* was to film himself in bed with a long-haired wench (seen from the back). Then he'd suddenly say to the camera, "Oh – pardon me . . . you caught me at an inopportune moment." While he said a few explanatory words about the first film, the "girl" would be revealed as a large collie dog.

We had fun playing with the Maugham parody idea for several days. Soon it was abandoned. Then he had an idea for a comedy sequence in pantomime. He didn't yet know which picture it was to fit in. But that's the way he worked. First came the sequences; then he'd devise a way of tying them up with a storyline.

The setting was a grocery shop. A goose is hanging from a hook. A bald shopkeeper gets into a fight with a woman customer; he tries to hit her with the goose, misses, and pushes her into a pile of eggs. The shopkeeper gives her the goose as a peace offering. She smells it and complains that it stinks. The shopkeeper pantomimes that she's smelling the wrong end.

Charlie had me roaring with laughter, and the more I laughed, the more gags he invented. Crazy ideas kept pouring out. But he also abandoned this idea.

For days we took long walks into Vevey and trams into Montreux, as Charlie bounced ideas off me. He was looking for another character to play. He toyed with reviving the Tramp, as an old man. But he rejected that. "The whole romance of the Tramp", he said, "lay in his litheness and acrobatic skills, his ability to escape quickly from any situation." No, he would have to find a different character.

For a while he thought of playing another character like the fastidious Verdoux, but Oona and I put our foot down. Then, inadvertently, he suggested a King. In Switzerland he had recently met several deposed monarchs, and became intrigued with their stories of how they had fled revolutions. The moment he mentioned a king, I

CHARLIE AND ME AT THE PING-PONG TABLE.

could visualize him playing a deposed monarch. I remembered an American comic-strip I used to love, "The Little King," drawn by Soglow, and I had a vision of Charlie impersonating him. I immediately said, "Yes, a king!"

The idea grew with Charlie. He began to feel comfortable with it. For days afterwards we sat on the lawn and I took notes as he improvised ideas and sequences. Where they were leading, he did not know. But he soon had an opening sequence.

A revolution outside a palace. Mobs storm in demanding the head of King Shadov. They charge up the grand staircase and search from room to room. But they can't find him. They open up the royal safe. Empty. King Shadhov has escaped just in time, with all the Treasury funds, and is now en route to America, the Land of the Free, the Home of the Brave.

We now had a character and an opening: the two key ingredients in Charlie's theory about writing movies. First, find a character you understand; then put him into a good opening situation that illustrates his character. Afterwards, get him into trouble and out of trouble; into more trouble and out of trouble. Keep this going for ninety minutes, and presto! – you have a full-length feature.

Charlie was now excited. He would write a satirical comedy set in America, and express in dramatic terms all the things he loved, admired and thought ridiculous about the States. But first and foremost, it would be a comedy. He would film it, probably, in London. Although it would feel strange being without his own studio and staff, at least there'd be no language difficulties.

As he developed King Shadhov's character and gave him funny quips, Charlie kept saying, "Bob Hope would be perfect in this part!" I don't think he was seriously considering him, but it possibly helped him visualize some of the King's smart-aleck asides.

CLAIRE, ME AND OONA, SNAPPED BY
CHARLIE IN SWITZERLAND (1953).

Right: Charlie in his Marlon Brando pose.

Far right: Oona having lunch on the veranda.

Below: Charlie and me about to leave for London. It was to be my first visit, and Charlie insisted on accompanying me. Oona took the picture.

Charlie satirized progressive schools where students are given free rein (Geraldine had once gone to one in Los Angeles). He also satirized the noise in New York, and – lo and behold – devised a sequence making fun of CinemaScope (plus the film industry in general). We were having such a good time; we couldn't wait to get to work every morning. But lunch times were the most fun, when we tried out the sequences on Oona. She was our sounding board and best audience. I always looked forward to lunch: when Oona was around there was so much gaiety and laughter, and a feeling of well-being and security.

My two weeks were coming to an end and I was getting nervous. Without being told to leave, I thought it was time to go. I remembered the old saying in Brooklyn: "House guests and fish begin to smell after three days." I told Oona and Charlie I was going home. With my return ticket I could visit either Paris or London on the way back; I decided on London.

Charlie insisted on coming with me to show me his London. Oona was still pregnant, and didn't wish to travel. Charlie's great excuse for the trip was United Artists business: the company wanted to sell their stock in the Odeon theater chain to obtain money to finance films. Charlie was furious. United Artists had not been set up as a financing company, he said. They were merely distributors, and he felt they would lose a fortune. A Board meeting was planned in London, and Charlie wanted to go to protest.

But once in London he was only interested in showing me the city. When I reminded him of the Board meeting, he brushed it aside. He had lost interest in the affairs of United Artists, and only wanted to get rid of his holdings. We stayed at the Savoy Hotel. Once again he took me on foot on what was to become a ritual walk through London.

Some vivid memories of my three days . . . Dining at the Caprice and rubbing shoulders with Sir Jacob Epstein, the sculptor; Sir Jacob trying to find out if we were related – "My brother is a dentist in West Seventy-Seventh Street. I'm sure we belong to the same family!"

. . . Along the Embankment, crowds spotting Charlie and shouting "Charlie Chaplin! Charlie Chaplin". Charlie became nervous: "Let's get out of here," he said. A sightseeing boat on the Thames was about to take off; we quickly hopped on. As we sailed towards Greenwich another boat passed us, blasting its sirens. People on deck were shouting "Charlie Chaplin! Charlie Chaplin!" It was the same crowd we thought we'd left on shore. They had obviously taken the next boat out and were still hunting their prey.

It was time for me to return to the States, but Charlie said, "You don't want to go yet. Come back to Switzerland. Wait until Oona has her baby." I really didn't want to leave, but I never knew with Charlie what he wanted. He would never make things clear, and I was always so self-conscious. But I was happy to return.

Back in Vevey, we rolled up our sleeves and began working on the new film in earnest. He wrote a lovely sequence where King Shadhov gets lost one night in Manhattan and is picked up by a taxi driver; not knowing his identity, the driver befriends the King and takes him back to his Bronx apartment. Charlie suddenly rejected the idea; "It's a cliché," he said. I later found out from his autobiography that the incident had actually happened to him in New York.

Charlie was always searching for original ideas. He would fight until he found one: "You must struggle until you find a fresh conception. That's what they expect from a Chaplin film. Original ideas." He was aware that others copied him; but his own work had to be original.

OONA, PREGNANT, ON THE SOFA THAT WAS FEATURED IN *CITY LIGHTS*.

RIGHT: SIDNEY BERNSTEIN, CHAIRMAN OF
GRANADA TELEVISION, VISITING THE
CHAPLINS.
BOTTOM LEFT: ALTHOUGH THE POOL
WASN'T FINISHED, OONA, ALONG WITH THE
CHILDREN AND KAY-KAY, THEIR NANNY,
PRETENDED IT WAS.
BOTTOM RIGHT: VICKY.

In between work sessions, Charlie put the finishing touches to the house. One big project was the swimming pool. Charlie wanted the pool hidden away in the grounds, so it wouldn't intrude on the landscape visible from the veranda. But the Swiss builders had other ideas. Arguments ensued, with Charlie trying his best to explain what he wanted in English.

No matter how hard Charlie tried, French did not come easily to him; in fact it never came. He was slightly irritated when I began to pick up certain phrases (I used to study late at night). Soon, at lunch I was saying *"Encore de fraises, s'il vous plait!"* (More strawberries, please). My first spoken words in French!

Charlie would have to pantomime to make himself understood. Sometimes mistakes arose. According to Syd, a painter one day didn't understand the color he wanted on the walls. To indicate an off-white egg color, Charlie pantomimed a chicken squatting and laying an egg. At first the painter looked confused. Then it suddenly dawned on him what the color was; he came back carrying a filthy dark brown can of paint.

A letter arrived from Constance! "The heat in New York is unbearable. We have an air-conditioner in my bedroom, and Phyllis and me and the parrot and the dog all sit there together and don't move outside. I think it's very strange that Charlie left the American public the top tune of the country. It is almost like a message. The *Limelight* theme is Number One on the Hit Parade. Vic Damone sings it all the time."

I laughed as I read the letter. Constance kept up with everything – even the Hit Parade.

Victoria was now two, Josie four, Michael seven, and Geraldine nine. They would usually join us on the verandah for lunch; then they'd be herded away by their nannies, Kay-Kay and Miss Pinnie, as Charlie and I would return to work.

Dinner for Oona and Charlie was at 6.45 p.m. sharp. The children had theirs an hour earlier in their own dining-room. As Oona and Charlie enjoyed a pre-dinner cocktail and nibbled on salted peanuts, the children were brought in to say goodnight. They would pounce on those peanuts, but Charlie would limit them.

Charlie had a sweet tooth, and See's chocolates from Los Angeles were his favorite candies: crunchy, chewy, and full of goodies inside. The children adored them also, but the chocolates were his, and they were carefully rationed out, just like the peanuts. Once he left them on the coffee table; when he opened the box, he found most of the chocolates gone or half-bitten and discarded by the children. From that moment on, they were firmly locked up.

RIGHT: CHARLIE AMUSING THE CHILDREN
WITH COBS OF CORN.

Occasionally, Charlie would do the dance of the rolls from *The Gold
Rush* for the children. But what delighted them the most was when he
went behind the sofa and pretended he was walking down a flight of
steps; he'd get smaller and smaller, and finally disappear. The children
would scream with laughter. The illusion was absolute; you'd swear he
was going down into the basement.

Oona and Charlie would retire for bed at about nine o'clock, leaving
me with nothing to do. I would read, but sometimes I wanted to get out
in the evening. But I knew no one in the area apart from the Chaplins,
and the Manoir was on top of a small mountain. There was no television
in those days to lull you to sleep. In desperation, after everyone went to
bed and the doors were firmly locked, I used to climb out of my
bedroom window, find my way down the cold mountain and walk into
Vevey, only to discover that all Switzerland went to bed at nine o'clock.

Another letter from Constance: "It must be so exciting living in
Switzerland. I know you are a good omen and mascot for Charlie and
keep him working ... Oona wrote me that if her next baby is a girl, it
will be called after me ..."

*Charlie giving her off-camera instructions:
"ACT frightened."*

ABOVE AND RIGHT: VICKY DISPLAYING HER
TALENTS AS A BUDDING STAR.

*"Imitating the tramp's 'shrug of
her shoulders"*

ACT sleepy ...

Right: The day after Eugene's birth, Charlie kisses Oona in the hospital.
Far right: The children take their first look at the latest addition to the Chaplin family.
Center: Oona holding Eugene, with proud father ogling him.
Bottom: Oona, Josephine and Eugene.

Opposite, left: Charlie and Josephine.
Opposite, top right: Michael after doing the imitation of his schoolteacher that led Charlie to write a part for him in *A King in New York*.
Opposite, center right: Charlie enjoying fresh strawberries.
Opposite, bottom right: Charlie recognizes the potential actor in Michael.

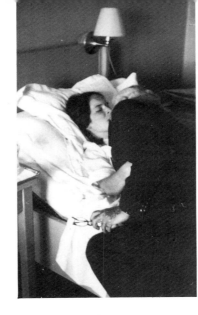

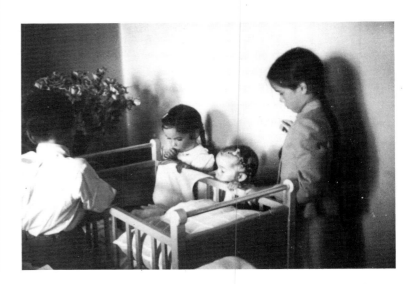

On August 23rd, Eugene Anthony Chaplin was born. "Anthony" was my suggestion. Charlie, the children and I visited Oona in hospital. I had my camera with me and recorded the event. My pictures had become a big part of the Chaplin family album. The moment Charlie saw my camera, he improvised gags in front of it, sometimes taking ten minutes to find the right pose. Charlie loved my pictures and called me his favorite photographer. One of the snaps I took of Victoria as a child was always on his bedside table. After returning home with Eugene, Oona said, "I love going to the hospital to have a baby. It gives me a chance to re-read *War and Peace* – in peace!"

The children were now speaking French and attending Swiss schools. Michael went to a local one in Corsier. One evening he told us about his very strict Swiss teacher. The man would speak very calmly at first and then work himself up into a lather, telling the children what their punishment would be if any of them got out of line. As Michael imitated the teacher, gesturing with his hands and becoming red in the face, Charlie looked at him amazed and suddenly realized there was a new actor in the Chaplin family.

During that hot summer, our daily dessert was large home-grown strawberries. As Charlie ate them he kept remembering an old vaudeville act he saw in America with Willie Howard, called "Comes the Revolution". Charlie, in a Russian accent, would imitate Willie Howard as a soapbox radical talking to bystanders: "Comes de rewolution, you'll eat strawberries and cream!" Then he'd take a heckler's part: "But I don't like strawberries and cream!" And Charlie, as Willie the rabble-rouser, would answer, "Comes de rewolution, you'll *eat* strawberries and cream AND LIKE IT!" Every time Charlie told this Willie Howard skit, he would howl with laughter.

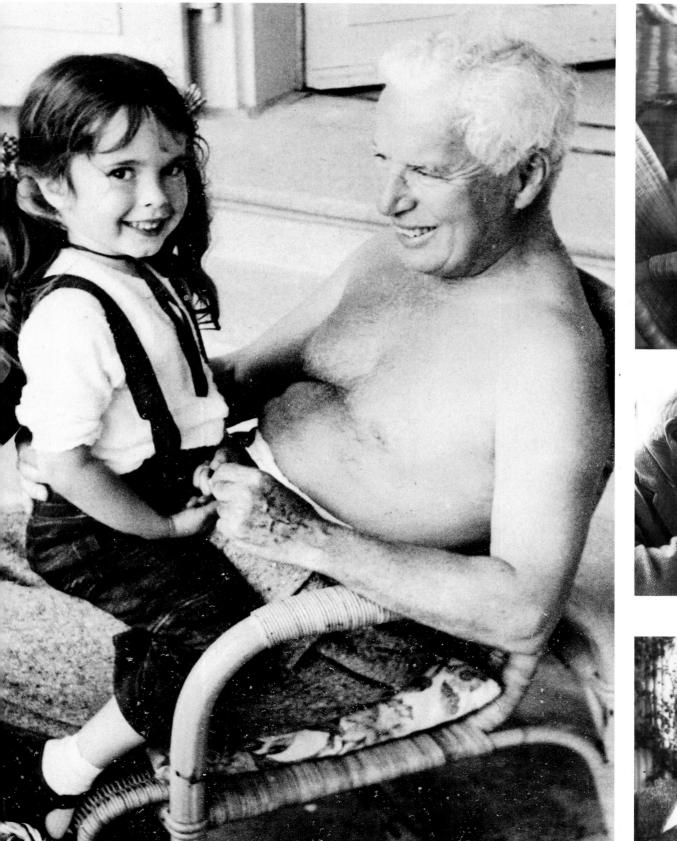

OONA DINING ON THE LAWN.

I feel Charlie must have been inspired by the Willie Howard routine and Michael's imitation of his teacher when he devised his progressive school sequence. The construction is similar. In Charlie's scene, a nine-year-old anarchist, Rupert, meets the King, and the two get into a political argument. Rupert attacks the King with a tirade against the loss of freedom and the evils of big business, and the King has difficulty getting a word in edgewise.

Substitute Rupert for Willie Howard as the soapbox orator: "Am I free to travel?" Rupert proclaims aggressively to the King. "*Only* with a passport! . . . And *free* enterprise – does that exist?" he continues, ranting.

Now substitute the mild King for the heckler: "We were discussing passports," the King says plaintively. But Rupert the anarchist presses on: "*Today* it's all monopoly! *Monopoly* is the menace of free enterprise!!" The King butts in: "If I can say something . . ." But it's no use. Rupert continues: "*Only* with a passport . . ." And so it goes . . .

When Charlie was creating, everything around him seemed to give him ideas – in this case, Michael's stern teacher and now fresh strawberries! Michael was eventually to play Rupert the anarchist, and the film was now entitled *A King in New York*.

But lunch on the terrace was not always that pleasant. Hordes of flies and bees would descend when they saw those strawberries. But Charlie had his eagle eye trained on them, and his faithful fly swatter was at the ready. The moment he heard the slightest buzz, he went up on tiptoe, followed the insect to its next port of call, swatter in hand. Bang! He got him. Charlie, contented, then went back to his strawberries and cream.

Once, to help the fly situation, Oona sprayed an aerosol can, just as Charlie moved. The spray went into his eyes, and he covered them with his hands. "My eyes!" he gasped, "I'll be blinded! They're so important to my career! I'm finished!" He gave a performance to match the moment in *Monsieur Verdoux* when Verdoux thought he drank a glass of poison by mistake. His eyes bulged in panic.

I was witnessing high drama. As he ran into the house and doused himself with water, Oona and I looked at each other fearfully. A moment later, he returned to the veranda, all smiles, his old self again. Oona and I sighed with relief. His eyes were fine. His career would continue.

Constance, meanwhile, was having problems with her own eyesight. "I am going into the hospital next Wednesday to have an operation," she wrote me; "I can't see a thing. Oh the relief to be able to recognize a friend again, or perhaps see a flower . . . Charlie could do a picture that would be really good for the world. I have a feeling his new film will be one of his greatest triumphs."

Charlie continued working on the progressive school scene. Over and over he would prune extraneous words or phrases. The dialogue had to be fast-moving and brittle. Once again he was determined to show he was still a force to contend with.

TOP RIGHT: CHARLIE, JOSIE AND ME AT THE KNIE CIRCUS.
BOTTOM: CHARLIE FEEDING A LOAF OF BREAD TO THE ELEPHANT — OR IS IT THE TRAMP?

In October, the Knie Circus – the Swiss national circus – made its annual visit to Vevey. It was run by the Knie family and was the best circus I ever saw. All the major circuses of the world – from the Ringling Brothers to the Cirque Médrano in France – looked up to the Knies. They always had the most exciting performers, the most amazing animal acts. The Knies used only one ring, so it was possible to concentrate on whatever act was performing. Oona, Charlie, and the entire family went, along with Lillian Ross and myself.

In honor of Charlie's visit, they had a dancing elephant dressed with the Tramp's Derby hat, tight-fitting coat and large shoes – the cane was held in its trunk. The audience cheered, and some cried out "Charlot!" Then Rolf Knie took Charlie by the arm and pulled him into the ring. Rolf handed Charlie a large loaf of bread to feed to the elephant. After Charlie gave the elephant the bread, they both exchanged bows.

When the show was over, we were all invited into the Knies' caravan. Charlie raved to the company about their circus, the skill and the wonderment of it all. He commented to Rolf Knie, "Dwarfs are the ones who work the hardest in a circus, and they're very sad." Rolf Knie nodded in agreement.

From that October onwards, the Chaplin family outing to the Circus became an annual event, and the arrival of the Knies in Vevey caused as much frenzy as any big Hollywood première. Recently, Oona put down her thoughts about the Knie Circus and sent me a copy:

Every October, for the last thirty years, an excitement has grown in our household as traditional as autumn itself: the Knie Circus is coming to town, coming to Vevey. It always has been, as it still is, a magic time, beginning with the animals' arrival, camels and elephants walking calmly through the streets as if it were an old story to them, as indeed it must be, though never to us, waiting happily on the sidewalk. What is an old story, however, is the friendship between our two families. The first time my husband saw the circus, he was overcome by the excellence and the charm and the enterprise of it; it was unique, and it's remained unique. Every year the rumor starts from Geneva – it's better than ever this year – and every year, if possible, it's true. Our children have grown up together, and we have an affection and admiration for the Knie brothers, fathers and sons, that is a pleasure that endures through time and change . . .

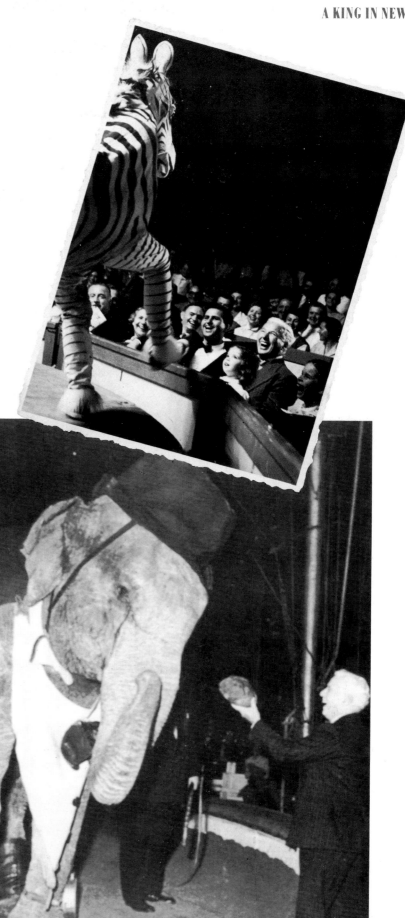

RIGHT: LEFT TO RIGHT: GEORGE, THE FAMILY DRIVER, ME, SYDNEY, LILLIAN ROSS OF *THE NEW YORKER* MAGAZINE (VEVEY, 1953).
BELOW: VICKY AND MICHAEL SORRY TO SEE ME LEAVE FOR PARIS.

Christmas was around the corner. Oona and Charlie were planning a trip to London. I didn't know what I was supposed to do. Should I stay at the house when they left? Was this Charlie's way of telling me to leave? I was confused. I was so afraid of overstaying my welcome. I was happy at Vevey with Oona and Charlie. I enjoyed the work, the children, the laughter and merriment when Sydney came. But I didn't think it was right to stay on while they were in London – being paid for doing nothing. If only Charlie had said something.

I took the bull by the horns and announced that I was leaving for Paris, then I'd be going home. I think Charlie was upset. I wish I could have spoken to him about the way I felt. If only I hadn't found difficulty in discussing certain matters with him.

I was on my way again.

EDDIE CONSTANTINE, WITH HIS BREEZY CHARM, BECAME AN OVERNIGHT MOVIE SENSATION THROUGHOUT FRANCE AND ALL OVER EUROPE.

I was met at the Gare de Lyon by Sydney and his current girlfriend, a beautiful young actress called Kay Kendall. After checking in at the Hotel Montaigne, where Sydney and Kay were staying, we went to a small bistro for dinner. It was good being in Sydney's comforting and relaxed company. He was such a tonic, with his great capacity for friendship and carefree attitude towards life.

I couldn't take my eyes off Kay Kendall. What a beauty! Large, voluptuous lips, half-lidded eyes, a tilted nose, and, most important of all, such charm and humor, and an ability to poke fun at herself. Nothing pompous about our Kay: her idol was Carole Lombard, and she behaved in the same zany way. She had just scored a success in the English comedy *Genevieve* and was becoming a hot property. Sydney and Kay were to leave the next day for Egypt to film *Abdulla the Great* under Gregory Ratoff's direction. Though our first meeting was brief, Kay was soon to become one of my closest friends.

The following day I was introduced to two Hollywood screenwriters at the hotel. Hal Bloom was writing a script for *Land of the Pharaohs* with William Faulkner and Harry Kurnitz. Lou Morhaim was working for Sheldon Reynolds on a TV series, *Foreign Intrigue*. I was unemployed.

That evening we went for dinner at Les Calvados Bar. Lou recognized someone in the distance and waved to him. It was Eddie Constantine, the new sensation of the French cinema. Eddie came to our table. Lou had a message from Eddie's mother in California. We were introduced.

Eddie was an American. Only yesterday he was an MGM chorus boy, singing in films like *Rosalie*, and receiving encouragement from Joan Crawford. Then he and his wife left for Paris, where Eddie sang in dives until Edith Piaf caught his act. He soon became her protégé, following in the footsteps of Charles Aznavour and Yves Montand. Now he'd just scored a huge success as an American private eye, Lemmy Caution, in a French gangster film.

Eddie was basking in his new-found fame. "I'm going to be the biggest star in France!" he told us. Hal and I looked at each other, amused. Eddie continued, "The French don't know how to make gangster films. For my next picture I want an American director who can give my film more tempo and humor." Eddie turned to Lou and Hal: "Can you suggest someone?"

Hal and Lou, knowing I wanted to direct, pointed to me. "Him!" they said. Eddie turned to me: "Would you like to direct my next picture?" Laughingly, I said "Yes". He asked where I was staying, saying he'd be at my hotel at eleven o'clock the next morning. When he left, we laughed and dismissed it from our minds.

At eleven o'clock the next day, Eddie arrived ready to make a deal. I didn't speak French, but I was keeping my mouth shut. Then he asked if I wrote scripts. I had never written a thing in my life. But in France, all French directors helped with the scripts. And I remembered Charlie telling me how he started to write – he knew that if he was going to find the kind of material he wanted, he would have to write it himself. And so he did. So when Eddie asked if I wrote, I said "Yes!" If I had to write to get the job, I would do as Charlie did – *write*.

At first, I think, the French producers confused me with the Epstein brothers who wrote *Casablanca*. When they found out I was another Epstein, they were frightened of hiring someone who had never directed a film and couldn't even speak the language. But Eddie was insistent. I was his boy. If I didn't direct, he wouldn't make the film. He fought everyone: the unions, the producers, the technical staff. You couldn't help liking Eddie – he had such enthusiasm and loyalty. But he couldn't avoid the tremendous anti-American sentiments prevalent in France. "U.S. go home!" was scrawled on the walls all over Paris. But they couldn't mean me, could they?

I was hired to direct. Elated, I called Oona and Charlie, and told them what had happened during my first three crazy days in Paris. They couldn't believe it; neither could I. Charlie giggled over the phone, saying it was marvelous, just marvelous.

I was introduced to a French writer, Jacques Vilfrid, who spoke no English; I spoke no French. What a team! But somehow the two of us began knocking out a script, with Eddie and his American pianist Jeff Davis acting as translators; we gave Eddie the part of an airline pilot, mixed up in a murder case on a brief vacation in Paris.

On weekends I took a train to Vevey, loaded down with Kleenex and Almond Joys for Oona and Charlie. Kleenex tissues were not available in Europe at the time; and of course Almond Joys were one of Charlie's great pleasures. These were supplied to me, almost by the carton, by Elliott Kastner – today a prominent film producer, then a GI stationed with the American Army in Paris.

In Vevey, Charlie would read me his latest sequence for *A King in New York*. Now he had to hear *my* screenplay, *Votre Dévoué Blake (Yours Truly, Blake)*. But this wasn't an ordeal for Charlie. He enjoyed listening to other people's work, giving advice and helping them with their script problems.

"Who's the murderer?" he asked. I had him completely baffled. But so was I, since we hadn't yet decided who the murderer was going to be. Charlie suggested some gags and ideas, all of which I put into the film. He soon became a Constantine fan – he loved his breezy manner and boyish zest for life. When Eddie came to Switzerland, Oona and Charlie took him to dinner at the Palace Hotel, Lausanne. Eddie gave an impromptu concert and Charlie requested one of his favorite songs, "Ol' Man River". Eddie gave it his all. Charlie's favorite line in any song was Oscar Hammerstein's "Ah'm tired of livin' an' skeered of dyin' ". He felt it was most profound.

Although Charlie had written isolated sequences for *A King in New York*, he still hadn't found the storyline that would tie them all together. But the *Votre Dévoué Blake* script was soon finished, and we were now ready for pre-production work. At the time there was high unemployment in the French film industry, yet here was I, an American, directing a French film. I began to feel an undercurrent of resentment from the technicians. What had I got myself into?

Eddie, at least, was confident. "I'm a big star!" he kept repeating,

"They can't make the film without me!" But in order to appease the unions I had to allow a Frenchman to sign the film as the credited director. (I felt like a blacklisted writer, writing under a pseudonym.) Even Eddie couldn't do anything about that, although he tried. My own credit would be technical director. But I was assured that if I went along with this arrangement this time, I would be given full credit on my next film. I was so involved in pre-production that I agreed.

Oona had just given up her American citizenship – in protest at the way Charlie had been treated in the States. She was now a British citizen, like Charlie. They were both due in London soon; Charlie was going to give a press conference. Casting for *Votre Dévoué Blake* would start the following week, so before the ordeal started I left for a weekend in London.

Without the Army's knowledge, Elliott Kastner followed me there, bringing more Kleenex and Almond Joys for Charlie. We both stayed in a sleazy hotel in Bayswater. As Charlie was holding a press conference at the Savoy, I arrived in his suite loaded down with my goodies. While he told the journalists about his new film, I gently laid the Almond Joys on the coffee table. At that moment a reporter asked him what he missed most in America. Spotting the candies, Charlie lifted one up and declared, "Almond Joys!" The cameras flashed.

When I repeated this to Elliott back in Bayswater, he panicked.

"That'll make the front pages!" he said nervously, and began to pack his valise. "They'll trace the Almond Joys to me and find out where I was, *and who they were given to*!" I think Elliott was in the Intelligence Service – and Charlie was still considered a Commie Red. In a flash, Elliott was on the next plane back to Paris. He was right about the newspapers. Next day a picture of Charlie holding up an Almond Joy made the front pages of the tabloids. Poor Elliott, how he suffered!

In Paris, I finished casting. From the Comédie Française, I chose the great French actor Robert Hirsch to play a film director. Carol Saroyan, Oona's best friend, was in town. No longer married to Bill, she was dead broke but looked more beautiful than ever. I knew she could act, and I wanted to get her a job. So Eddie and I told the producers that she was a big American star and could only enhance the film's grosses. So Carol Saroyan – a complete unknown – made her movie debut in a French film, portraying a film star in a scene with the great Robert Hirsch.

As soon as Colette Doréal walked into my office I knew I had found the right actress for the sultry villainness. Her Romanesque nose intrigued me. It made her look quite beautiful. Six weeks later, when she reported for shooting, I didn't recognize her. She had a tiny nose. I guess she now had enough money to pay for the nose job she'd always wanted! All actors' contracts should have a clause: their nose stays, as is, at the time of signing.

OPPOSITE: OONA AND CHARLIE ENJOYING AN EVENING OUT.

RIGHT: ON THE SET OF *VOTRE DÉVOUÉ BLAKE*, CAROL SAROYAN (NOW MATTHAU) MAKING HER FILM DÉBUT. SITTING NEXT TO HER IS ROBERT HIRSCH OF THE COMÉDIE FRANÇAISE.

ABOVE: WHEN JOSIE AND VICKY STARTED BALLET LESSONS, CHARLIE GOT IN ON THE ACT TOO.

OPPOSITE: I'M TRYING TO DIRECT FRENCH ACTORS IN PIDGIN FRENCH. LEFT TO RIGHT: DORA DOLL, EDDIE, ME, JEAN LAVIRON AND AN UNIDENTIFIED ACTOR.

We filmed all over town. Sometimes we'd rewrite scenes two minutes before shooting. Eddie couldn't remember all the new dialogue. But he took it in his stride. "Don't worry, Jerry, I'll pretend I'm chewing gum and keep my mouth moving – we'll dub in the words afterwards."

I had worked out so many funny gags and sequences for the film. But no one on the set laughed – not even at the gags Chaplin had given me. The French assistants would come over and say, *"Ce n'est pas drôle!"* (It's not funny) or *"pas logique!"* Everything in France had to be logical. They let me know in no uncertain terms that the French would never laugh at my gags. I told them: "But I laugh at French films; and I know from seeing movies on the Champs Elysées that they laugh at American films."

My argument didn't convince them, and their antagonism began to reach Eddie. I could see he was being swayed: his opinions always depended on the last person he spoke to. If a cab driver told Eddie he was making a mistake over his career, he would immediately take this unknown person's opinions as gospel, call up his agent, and give him hell. I sensed Eddie was beginning to wonder how he had ever got involved with me.

One morning, before I left for the studio, I received a letter, in French. I stuffed it into my pocket, planning to have it translated during the day. As we were shooting, I felt mounting tension on the set. But I dismissed it from my mind and continued arranging the next set-up. Then, as I was walking down the stage, a tremendous sandbag hurtled toward me. Eddie yanked my hand just in time.

I was shaken. It obviously wasn't an accident. Instinctively I took out the letter. Eddie translated: "Don't come on the set today. If you make an appearance, you will be killed." After that, though, the crew left me alone. They believed I had read the letter and still came on the set. They had new respect for me!

Just as Charlie needed his walks into the past, I seemed able to replenish my spirit by spending weekends with Oona and Charlie in Vevey. One particular weekend, Charlie, little Josie and I were driven into the village of Vevey. From his car, Charlie looked at the swans on Lake Geneva; Josie went out playing. Charlie was suddenly recognized by a group of children. They all rushed to the car and handed in slips of paper for his autographs. He happily signed. Then he noticed Josie crammed in amongst the children, also wanting his autograph!

I usually returned buoyed up from these trips. But when I came back to Paris this time, my high spirits were quickly dashed. The rumor spread that the film was a disaster. Eddie was now beginning to feel he had made a big mistake. "Why did I hire you?" he snarled at me.

With the shooting finished, I was eager to begin editing, but I was forbidden to enter the cutting room. And this time Eddie would not back me up; he had completely written off the film. I felt like an unwelcome guest in Paris – "U.S. go home!" really *was* meant for me.

By coincidence, Sydney and Kay had now returned from their labors on *Abdulla the Great*. I was temporarily able to forget my troubles as I listened to Sydney's hilarious stories about working in Egypt with Gregory Ratoff. By now Kay was madly in love with Syd, but their romance was tempestuous. Sydney appeared more interested in his golf strokes (which he continuously practiced in his hotel room), while Kay desperately tried to make contact with him by whacking him on the head with one of his clubs.

Sydney was anxious to introduce Kay to Oona and Charlie. We all traveled together on the night train to Vevey. At the Swiss border, the customs official asked if we had anything to declare. We all replied "No". Then they noticed Syd's enormous valise, and asked us to get off the train. As we saw our train depart, the Customs men attacked Syd's suitcase.

Kay was fuming, and acted the part of the haughty, affronted traveller. "Do you know who we are? I'm a famous film star," she insisted, "and this is Charlie Chaplin's son. I'll have you all reported to the British Embassy. Do we *look* like smugglers?" They had now opened up Syd's valise. Out rolled large bolts of the most expensive, exquisite Egyptian silks, purchased in Cairo – a present for Oona.

Silks or not, Kay kept ranting: "I want all your names. Who are you?" I kicked her in the shins. If we weren't careful, we'd put the whole Chaplin family in the clink. In order to calm Kay down, Syd had to fork out ten times more than the bolts were worth.

CHARLIE AND VICKY.

Syd and Kay had a running argument. Kay had reminded him more than once that she too came from a famous theatrical background: her grandmother was Marie Kendall, a star of the English music-hall. Sydney dismissed her: "Who the hell ever heard of Marie Kendall? My father's Charlie Chaplin!" Although the argument was pursued with light banter, underneath Kay was annoyed.

In Vevey, Oona and Charlie were introduced to Kay, and Charlie quickly became entranced. He asked her about herself. When she mentioned who her grandmother was Charlie's face lit up, and he looked at her with awe. "So you're Marie Kendall's grand-daughter!" Kay nodded modestly. "Oh she was just marvelous!" Charlie continued, "What a great star!" Kay was in seventh heaven, and turned to Sydney; "See?" she said, and stuck her tongue out.

Charlie became very fond of Kay and soon devised the leading lady's part in *A King in New York* with her in mind. The character (a brash television personality) was even to be called Miss Kay.

Soon afterwards I left for London. With *Blake* finished at last, there was nothing in Paris for me any more. I was distressed to learn a little later that Sydney and Kay had broken up because of Syd's dalliance with Joan Collins. Kay was now seeing Rex Harrison, who was in London appearing with his wife Lilli Palmer in *Bell Book and Candle*. People in the know referred to the play as *Bell Book and Kendall*.

Kay put me in the hands of her agent George Routledge, who found me a one-roomed apartment at 166 Sloane Street, Knightsbridge. This turned out to be an apartment of intrigue. In that small room, above a furniture shop, so much went on: all-night parties with the likes of Ken Tynan, Irene Worth, Claire Bloom and Huntington Hartford. There were no chairs – everyone sat on the floor. Eventually that apartment became the secret rendezvous for Rex and Kay.

Sidney Bernstein, Alfred Hitchcock's great friend, invited me to see Ingrid Bergman at the Stoll Theatre in Paul Claudel's oratorio *Joan of Arc at the Stake*. Constance arrived in town. She was here to coach Marjorie Steele – our Viola in *Twelfth Night* – in the leading role in *Sabrina Fair*. We had lunch together at the Connaught Hotel. I told Constance I had just seen Ingrid Bergman in *Joan of Arc*; this was the third time she had played Joan (once on Broadway, once in a movie, and now in this dramatic oratorio). Constance looked at me. "That woman thinks she *is* Joan of Arc!" she said, disdainfully.

RIGHT: SYD WITH HIS LATEST GIRLFRIEND, SOMEONE CALLED JOAN COLLINS, AT THE CHAPLIN POOL.

Philip Langner visited me. He still wanted to make films, so we decided to find someone to write a screenplay. After reading scores of submitted material, we both found an unknown writer, Abby Mann. (He subsequently won an Academy Award for *Judgment at Nuremberg*.) Later, through Abby, Philip finally entered the film business; Abby also became a major stepping-stone in launching my friend Elliott Kastner as a top-notch MCA agent.

Oona and Charlie kept in touch by phone. One day, Charlie insisted I visit them. I usually knew what this meant; he had finished another sequence for *A King in New York* and wanted me to read it. When I arrived he was bubbling with joy. He had just written the scene where Miss Kay, the television personality, entices the King to a banquet in New York. Unknown to him there are hidden cameras, and he is being televised as she sells deodorants. It's one of the most hilarious sequences in the picture. Yet with all these scenes written, Charlie still didn't know where the story was heading.

It was almost Christmas. 1954 wasn't my year, what with the fiasco of my French film; I was glad it was ending. Then, to my surprise, I received a call from Eddie Constantine. He was excited. *Votre Dévoué Blake* was a smash hit! It had opened at a theater off the Champs Elysées, and the lines stretched round the block; audiences were screaming with laughter. "You were right!" Eddie told me, "Everything you said about the gags was true. I want you for my next picture!" I was ready to celebrate.

Oona and Charlie invited me for the holidays. I was happy to go. That Christmas in Vevey started a tradition; I was to spend at least eighteen Christmases with them over the years. The pattern was usually the same. On Christmas Eve, everyone wrapped their packages and decorated the tree. This was Oona's domain, and she insisted we all help. While all this was going on, Charlie would sit in the living-room reading, always unconcerned. Christmas depressed him; he thought Oona was spoiling the children with all her lavish presents (he'd remember his orange). Usually, the day after Christmas he'd get ill with a cold or the 'flu.

This Christmas, he just wanted to talk about his next movie. We both wanted to talk about our projects. But at seven in the evening the doorbell rang, and in walked the kindly Mayor of Corsier, dressed in a Santa Claus outfit. In America, Santa Clauses are usually fat, jolly men; our Father Christmas was tall, thin, and serious, and his costume hung loosely. He sang Christmas carols in a high tenor voice. Charlie took this event very seriously and insisted everyone go into the hallway and listen. The Mayor's visit became an annual ritual.

LEFT: SYD WITH KAY KENDALL, MICHAEL AND, WITH HER BACK TO THE CAMERA, GERALDINE, IN LAUSANNE.

At 6 a.m., Christmas morning, squeals from the children resounded through the house. Within a flash all the paper from the carefully wrapped packages was ripped open. Charlie would come down hours later, after the commotion had subsided. Then he would open his gifts – as delighted as one of the children when he liked something. I usually bought him recordings of old-time English music-hall artists, or picture albums of Victorian London. He was always fascinated by anything that evoked old memories.

After lunch and more champagne, we watched one of his films. By six o'clock everyone was falling off their feet. The help were relieved when we all went out to dinner.

The routine changed one Christmas. Clara Haskil, the great pianist and exponent of Mozart and Haydn, came for lunch. Her visits were to become an annual event. In the afternoon she would play at the Steinway piano Charlie had bought especially for her. It was the first time I ever saw Oona and Charlie like worshipping fans.

I left for Paris in high spirits and began working on a new screenplay for Eddie with an American collaborator, Joe Morhaim. We concocted a romantic comedy about an American Don Juan who runs a sight-seeing launch on the Côte d'Azur and gets entangled with an American lady evangelist.

In March a long chatty letter arrived from Constance:

Thank heaven! You are having such splendid success! It must be so interesting. Why not stick to Paris as you have done so well there? You can't make roots if you change ground . . . I have a very strange group of pupils – Kate Hepburn, Margaret Truman [the President's daughter], Marilyn Monroe, Linda Berlin and lots of others! I have just finished with Paulette [Goddard]. But it is so tiring – as I teach them individually. If only I had started a school. I could have had an income in my old age.

Six weeks later, she died. Dear Constance, she was so brave. Despite all her infirmities, next to Charlie she always seemed the youngest person in the world. She never gave up. Afterwards, Phyllis showed good sense and went to work for Katharine Hepburn. They're still together.

Opposite, top: Pablo Casals, Clara Haskil and Charlie.

Opposite, bottom: Charlie ready for lunch.

Right: Oona, Charlie and their growing family at the pool.

Errol Flynn was looking for a writer for a movie about the legendary Swiss hero William Tell. Flynn had already made one abortive attempt at filming the story; now he wanted another shot. The swashbuckling role, he thought, could revive his flagging career. My English agent called me and suggested I meet Errol in Monte Carlo. Perhaps the job would be mine.

Before going to see Flynn, I visited the Manoir. When I arrived, Charlie was most excited. He'd broken the storyline of *A King in New York*. He knew how he'd tie his isolated sequences together. The young boy Rupert, whom Shadhov met at the progressive school, would now re-appear later in the film; he was to be the key to the story.

Shadhov finds Rupert shivering in a snowstorm outside his hotel, takes him in, and discovers that his parents are under investigation by the Un-American Activities Committee. Since the parents won't co-operate, the investigators are searching for the boy to question him about his parents and their friends. The King feeds and looks after Rupert in his suite. By performing this simple act of kindness, Shadhov is now labelled a Communist sympathizer and brought before the Committee.

After he's cleared, he visits Rupert. In a devastating scene, Rupert, to save his parents from jail, informs on them. To the King's chagrin, the young spunky anarchist has become brainwashed and is now a mere whisper of his former self.

The last scene in *A King in New York* shows Shadhov flying back to Europe. He has had enough. Originally, Charlie planned to end the film with a shot of the plane flying over New York. In the background we were to see the Statue of Liberty growing smaller and smaller – a metaphor for Liberty slowly fading away. But the scene was never shot. Charlie decided the film was sufficiently hard-hitting. Why rub it in?

Charlie always denied that the Rupert storyline was based on the Rosenbergs and the plight of their children. And I believe him. But the tenor of the times obviously played a part. I was proud of Charlie. Here he was, in political hot water because of his so-called Communist sympathies, living in exile. But instead of taking the easy way out by making a sure-fire comedy, he was back in the forefront of the fight, thumbing his nose at his critics by making a film with strong political overtones. Charlie was the only film-maker at the time to have the guts to tackle McCarthyism head on.

ABOVE: I'M LAPPING UP THE SUN IN SITGES, SPAIN, WHILE WAITING FOR ERROL FLYNN.

OPPOSITE: ERROL IN HIS ROBIN HOOD DAYS.

Once again, Charlie was hatching a film destined to be provocative. I didn't want to leave – I was so excited; but I had this rendezvous with Errol Flynn.

In Monte Carlo, Flynn and I walked towards the Casino. Flynn was heavier than the youthful hero of his wonderful adventure films, and becoming jowlly in the face. A little tipsy, he turned to me and said, "Let me tell you about myself. If I wasn't an actor, I'd have been a con-man. Watch me carefully." I should have taken him seriously.

Errol was living in Europe to avoid the American tax man. He was broke. But somehow he found enough money to gamble. Inside the casino, crowds gathered to watch the dashing Errol at the roulette table, smoking a cigarette in a long holder. Whatever number he played, he missed by one notch. But he kept on going to the cashier for more chips. He was losing heavily, and I was dying inside.

Errol kept mumbling under his breath, "Keep smiling, Errol, they're all watching you!" In front of the crowds, he had to be the same carefree, devil-may-care hero of his films.

After losing even more, he asked my birthdate. I told him January 17th. He then kept gambling on the number 17, and still kept losing. I couldn't look. I pleaded with him to let me hold some of his money, so he wouldn't leave empty-handed. But Errol wasn't satisfied until the last chip was gone. He finally left the casino without a *sou* but full of bravado, waving and smiling to his fans. You'd think he'd just broken the bank, instead of the reverse.

The writing job was mine. Joe Morhaim joined me in Spain to collaborate; Errol was filming Ivor Novello's Ruritanian musical *King's Rhapsody* in Barcelona with Anna Neagle – an odd combination. Joe and I were put up in Sitges, a small fishing village about twenty-five miles to the south. Once a week I'd visit Errol with the script. "Read me the scene with the apple!" he kept saying. As I read, he'd pantomime pulling the bow, and half-choke with emotion as he prepared to release the imaginary arrow into the apple on the boy's head.

At his hotel, Errol always prepared for filming with a massage to clear away the previous day's hangover. As he lay on his stomach, being worked over by hulking brutes, he'd take generous gulps from what looked like a glass of water. It was actually straight gin. Then he'd stagger onto the location for his scenes as Richard, King of Laurentia.

Errol was killing himself. His wife, Patrice Wymore, approached me and asked if I'd speak to him about it. She was desperate: she was very much in love, but no longer knew how to help or cope with him. "He won't live much longer if he keeps this up – someone must get to him!" I did my best. But it was impossible to reach Errol. He had to play the role of the reckless knight errant to the end.

Errol kept asking me about Charlie. He was fascinated by him. He wanted to know all about his new screenplay. He couldn't believe that Charlie was about to embark on another film at his age. I told Errol the film was about a boy who gets into trouble when he tries to shield his parents from a Government investigation. "Jesus!" Errol cried, "We can use some of this in *William Tell*!"

"Don't you dare!" I replied. But I knew Errol wouldn't touch any line or situation devised by Chaplin. Errol had a close friend who served as his adviser; they were both afraid of anything they thought smacked of Communism. In our *Tell* script, we had a scene where a young girl working for the downfall of the tyrant Gessler goes about at night daubing on the walls "DOWN WITH GESSLER!" Flynn's friend was always suspicious of my connection with Chaplin and told me pointedly: "This is what the Reds do. It's blatant pinko propaganda!" I never saw it that way, and luckily neither did Errol.

Philip Langner visited me in Barcelona, and Errol invited us to lunch with Anna Neagle. Years before she had been at my theater with her husband Herbert Wilcox. But I never mentioned it; the Circle seemed so long ago. Anna was now about fifty, and always held her head stretched up like a giraffe; she never lowered it for a second. Anna had made a career of playing queens; sitting with her, you felt you were actually with royalty, and treated her likewise. But not playful Errol; he enjoyed goosing her.

Trying to make conversation, I asked Anna how she went about portraying royalty. Anna replied majestically: "A queen never uses a contraction." This was the entire basis for her characterizations of royalty, saying "shall not" instead of "shan't", "can not" instead of "can't". I told this to Charlie before he played Shadhov in *A King in New York*. I thought he'd laugh, but he listened seriously. "Makes sense," he said.

One night Errol invited me for dinner. "You're going to have the best meal you've ever eaten!" Errol's chauffeur-driven limousine drove us to the outskirts of Barcelona, and stopped before an illuminated adobi. Errol sat with the window open. Suddenly crowds of young girls rushed to the car. "Errol! Errol!" they shouted. Errol, pie-eyed, put his hand out of the window as though he were going to shake their hands. Instead, he began fondling the girls' breasts.

I accompanied Errol into the adobi, looking forward to this great feast. We were in a high-class brothel! The girls went wild when they saw Errol and rushed out of their rooms, abandoning their disgruntled clients. He was obviously a tried and true customer. Everyone was on first name terms . . . Incidentally, they also had a fine restaurant . . .

The *King's Rhapsody* unit moved to London for interiors at Shepperton Studios. I went on the set, and watched the same brutes massaging Errol and trying to sober him up behind a stage flat, while Anna made a regal entrance down the steps of a large palace. They were desperate to get him ready to shoot, but he could hardly stand.

Seeing me, Errol gulped down another glass of "water". He knew I was there to collect my money. Luckily I had everything in writing, countersigned by Herbert Wilcox, the film's producer. But they still ignored the facts of life. I had to sue. The day before the case was due to be heard, they settled out of court. In spite of everything, I still have fond memories of Errol. He *was* a charming, confused con-man.

Eddie Constantine wanted me to write a script for another film. Inspired by my adventures with Errol, I devised a screenplay called *Le Grand Bluff* about an American con-man who comes to Paris. Somehow the script wrote itself; Errol was a great inspiration.

During a weekend with Eddie and Hélène on their farm, I directed a home movie featuring Eddie and myself. I improvised many crazy gags. Eddie howled with laughter; he was a great audience. *Blake* was such a big hit, he'd laugh at anything I said now; he wasn't taking any chances. Because of this home movie and my mad antics, Eddie thought I would be great in his next film, playing his buddy. I didn't want to – acting made me nervous. But Eddie kept looking at my face. "You could be so good-looking. You've got the personality for the screen – if only you'd have a nose job and shorten the tip!"

"Oh, Eddie," I replied, "it doesn't bother me!" But he wouldn't give up. "Put your index finger over the bottom of your nose, and cover it

up!" I obeyed. "My God," he cried, "you look like Cary Grant! Get your nose fixed. I'll pay for it, and put you in my next film!"

I weakened. After a couple of visits to the plastic surgeon the big day finally came. I sat nervously in the waiting room with the other patients. We surreptitiously examined each other, wondering what each of us were going to have fixed. Now it was my turn to go in. After showing me again how my new nose would look and explaining the surgery with diagrams, the doctor thrust me onto a table, and covered my face with plaster of Paris. As it grew hot and hardened, I thought I would suffocate. I smashed the plaster off and bolted for the door.

Charlie loved the story of my nose-job. Shortly afterwards, he worked a hilarious face-lifting sequence into *A King in New York*. Miss Kay approaches the King before he's due to appear in a TV commercial, and suggests he has his face lifted and his nose shortened. "You'd be surprised the youthful effect it will give you!" she says. The face-lifting sequence is a show-stopper.

By early 1956, *A King in New York* was ready for pre-production in London. Charlie and Oona arrived at the Savoy; I had an apartment in Pont Street. I was employed, but my good work on *Limelight* was apparently forgotten. It seemed I had to prove my worth all over again. But soon the entire production was thrown into my hands – finding the right studio, hiring the production manager and crew, casting, and generally setting up the film.

Charlie and I traveled around looking at the various studios – Shepperton, Pinewood, Elstree, Walton-on-Thames. Everyone treated us cordially and seemed to want us to shoot at their studio – after all, this was to be Chaplin's first film in his own country. Everyone, that is, except Pinewood. There an aura of snobbery hung in the air. You felt they regarded Charlie as a mere music-hall comic. And yet, some ten years later, with *A Countess from Hong Kong*, we loved working at Pinewood: a different climate and new personnel now prevailed. Gone was their Establishment attitude.

At Walton-on-Thames, they bent over backwards to get Charlie to shoot his film with them. We visited the set of *Child in the House*, with Eric Portman and Phyllis Calvert. Directing the film was Cy Endfield – like Charlie a refugee from the American political scene. But, much as he liked Walton, Charlie felt the stages were not large enough.

Anna Neagle and Errol Flynn in
King's Rhapsody. Such acting must be
seen to be believed!

IMP.114.

133

I liked Elstree Studio the best. In charge of production were Robert Clark and James Wallis. This was my first encounter with hard-headed, dour Scotsmen. I had formed an affection for the breed during production of *What Every Woman Knows* at the Circle; now I was meeting their real-life equivalents. Although they were tough, I felt them to be honest and trustworthy. Besides, they proposed a deal that I thought impossible to turn down.

They gave us everything I asked for; the price was right, the stages were perfect, and they threw in many perks. After months of negotiations the contracts were ready to sign the next day. I told them they had a deal. That night Charlie must have met someone at a dinner party who said, "Don't go to Elstree – Shepperton is the place for you!" That did it. No matter how hard I tried to convince him that we had a better deal at Elstree, Shepperton was in and Elstree was out. It was just like Eddie listening to the cab driver; all it took was someone to throw in a monkey wrench at the last moment, and my months of negotiations crumbled. Today, Elstree is the studio preferred by Steven Spielberg, George Lucas and Stanley Kubrick.

Charlie was financing the film himself. We had no distribution deal, but the hierarchy of United Artists – Max Youngstein and Arnold Picker – flew over from New York to meet with Charlie at the Savoy. For two hours they sat in his hotel suite while I read them the *King in New York* script. They looked pale when I finished; they were obviously disturbed by its content. They were hoping for another *Limelight*, which put millions into their coffers. They bade farewell, and said they would make their decision when they saw the finished film.

We knew the picture would be controversial, so we had to economize. This was no hardship for Charlie: to him, economizing was part of the fun in film-making, because it forced you to be more imaginative. He always said, "Anyone can hire twenty thousand extras for a scene – that doesn't take talent!" But it took real talent to give the illusion of twenty thousand through the tricks of a camera.

In *A Woman of Paris*, Charlie created the effect of a passing train by keeping the camera on Edna Purviance, and showing lights playing across her face – as though the lights came from the carriages of a train arriving at a station. The effect has since been copied many times.

Charlie also used all his ingenuity on the mob scenes in *The Great Dictator*. If a major studio had mounted the film, he once told me, they would have had ten thousand extras listening to the dictator's harangue. Charlie staged the scene with fifty extras standing in the foreground in rapt attention. Beyond them stood midgets, and beyond that, small wooden figures with moveable arms that could rise in salute. Beyond that, Charlie later superimposed a tray full of popcorn; once the popcorn was heated, they looked exactly like human heads popping up and down. On the screen, you'd swear Hynkel had an audience of one hundred thousand flesh-and-blood people. Figuring out visual effects and making illusions were what intrigued Charlie about movies; he was like a magician with a bag of tricks.

We were scheduled to begin filming in May, though we still had to cast most of the parts. Michael was set for Rupert, and Kay Kendall had been inked in as Charlie's leading lady. Kay was now being courted by Hollywood (she eventually signed with MGM). I thought she might be apprehensive about appearing with Charlie, since he was still *persona non grata* in the States. But this didn't matter one iota to Kay. She just wanted to work with him.

In my enthusiasm, I suggested to Charlie that we look at Kay in her film *Genevieve,* to get an idea of how to photograph her. I arranged a showing at the United Artists projection room. The film was a great success with the public, but it bored Charlie to tears. More importantly, he began to think Kay was wrong for the part in *A King in New York*. I almost died. "She's too English," Charlie complained. "She has to be American."

One of the hardest things I had to do was call Kay and tell her the part was not hers. I hesitated several times before I dialled; she was so looking forward to the film. But sweet Kay made it very easy for me. Happily, her career was taking off.

When it came to casting smaller parts, Charlie didn't like to feel I was pushing friends. So when I auditioned actors whom I knew personally and who were right for the part, I always told them: "Whatever you do, when you come to read for Charlie and myself, don't acknowledge me. Charlie will always ask me afterwards what I think. Then I can say you were very good. But if he suspected we were friends, he'd doubt my judgment." Once, when an old friend came to audition, Charlie and I both thought he'd be excellent. Just before he left, my pal turned to me and said, "What time shall we meet for dinner?" Our cover was blown. He didn't get the part.

CHARLIE AND OONA WITH PRODUCER
MARSHALL YOUNG AND MY CLOSE FRIENDS
MARILYN AND PHILIP LANGNER OF THE
NEW YORK THEATRE GUILD.

But who was to play Charlie's Queen? Although the part took only a day's work, it gave substance and body to the film. The process of casting went on for a couple of weeks. Sometimes we thought we'd found the actress, then suddenly she wasn't available. This small role, which we thought would be easy to cast, was now draining our energy.

The person we were both sold on was Margaret Johnston, married to Charlie's old Hollywood friend, the director Al Parker (then working in London as an agent). I showed Charlie a film she had made, *Monsieur Ripois,* with Gérard Philippe. Maggie was lovely. But she was tied up playing Lady Macbeth. So the search went on and on.

In a small lounge off the main lobby at the Savoy Hotel, I interviewed and read most of the top 35-year-old actresses in London. Those that I thought had possibilities, I sent up to Charlie's suite to meet him. After days of this, Charlie sent me a message via the telephone operator that he was exhausted and didn't want to see any more Queens. By the time the message was filtered through to me by an old retainer on the switchboard, the lobby rumbled with noise and consternation. I asked the receptionist what was going on. The Queen was coming to visit Mr Chaplin, he said, and Chaplin had refused to see her! The controversy was quickly sorted out. But if Louella Parsons or Hedda Hopper had got hold of this story in Hollywood, Charlie would have been nailed to the cross. Eventually we found our Queen in Maxine Audley.

While waiting for production to begin, Charlie and I walked around London. We had a big search in mind. We went from Lyons' Tea Houses and ABC Express Dairies to various snack bars in our quest for – cottage cheese! No one in England had heard of it. We kept telling the proprietors they should find out about it – we were sure it would do well here. And lo and behold, one day when we went into an Express Dairy near Whitehall, we couldn't believe our eyes – there we saw a carton of our beloved cottage cheese. It had reached England! I felt that we introduced it into the country through our constant requests!

Philip Langner was in London, along with Marilyn Hollywood. She was now divorced from her husband. One Saturday we went to see the pantomime *Aladdin* at the Golders Green Hippodrome. We loved the show. I told Charlie about it, and the following Saturday he and I took the tube out to Golders Green. Charlie was also wild about the show and went overboard for the comedians; he rolled in the aisles at Dick Emery's Widow Twankey, and George Truzzi and Laurie Lupino Lane's window-cleaning routine. He loved Shani Wallis, whom he considered a young Judy Garland. Afterwards he told me to sign them all up. Alas, the only one not available was the very funny Dick Emery.

Our casting was falling into place. But we still needed a replacement for Kay Kendall's role, Miss Kay. Several months earlier, Oona and Charlie had been invited to Dawn Addams's wedding. Dawn was a young MGM starlet when Charlie had met her briefly in California. Now she was marrying Prince Massimo in a local village church in Italy. The Prince stood at the altar waiting for his bride. But where was she? Eventually, Dawn stormed down the aisle, gesticulating with her hands as she argued in Italian with various guests. Charlie always laughed as he recounted the story of this wild creature fighting with her guests while her husband waited at the altar. Dawn was cast as Miss Kay.

The sets were now built at Shepperton, and in early May we started filming. First we shot all the scenes in the King's hotel suite. Once again, they were well rehearsed. Charlie and I played all the parts weeks in advance; we knew the blocking and the staging by heart. On the floor, we used our old tricks from *Limelight,* filming all the long shots together. Shooting went very fast. Oona never left the set; she watched the filming, and started to embroider a rug. We were all interested in her progress as she fetched various colored wools from her large knitting bag. Which would get finished first, the rug or the picture?

Dawn Addams sat on the set one day studiously reading Stanislavsky's *An Actor Prepares.* I felt like telling her, "Just know your lines, and do what Charlie says – that's all the preparation you need!"

RIGHT: DAWN ADDAMS TRIES TO PERSUADE CHARLIE, AS KING SHADHOV, TO HAVE HIS FACE LIFTED: "YOU'LL BE AMAZED HOW MUCH YOUNGER YOU'LL LOOK."

BELOW: AFTER HAVING HIS FACE LIFTED, CHARLIE HAS BEEN TOLD BY HIS DOCTOR NOT TO LAUGH, AS HIS STITCHES MAY GIVE. HE GOES TO A NIGHTCLUB, CAN'T CONTROL HIS LAUGHTER AT TWO COMEDIANS . . . AND – OOPS – EVERYTHING FALLS APART!

In the projection room, Charlie noticed light reflecting off Dawn's lips. He discovered she was putting vaseline on them before every shot, to draw attention to herself and make her appear more sexy (an old Hollywood trick). Charlie was furious. When Dawn next went before the cameras, he handed her a tissue to wipe her lips dry. "You look as though you've just eaten herring," he said tartly. "There's nothing sexy about greasy lips." Like all actresses, Dawn obeyed at first, but as time went by, the vaseline slowly crept back.

Charlie felt like a displaced person working at Shepperton. He was used to his own studio and his own staff: his office manager, gateman, even his studio cat – everyone who had made the Chaplin studio in Hollywood so friendly. Here, I was the only familiar face. The spring and summer of 1956 were very cold (it actually snowed one day in July), and Shepperton Studios seemed even colder. *Limelight* had been such a happy experience; with *A King in New York,* the atmosphere was frosty and strained. There seemed to be no heart at Shepperton. We felt we were *all* in exile.

In Hollywood, if Charlie thought of a last-minute gag and needed a string of phony sausages, the prop people would immediately scurry to make them. At Shepperton, the reply was always, "But they weren't on the prop list!" And that was that. It infuriated Charlie. "In Hollywood," he'd say, "if I asked for the Eiffel Tower at the last minute, they'd give me three of them in a flash, all different sizes."

One day, Charlie rearranged a chair on the set to his own liking. Suddenly a strike was called. Charlie was told he was taking the prop man's job away by moving the chair. "You don't do those things here. If you want a chair moved, ask a prop person to move it." "They're going to kill the goose that laid the golden egg," Charlie kept saying to me.

The Shepperton canteen was like an old army barracks with hard wooden tables and a counter. Most of the food was inedible. Every day the menu featured paper-thin slices of dried, overcooked roast lamb smothered in indigestible gravy. Dessert was always rice or bread pudding. The poor actors, trying to watch their diets!

We would sit and complain how slowly the shooting was going. Jack Benny, seated at the next table (he was filming a television special), overheard Charlie one day. "I came here to shoot *Richard II*," Benny told Charlie, "and now I'm filming *Richard III!*" He managed to make some of the gloom disappear.

RIGHT: The beautiful, historic Great Fosters Hotel in Egham, Surrey, where Oona and Charlie stayed during the filming of *A King in New York.* In the foreground are the hedges, designed like a Persian carpet, that Joan Crawford wanted removed.

BOTTOM LEFT: The dining-room at Great Fosters.

Life was no better outside the studio. Charlie was staying at the Great Fosters Hotel in Egham. This was a great Elizabethan mansion – Henry VIII supposedly had it built as a hunting lodge for Anne Boleyn. Even today it looks much as it did in the sixteenth century. The interior is decorated in somber, varnished oak; Hammer horror films were sometimes filmed there. It's a marvelous place to go for afternoon tea. But living there took its toll: it's no joke making a comedy and coming back at the end of the day's shooting to a spook house. This went on for three months!

To make matters worse, all the hotel's other guests looked like displaced persons. The dining-room was enormous, cheerless and empty, like an aircraft hangar. No one else seemed to eat there except us. I guess they knew something we didn't. There was a communal

room where you could watch TV – the only set in the building. Charlie, Oona and the children sat alongside the other guests, engrossed in whatever the majority wanted to watch. It was as though they had booked themselves into a seaside boarding house. At times like this, Charlie became shyer and tried to vanish into the background. After dinner, it was difficult to discuss the next day's shooting. You simply wanted to get to bed and forget where you were.

Shortly after we finished filming, Joan Crawford, who was working at Shepperton on *The Story of Esther Costello,* moved into Great Fosters. *She* soon shook up the old fuddy duddies. The first thing she demanded was that all the hedges behind the lodge be torn down. The hedges were a tourist attraction – part of an elaborate maze built four hundred years ago by Henry VIII. But Crawford didn't give a goddamn. All she knew was that mosquitoes were biting her, and the hedges had to go! Mention Joan Crawford today to the old retainers at Great Fosters, and they shake and tremble with fear.

Every Sunday, Charlie and I rehearsed the following week's scenes at the deserted studio. We looked like two survivors of the nuclear holocaust. No one else was around. How we craved a cup of black coffee! But this was Sunday in England: *nothing* was open.

We were now shooting the progressive school scene. Charlie rehearsed Michael over and over in his lines. Michael knew them backwards, forwards, inside-out and upside-down. But Charlie was relentless, and kept after his governess, Miss Pinnie, to go over his lines just once more.

Our French cameraman, Georges Périnal, was considered one of the best; he photographed classics like René Clair's *Le Million*. But was he slow! Molasses were fast next to Périnal. Even Oona's embroidery was moving faster. Charlie would boil, waiting for him to announce he was ready to shoot. Even while filming, Charlie could see him fiddling in the background, perfecting his lights. It drove Charlie mad.

Finally, he couldn't take it any more. "Turn all the lights on!" he shouted. "I have to give a performance! I don't give a goddamn about your artistic effects! It's a comedy! We need light! Besides, they're coming to see Charlie Chaplin, not your goddamned lighting!" But while Charlie burned, Périnal, like Nero, just kept fiddling.

They say in England that the war couldn't have been won without the afternoon tea-break. It was the same with *A King in New York*. At about two-thirty every day, the crew and cast always succumbed to a certain lethargy. Long, anxious faces started scanning the horizon, waiting for the arrival of the tea trolley. If it hadn't come by three o'clock, not only would there be a mutiny, there'd also be bodies collapsing over the floor. After a while, even Oona and I began to wait for that blessed tea trolley.

John Frankenheimer, the director, tells a funny story about shooting crowd reactions in the studio for *Grand Prix*, a racing film. He needed the extras to pretend they were excitedly watching the racing cars zoom by. He also needed a big reaction when one of the cars exploded. The extras wouldn't react: their eyes were focussed on the tea trolley in the distance. They were practically fainting. But Frankenheimer refused to let them have their tea until he got his shot.

The going got tougher and tougher. In desperation Frankenheimer whispered to the special effects man to wire up the tea trolley. He then told the cameraman to secretly roll the cameras on the extras. As the cameras turned, he gave a signal, and without the extras knowing, in front of their eyes the trolley blew to smithereens!! The extras reacted with shocked horror. Their precious tea was blown all over the set, but Frankenheimer secured the reaction he wanted!

In one of the scenes in the film, Charlie, at his hotel, peeks through the bathroom keyhole into the next suite. There, he sees Dawn Addams taking a bath, and becomes so excited that he performs a cartwheel and lands in his own bath tub. We did several takes. Charlie kept looking at me for my reaction. I didn't think the gag came off.

CHARLIE DIRECTING MICHAEL AS RUPERT IN *A KING IN NEW YORK*.

CHARLIE ON THE POINT OF LEAPING INTO
THE BATHTUB – AND HITTING HIS HEAD
AGAINST THE PORCELAIN.

He was getting annoyed. "Get yourself another actor," he shouted. "That's the best I can do." He repeated the cartwheel once again to please me. This time, when landing in the tub, he hit his head hard on the porcelain.

There was a loud crack. You could have heard a pin drop on the set as he lay there, prostrate. I died inside. It was all my fault. I killed Charlie Chaplin! Then he stood up, rubbed his head and said, "That's it. Good or bad, it goes." It was good. I was relieved.

The American actor Sam Wanamaker – another refugee from the blacklist – was cast as an advertising huckster who tries to sell Shadhov on the idea of doing a television commercial. We rehearsed the scene many times, and Charlie seemed satisfied. Wanamaker was thrilled to be working with Chaplin. But when Charlie saw the rushes, he didn't think Sam was right for the part. We hired another actor, Sid James, and reshot the sequence.

But no one had told Wanamaker. At the London première, I saw him arriving proudly with his wife and children to show them his performance in *A King In New York*. I was so embarrassed. I didn't want to see him. I hid. I often wondered about Sam's reaction, waiting with his family for his big scene, only to find another actor playing the part.

We were now shooting exteriors. We slogged along, day by day, trying to get more film in the can, so we could make a quick getaway. Charlie hated shooting on location – you were at the mercy of the elements. He liked the control that a studio gave. We hurriedly filmed the outside of the Tate Gallery as a New York courtroom; for New York streets we shot on Berkeley Square, with a Rolls-Royce showroom in the background. And for Broadway at night, we shot in Leicester Square with a hidden camera in front of the Warner cinema. In the background, you can see a poster reading "Richard Attenborough in THE BABY AND THE BATTLESHIP" – a film that would never have played on Broadway.

We were all happy in July when the picture was in the can. Charlie and Oona left London immediately; for tax reasons he could only remain in the country for six months. I prepared all the tins of film for shipment to France, where the editing was to be done.

In Paris, Oona and Charlie were ensconced at the Georges V Hotel; I returned once again to the Montaigne. Paris was beautiful that summer. Some afternoons, we ate in the Bois de Boulogne under lovely chestnut

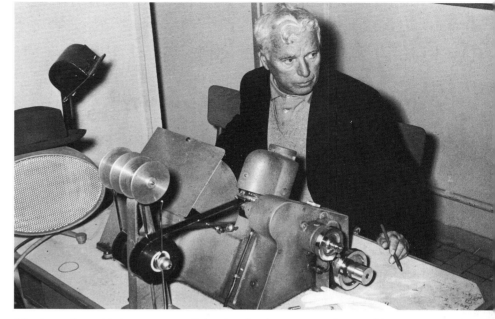

CHARLIE EDITING *A KING IN NEW YORK* IN PARIS.

trees. One day Paulette Goddard and her husband-to-be Erich Remarque were dining at the next table. Oona and Charlie went over to greet them. How civil, I thought.

We now had a rough cut of the film. The United Artists hierarchy flew in to view it. They emerged from the projection room shaken. They were frightened, and said they couldn't distribute the film. It was a hot potato as far as they were concerned. Arnold Picker, the new vice-president of United Artists, took me aside and advised me not to have my name on the screen. It would only give me trouble, he said. But none of that bothered me.

I thought the film was great – I still do – and I could never understand why people thought it was a bitter attack on the United States. I always felt the great virtue of being an American was that you could criticize, satirize and point out wrongs in the system – even if it was witch-hunts and blacklists – without being condemned. I never thought *The Grapes of Wrath* anti-American for depicting the plight of the farmers, or *Mr Smith Goes to Washington* for showing corruption in the Senate, or *I Am a Fugitive from a Chain Gang* for criticizing the penal system in the South. No one took umbrage at these movies. To me these films were pro-American, and showed the world what democracy was all about – freedom of speech and thought. And so with *A King in New York*. There was no anti-Americanism in the picture; it simply depicted what was going on in America at the time.

But McCarthyism was still rampant. Arnold Picker advised Charlie to sell the film on his name alone, territory by territory, sight unseen. Then Art Buchwald, the American columnist, saw the film in London before it was shown to the press, and blasted it in the *Herald Tribune*. And it only took one to start the band wagon rolling.

Charlie was very tense during this stage. Who could blame him? His own money was tied up in the film; and the outlook appeared bleak. Charlie's nerves began to affect me. I was given pills by a friend to relax; and when I'm nervous, I put on weight, so another friend gave me diet pills. Later I was to find out I had been on heavy doses of benzedrine. As my weight fell off, my equilibrium collapsed. I was heading for a nervous breakdown. I didn't feel I had much to offer any more. So I decided to quit. I don't think Charlie understood what was happening to me; not even I understood.

I holed myself up in a dingy hotel on the wrong side of the Champs Elysées and wouldn't see anyone. Being in a foreign country, I never felt so alone in my life. Eddie Constantine and Jeff Davis tried to get me back on my feet. Eddie offered me another film. But I couldn't do anything. I was still on those pills, and in those days we didn't know the effects of these drugs; I was unaware of what was happening to my psyche.

Sydney Chaplin located me and called from New York. He was starring opposite Judy Holliday in *Bells are Ringing*, written by Sydney's pals Adolph Green and Betty Comden. The Theatre Guild was presenting it on Broadway. He insisted I get over there immediately and help restage the show. I always had the feeling he heard the state I was in and was trying to help. I thought perhaps it would do me good to get away for awhile and be with my old pal. Syd would be a tonic.

Although *Bells* had just opened under Jerome Robbins's direction, and was doing big business, Judy and Syd were unhappy. Judy threatened to leave if the musical wasn't restaged. And without Judy, the headliner, they had no show. It would be my first trip back to America in three and a half years.

I went to say goodbye to Oona and Charlie. He had just finished writing the music for *A King in New York* and was about to work on the scoring. He was in a wonderful mood. Recording his music always dispelled any of his anxieties. He wished me luck. As I was about to leave, news came through that Humphrey Bogart had died of cancer. Charlie was upset. "He was so young," he said.

On arrival in New York I immediately went to the Shubert Theater to see a Saturday night performance of *Bells are Ringing*.

THE **6** CHAPLIN REVUE

SYDNEY CHAPLIN TRIUMPHS ON BROADWAY IN *BELLS ARE RINGING.*

New York City,
January 21st, 1957.

Dearest Oona and Charlie,

So much to tell you. Sydney is marvelous in the show. He has such charm, and he's so relaxed. The part fits him like a glove. When he makes his first entrance, you can hear a loud whisper over the entire theater, "That's Charlie Chaplin's son!"

The audience adores Judy Holliday. She can do no wrong. Judy too has great charm, and a dazzling smile. Yet offstage she's rarely happy. She lives with her mother in the Dakotas, a somber, bleak Charles Addams-type apartment house off Central Park West. She has a young son, Jonathan, from a former marriage. Her mother still treats her like a child, waits up for her at night, and is always concerned about whether or not she's eaten. And she always greets her with bad news: "Jonathan's not feeling well, he's been asking for you."

Judy seems to wallow in misery. One evening, after a performance, she said to Syd, "Let's visit Cyril tonight ... He's depressed." And Syd replied with a sigh, "Aw, honey, can't we visit someone who's happy for a change?"

Syd got the part because Judy played cards with him in Los Angeles, and naturally he was very funny. He still can't read a cold script, but Judy remembered how amusing he was at that card game. She fought the Theatre Guild and everyone else concerned, and insisted he played opposite her. So Syd is very grateful, and I think she's mistaking his gratefulness for love.

I haven't started working on the show yet, but I feel it's going to be an impossible task. It would be different if the play were a flop, but it's doing big business. So why tamper with a hit?

Sydney is enjoying his success. I bought him a tiny television set for his dressing-room, and his eyes are firmly glued to it as he makes up. Without ever breaking his concentration from the program he's watching, Harry Edwards, his dresser, gets him to stand up, slips him into his pants, then pulls his arms out and pushes him into his jacket.

There's his cue; he rushes onstage. He sings "Just in time, I found you just in time", rushes to his dressing-room, and goes straight back to the television. Now he switches to the basketball game as Harry forces him into his next costume, his eyes again never leaving the screen. When Harry wasn't around one night, Syd was so absorbed by a quiz game that he ran on stage with a hanger still inside his jacket. He wondered why he couldn't dance so well!

When the show is over, Judy and Syd usually dine at Sardi's, and Syd is able to discuss with Vincent Sardi every show on television that night. "But you were performing!" Sardi tells him; "How can you have seen all these shows?" Sydney just smiles enigmatically.

Rumor has it that Syd will win the Tony award this year . . .

How's the music for *A King in New York* coming on? Tell me all. Miss you.

Love,

Jerry.

A couple of weeks later, Oona wrote that Charlie was about to score the music – that he'd written some beautiful songs, and she couldn't wait until I heard them. And Charlie was so proud of Sydney's success that he was thinking of writing a musical for him. She also wanted to know whether or not I was working on the play.

New York City,

February 15th, 1957.

Dearest Oona and Charlie,

I've pulled out of *Bells*. Although Judy claims she wants to be re-directed, she is very set in her ways. When you ask her to walk somewhere, it's like trying to move the *Queen Mary* into its berth. I think she was simply trying to keep Sydney happy. He feels strongly that the show could be improved – and she's fallen madly in love with him and goes along with anything he wants. So I'm in the middle.

You should be glad you're not living in New York. Maybe it's the times – McCarthyism – everyone seems so unhappy. No one knows who's going to be named next by their "best friends". Judy was called to Washington by the Committee. I hear she played her *Born Yesterday* role – the dumb blonde – to perfection. I asked her about the experience, but when I saw her fearful expression, I didn't pursue it. A black cloud seems to be hanging over everyone.

I went with Judy and Sydney to a party at George Axelrod's the other night. Lauren Bacall was the guest of honor. Friends called it the "Help Betty Forget Bogie Party". Every name from the New York theater was there. People were dancing. But there was no merriment. All you felt was tension and depression.

But I was having a good time. Arthur Kober, the playwright, saw me smiling and came over. "Why are *you* so happy?" he said. Taken aback, I replied, "Well, it's a party!"

Then he pointed to Moss Hart, who'd just directed *My Fair Lady*. "Do you think *he's* happy?" Kober asked. "He should be," I said, "he has the biggest hit on Broadway." Kober replied, "But who's getting the credit? It's all Lerner and Loewe. No one even realizes he's the director."

I left him to speak to another misery who wanted to know about Charlie's new film. When I told him that it satirizes American mores and deals with informers and the Un-American Activities Committee, he tensed up and quickly vanished. It's sad.

Audrey Wood (she's a top New York agent who discovered Tennessee Williams) is now handling me. I'm crazy about her and her husband Bill Liebling. They're determined to find me a play to direct. What's happening with the film? Write!

Love and kisses,

Jerry.

Shortly afterwards, Oona wrote that Charlie could use me for a couple of months. *A King in New York* would be opening in England in forty theaters and he'd want me to check on all the details. But Oona didn't go into it too much; she simply stated that Charlie needed me if I were free.

I was in a quandary. I had a strong desire to see Oona and Charlie, but part of me thought it wiser to remain in New York. I felt things were

LEFT: CHARLIE DESPAIRING OF HIS LATEST HAIRCUT — OR IS IT A BIRD'S NEST? BELOW: CHARLIE WITH HIS CHILDREN, HIS BROTHER SYDNEY AND SYDNEY'S WIFE GYPSY, PICNICKING ON THE LAWN AT THE MANOIR.

opening up for me; yet, like a magnet, I was being drawn back to them. For a while, I cast the decision from my mind, hoping things would resolve themselves. But Charlie was impatient. Oona sent a telegram wanting to know my plans. I made my decision; I would return.

But I guess I had pondered too long. When I arrived in Switzerland, Charlie had lost interest. I left Vevey the following day and went to London, too embarrassed to return to New York after friends had thrown me a farewell party. Shortly afterwards, on May 23rd, Oona gave birth to another daughter, Jane Cecil.

Sidney Bernstein, the head of Granada Television, had invited me several times to join his company. He had seen my work at the Circle, and asked me to start an English equivalent. I was hoping this would be in London, but Sidney was thinking of Manchester (Granada's headquarters), and I felt I hadn't left Los Angeles to live in Manchester. But I took him up on his offer of TV work in London. First, I directed William Saroyan's *My Heart's in the Highlands*. It was transmitted live, and I was nervous as hell; but luckily for me, the play received excellent reviews.

Charlie was impressed when he saw my notices. *A King in New York* had just opened in London. The reviews were largely favorable. J. B. Priestley wrote: "Chaplin seems to me to have brought off something very difficult just as he did in *Modern Times* and *The Great Dictator*. He has turned film clowning into social satire and criticism without losing his astonishing ability to make us laugh."

Charlie gave an interview to the London *Observer*. "My film isn't

political. The picture is a satire," he said. "A clown must satirize." Then he added: "This is my most rebellious film. I refuse to be part of this dying civilization they talk about."

Charlie received many deeply felt fan letters. But the letter that touched Oona and him most was from the poet C. Day Lewis. We had met him through the novelist Elizabeth Jane Howard. His letter was so moving. He exalted both Charlie and the film's brilliance. But on the whole British audiences didn't fully understand McCarthyism or what was going on with the Un-American Activities Committee. The film wasn't to receive its proper due until the 1970s, when it was released for the first time in America. The young were surprised by the film's boldness. They didn't find it controversial, just funny. Charlie was simply twenty years ahead of his time.

My second Granada play was to be Sartre's *The Respectful Prostitute*. As I went into the first day's rehearsal, Judy and Sydney arrived at our cold, unheated rehearsal hall in Acton. They had both won Tony Awards for their parts in *Bells* and were now on a week's holiday from the show. The New York papers were full of stories about their imminent marriage; Sydney, they said, was bringing Judy to Switzerland to get Charlie's approval. What nonsense. Sydney, unfortunately, was not in love with Judy. But Judy was more in love than ever, and clung to him. Poor Syd was in a dilemma.

At the rehearsal Judy and Syd sat in a corner, tired and worn out from the flight. No one in the cast realized that the lady in the mink and dark glasses was the toast of Broadway, or that the handsome young

TOP: JUDY HOLLIDAY WITH CHARLIE, SYDNEY, THE CHILDREN AND ME ON THE VERANDA. THAT WONDERFUL HOLLIDAY SMILE WASN'T TO LAST VERY LONG.

BOTTOM: THE STRAIN IS BEGINNING TO BUILD UP BETWEEN SYD AND JUDY. IF LOOKS COULD KILL.

man was Sydney Chaplin. At the end of the day, I received a call from Bernstein's office. The Independent Television Authority had pronounced that the play and its title were too hot for British television. We were all paid off.

I decided to go to Vevey with Syd and Judy. Before we left, Syd went on a shopping trip while Judy and I walked around Piccadilly Circus. We stopped across the street from the London Pavilion movie theater, where the marquee stretched along the entire front of the building. Workers were putting up the name of the new attraction in blazing electric lights – "JUDY HOLLIDAY in FULL OF LIFE". We looked up as the last electric bulb was screwed into position. I was excited. But Judy turned to me and said, "Let's get out of here. It's *depressing.*"

The next day we were in Vevey. This was to be Judy's big moment.

Oona and Charlie were very gracious, but had no intention of getting involved in one of Sydney's romances. There had been too many: Kay Kendall, Marjorie Steele, Gloria de Haven, Evelyn Keyes, Joan Collins . . . The list was endless. Judy hoped Charlie would be so overwhelmed by her that he'd nudge Sydney and say, "That's the girl for you, my boy." But Charlie and Oona treated Judy civilly, charmingly, but like any other guest.

Sydney was now anxious to get to his beloved Paris, which he adored more than any other city: it suited his night owl temperament. The three of us took the train and stayed once again at the Hotel Montaigne. Sydney wanted to be with his old cronies and left Judy to her own devices.

She went into a decline. She wouldn't get out of bed and kept crying, calling for her mother. I tried comforting her, but all she wanted was Syd. Finally I found him in a bar, concentrating on a pinball machine with the same intensity he gave his television set. I pleaded with him to see Judy, but he was furious. "She's spoiling my holiday! She's no fun to be with. All she's done is drag along, telling everyone we were getting married."

It was Sunday. Judy had to be back in New York for the Monday night performance of *Bells.* I saw her off at the airport, and Sydney took the next plane back.

That same Sunday, the Theatre Guild had taken out an advertisement announcing that Judy Holliday and Sydney Chaplin had returned permanently to their original roles in *Bells are Ringing.*

THE AD THAT APPEARED IN THE SUNDAY *NEW YORK TIMES* THE DAY JUDY FLEW BACK FROM PARIS. ALTHOUGH IT WELCOMES SYD AND JUDY BACK "PERMANENTLY" TO THEIR ORIGINAL ROLES, SYD LEFT THE SHOW IMMEDIATELY AFTERWARDS.

CHARLIE SATIRIZED LIVING CONDITIONS IN THE ARMY IN *SHOULDER ARMS*. HERE HE IS TRYING TO SLEEP IN THE TRENCHES, KNEE-DEEP IN WATER.

In New York, Judy announced she would not continue with the show unless Sydney was OUT. He happily left, and Hal Linden, his understudy, replaced him.

With *A King in New York* out of his system, Charlie was getting restless. He couldn't decide on a film project, so he started to make notes for an autobiography.

In the meantime he returned to the idea he'd developed during my first summer at Vevey. He would release three of his old films – *A Dog's Life, The Pilgrim* and *Shoulder Arms* – under the title *The Chaplin Revue*. But instead of introducing them with a Somerset Maugham spoof, Charlie decided to lead into the films with some footage found in his vaults. There were scenes never shown in public before, depicting Charlie at work and play – dressing up as the Tramp, performing a routine with Harry Lauder, and receiving a visit from Winston Churchill. Later, Charlie told me to destroy this material, but I refused.

We couldn't find the proper footage to introduce *Shoulder Arms,* which was set in the First World War. At the Imperial War Museum in London we viewed actual combat scenes. We were told that the museum was originally the Royal Bethlehem Hospital – an institution for the insane, popularly known as Bedlam (a corruption of Bethlehem). When I heard this I wondered whether the museum had been one of the asylums where Charlie's mother had been sent. It was located just a few streets away from 3 Pownall Terrace, Kensington – the family garret. But Charlie never said a word about it.

Through Oona and Charlie I had met two of their closest friends – Don and Ella Stewart. Donald Ogden Stewart – a famous humorist, and brilliant screenwriter – had been one of Charlie's few champions on the night of the *Monsieur Verdoux* screening in New York. In the 1920s, Don had lived in Paris and hobnobbed with Hemingway and Scott Fitzgerald in the 1930s and 1940s, and had written top MGM films starring Katharine Hepburn, Spencer Tracy, Norma Shearer, and Joan Crawford. But the political troubles of the late 1940s had ended his Hollywood career, and he now lived in London with his wife Ella Winter.

Ella – a born fighter and firebrand, with large, black, aggressive eyes – was a force to reckon with. Like her first husband Lincoln Steffens, she was a well-known political writer. She had traveled with American troops across the Atlantic in a munitions boat, and interviewed Stalin and the Roosevelts. Wherever there was a demonstration, Ella was sure to be there, waving her banner.

LEFT: CHARLIE AS THE GREAT WHITE HUNTER, ON A TRIP TO KENYA WITH OONA.

ABOVE: OONA AND CHARLIE FREEZING AT THE EQUATOR.

REMEMBERING CHARLIE

RIGHT: DON AND ELLA STEWART IN THEIR
HAMPSTEAD HOME.
BOTTOM LEFT: A PORTRAIT OF ELLA.

OPPOSITE: CHARLIE IN THE TITLE ROLE OF
THE PILGRIM.

The Stewarts lived in a large Hampstead house at 103 Frognal, the former residence of Prime Minister Ramsay MacDonald. It almost became a second home to me; I became friendly with all the family, and began writing a film script with Don and Ella's son, Don Stewart Jr.

Don and Ella eagerly anticipated Oona and Charlie's visits. "When are they coming?" Ella would ask impatiently. But Ella had other reasons for wanting to know Charlie's movements. She usually had a petition for him to sign. She wanted Charlie and Oona's name attached to every cause she supported, whether it was Stop the Arms Race, Support the Aboriginals, or the protection of Abyssinian cats. Charlie, though sympathetic, could never be drawn. There were just too many causes: it was like getting junk mail every morning.

On Sundays Ella and Don held open house to names in the literary world and showbusiness. Ella called me one day saying she was terribly

depressed – no one visited the house any more. I quickly drove over. As Ella lay ill in bed, a woman arrived and asked how she could get her relatives out of the Soviet Union. Ella became her old self: "Don't contact the Soviet Embassy – speak to my hairdresser!" A minute later, Katharine Hepburn swept into the room with Phyllis, and immediately took over. "Get rid of all those pills. I'm sending my doctor over from New York to examine you." So much for no visitors!

One Saturday afternoon, Oona and Charlie visited Ella and Don. Ella expressed disappointment that they were returning immediately to Vevey. They would miss a great treat on Sunday. A group of Americans were coming, and she was going to make "good old American hamburgers".

I arrived on Sunday for the hamburger lunch, and looked into Ella's kitchen. As usual it was a mess, with dogs, cats, parrots and her monkey wreaking havoc. (One day the monkey bit her; she bit him back!) One old poodle, Fidget, had a slightly paralyzed tongue that hung lopsided out of its mouth with saliva dripping down. As Ella prepared her "good old American hamburgers", her refrigerator door swung open, and I saw Fidget jump in and begin nibbling at a large leg of lamb. Ella threw him out, shouting, "Get out of there Fidget, that's tonight's dinner!" I began to feel squeamish. What were those burgers going to be like?

Ella proudly carried her sizzling hamburgers into the dining-room. The guests eagerly bit into them, then suddenly stopped in their tracks. Someone said the meat tasted like fish. "Oh for Chrissakes," Ella said, "I got the tin of cat's food mixed up with the hamburger meat!" Wise Oona and Charlie had left town just in time!

In the autumn of 1958 Charlie and I hired cutting rooms in Hammersmith and began making trims on his three silent films for *The Chaplin Revue*. Oona often joined us for lunch. Hammersmith in those days was a depressed area. (It's not much better now.) There was no place to eat except a Wimpy bar across the street, we were grateful for small mercies.

Charlie was also busy composing two hours of original music to accompany the films. With the music attached, these films took on a new life. Charlie had a flair for watching the action on screen, singing to a pianist or into a tape recorder, and composing melodies to accompany each scene. He always found writing music "a cinch", and never understood the difficulties other composers experienced.

When he was at the piano, he always started at the beginning of the scale – C, D, E, F, G. Out of these same notes, with slight variations, he composed the *Limelight* theme, the theme for *City Lights,* the "Smile" tune from *Modern Times,* and "Love, This is My Song" from *A Countess from Hong Kong*. All of those melodies derived from a song that Charlie remembered as a child from the London streets – "Who Will Buy My Pretty Violets". Charlie went along with Irving Berlin's theory: "All that any composer has in him", Berlin told Charlie, "is one song. Every song he writes after that is a variation on the original."

Charlie hated "funny" music for his comedies. He always composed elegant, romantic melodies that were in counterpoint to the Tramp's antics. They gave his films an extra emotional dimension. Years later, when we talked about "The Countess from Hong Kong Waltz" – which we both liked better than the hit tune, "Love, This Is My Song" – he'd wink at me and say, "That's the *Merry Widow* waltz transposed!" But the best music he ever wrote, I felt, was the theme for his last projected picture, *The Freak*. "This", he used to say, "is real Puccini!" Charlie was cheeky about his music and never took it seriously – his films were more important. But he was deeply flattered when he heard that John Huston told a composer "I want the same kind of music that Chaplin composes for his pictures."

Ella was having an exhibition in her house for a struggling Indian painter. She was an avid collector – every nook and corner at 103 Frognal was crammed with antiques, artefacts and paintings. She discovered Klee when he was unknown, and had so many of his works

OONA AND CHARLIE EXPLORING LONDON.

that the Tate Gallery stored them for her. Oona, Charlie, their young daughter Vicky and I were invited to the showing. Charlie didn't care for the paintings, and didn't buy any. Back at the Savoy, Victoria showed her father a painting Ella had given her as a gift. Charlie disliked it, but thought the gesture was nice.

Shortly afterwards, Ella phoned Vicky and asked her to get money for the painting from her father. "He can afford it." she said. Charlie was furious, and sent the picture straight back with a driver. "You don't use a child like that," he said. But Ella took it all in her stride – just as she did when Oona discovered her own luxurious bath towels, embroidered with her initials O.C., hanging in Ella's bathroom. Ella must have helped herself when she was at the Manoir. When Oona pointed it out, Ella replied, "Oh, you've got plenty!"

Work on *The Chaplin Revue* continued. One Saturday afternoon, while we were waiting for the editor to finish some splicing, Charlie and

Top: Oona and Charlie on London Bridge.
Center and bottom: Oona and Charlie in the courtyard of the George Inn, South London.

I took a walk from Hammersmith to Kensington. Having time on our hands, I mentioned to Charlie that Peter Brook, the director, and his wife Natasha Parry lived in Kensington and had invited me that afternoon for drinks. "Why don't we drop in?" I suggested. Charlie hesitated: "But I wasn't invited." "I'm sure it'll be all right," I said.

The living-room was packed with Peter and Natasha's theater friends. No one recognized Charlie. As I said hello to various guests, I introduced them to Charlie, who was standing behind me – "Oh, by the way, you know Charlie Chaplin …" I said. The guests stood open-mouthed. They couldn't believe that Chaplin was standing there, shy and unobtrusive.

I left him alone for a moment to speak to people at the other end of the room. Charlie simply stood there – unattended and feeling awkward, too reserved to speak to anyone. Afterwards he said, "How can you talk to all those people who you don't know?" I never left him alone after that.

The next weekend, we were invited to Sandra and Sidney Bernstein's farm in Kent. In the morning Charlie and I worked in the cutting room. Later, we were to meet Oona at Waterloo station. Having time to kill, we went for coffee at Lyon's Corner House on Coventry Street, off Leicester Square. This was Lyon's showcase: everything was very posh, the *Maitre d'* wore tails. Yet they still catered for everyone.

As we sipped our coffee we noticed an old, poorly dressed woman with bedraggled hair staring at Charlie from the next table. He's been recognized, I thought. Sure enough, she leaned over and whispered to Charlie: "Do you know, if you pretended you were Charlie Chaplin, I bet the head waiter would give you a free cup of coffee. You're a double for him!" Charlie smiled awkwardly and turned away. The woman continued, "Do you know, I see doubles all the time. Last week I saw a double for Earl Mountbatten. The week before I saw a double for Prince Philip."

Charlie and I continued sipping our coffee, trying not to encourage her. But the woman wouldn't let up: "How do you like that Charlie Chaplin marrying that young girl! You've got to hand it to him." Charlie whispered to me under his breath, "Call for the check. Let's get out of here." I signalled the *Maitre d'*. As we left, I said, "Why don't you tell her who you are? She'd be thrilled!" Charlie shook his head: "No, she's happier seeing doubles."

CHARLES CHAPLIN présente

LA REVUE DE CHARLOT

UNE VIE DE CHIEN   CHARLOT SOLDAT   LE PÈLERIN

Eddie Constantine came to London to make a film. We'd dine together every night, along with Simone Signoret and Laurence Harvey; they were then shooting *Room at the Top* at Shepperton. Although I had met Simone in Paris, we became good friends in London. I'd watch the filming, and on weekends, Simone and I drove around town. She had no idea that *Room at the Top* was going to make her an international star. To her, it was just another film.

Simone had to know everyone's story, and the more painful and full of tragedy the better. How she suffered with you! When I saw *Room at the Top* I thought she was wonderful. But I also thought, "She's not acting – that's Simone."

Simone was dying to meet Charlie. But he wasn't in town. I told her that he was due shortly, and promised that as soon as he arrived, I'd try to arrange something.

One Sunday, on her vast lawn, Ella was having the Moscow Art Theater Company over for lunch. A week earlier I had seen them in *The Cherry Orchard,* and found the experience overwhelming. I wanted to meet them, but Ella had made a point of not inviting me. As I drove around London with Simone I asked if she'd like to meet the actors from the Moscow Art Theater. Of course she was dying to.

I called Ella from a telephone box. "You can't come," she insisted. "I would have invited you, but there's just no room." "What a pity," I replied, "Simone Signoret will be so disappointed. I'm with her, and she's dying to meet them." "WHAT?" exclaimed Ella, *"SIMONE SIGNORET!!!* Bring her over at once!" Ella was a great collector of celebrities. No matter how ill she was, she always perked up in front of luminaries.

On our arrival Ella pounced on Simone. She ignored all the Russians. Simone was her latest conquest. Besides, Simone was her soul-mate, a fellow left-winger, a fighter for causes. I never saw Ella sparkle and glitter so much; to her, Simone was now the star attraction. To hell with those Russians. They didn't exist any more!

OPPOSITE: *A DOG'S LIFE* (1918). EDNA PURVIANCE WAS THE LEADING LADY IN ALL CHARLIE'S EARLY SHORTS. LATER, WHEN SHE WAS OLDER, HE STARRED HER IN A DRAMATIC ROLE IN *A WOMAN OF PARIS.* ALTHOUGH THE FILM WAS A CRITICAL SUCCESS, AUDIENCES WERE DISAPPOINTED THAT CHARLIE DIDN'T APPEAR HIMSELF. EDNA RETIRED FROM THE SCREEN SOON AFTERWARDS.

Several days later, I went up to Ella's. There in the kitchen were Ella and Simone washing dishes. The next night I saw them together in a restaurant. Ella ignored me; she had completely taken over Simone's life.

Charlie came to London to check the progress on *The Chaplin Revue.* This was Simone's big chance to meet him. I spoke to Charlie. He had never heard of her or her husband Yves Montand, but he finally gave in. I arranged for them to come over to the Savoy for drinks. Simone was tongue-tied in front of Charlie. Usually she had an opinion on every subject; now she was quiet as a mouse. In France, they revered "Charlot" like a god, and here she was sitting next to God himself.

I remember Sydney telling me about a party he went to the first time he ever visited Paris. He was introduced to a man; and when the man heard that he was Charlie Chaplin's son, he burst into tears and began kissing Syd's hand. In order to get rid of him, Syd told the man that his father had just suffered a heart attack. The poor man went completely to pieces, and threw himself on the floor, sobbing. Simone wasn't quite that bad, but she came pretty close.

Charlie and Simone began discussing films. Simone told him that for her the hardest part in movie-making was establishing the character. "It's not *that* difficult," Charlie replied. "But it's easy for you," Simone said; "Your character's already been established. The minute you come on the screen, they know who you are – the Tramp." Charlie smiled. "You're right," he said. "I *have* got it easy. When I play the Tramp, all I have to do is raise my little pinkie, and they scream with laughter." There was a knock on the door; Yves Montand entered. He was shy and polite, and didn't want to intrude. Charlie liked him.

I think Simone expected Charlie to be political, but Charlie was only political when issues came up that he felt strongly about. Otherwise, political discussions did not excite him, and his interest in politics had waned since his move to Switzerland. Now he was only concerned with his work.

I had been seeing a lot of Rex Harrison and Kay Kendall. Rex was the sensation of the London stage in *My Fair Lady*. Before one Saturday matinee, Kay and Rex invited Charlie, Oona, Josie, Vicky, and me for lunch. They had just seen *My Fair Lady,* and, like everyone else, raved about it. Rex was so flattered. During the meal, Kay's pug dog suddenly began choking at her feet. Everyone noticed. Kay turned to the dog and reprimanded him: "Don't make that ugly face, darling – you look just like Joan Collins!" (Syd had jilted Kay for Joan.)

Rex and Kay's relationship was straight out of a 1930s screwball comedy. One minute they were lovey-dovey; the next, they fought like cats and dogs. When I first met Rex, he was playing in *Bell Book and Candle*. "You'll like him," Kay said to me, "he's so sweet." I'd also heard he could be difficult. In those days, Rex and Kay couldn't be seen together (Rex was not yet divorced from Lilli Palmer), so Kay arranged for us to meet in an Italian restaurant off Lowndes Square. She knew the proprietor, and he fixed up a table in an alcove near the kitchen.

Rex bounced into the restaurant. Next to Charlie, he was the most charming person I had ever met. "Dear boy," he said, "I'm so happy to meet you; I've heard so much about you. Do sit down and let's order!" I

sat between them. Rex looked at Kay. "You haven't been drinking, have you?" he asked. She pinched me under the table.

Within five minutes, Rex and Kay began arguing. It was very personal. I was embarrassed. I wanted to get out of there. I rose and apologized that I had to leave. Rex insisted firmly that I sit down, and not let Kay spoil the evening. I dutifully obeyed.

The argument intensified. I felt so out of place. I rose again to leave. Now Kay turned to me: "Sit down!" she said, even more firmly. "You're *my* guest, and he's not going to spoil our evening." I sat.

The argument accelerated. I didn't know what was going to happen next. Sparks were really flying. I rose. "I must go to the men's room. I'll be right back." The argument had reached such a pitch that I don't think they heard me. And although I didn't return, I'm sure I wasn't missed.

That was my first meeting with Rex Harrison. Everything after that was easy.

One night, Kay and I watched *My Fair Lady* from the wings. Kay had her two pugs under her arms, and was trying to break up Rex's concentration by waving and throwing kisses. But he didn't see her. So she shoved the pugs onstage. Out of excitement they leaped into Rex's

LEFT: KAY SUNNING HERSELF.

BELOW: REX AND KAY LEAVING THE MANOIR AFTER A WEEKEND VISIT.

ABOVE: TWO BEAUTIES – OONA AND KAY KENDALL.

BELOW: AT THE MANOIR POOL: REX HARRISON, CHARLIE, ME AND KAY.

arms. He completely dried up.

If you admired anything Kay had, she quickly gave it to you. "It's yours!" she would say. Once Rex, Kay and I were in Vevey for a weekend. She had a beautiful mink-lined coat that Rex had just bought for her. Oona saw it and admired it. Kay took the coat off and handed it to her: "I want you to have it. It's yours," she insisted. Rex's face dropped to the floor. I think if Oona had accepted it, he would have passed out.

Oona and Charlie came to London for the recording of the music for *The Chaplin Revue.* I went to pick them up at the Savoy. Besides the score, he would be recording his song "Bound for Texas", to be used in *The Pilgrim.* On a previous visit I had found him two singers; one was Billy Fury, whom I thought could do it. But Charlie preferred the second one – a new, promising vocalist: Matt Munro. Charlie liked the sound of his voice; it had a Bing Crosby feel, he said.

It was winter. Usually Charlie was very prompt when I came to pick him up, but this time I found him casually sitting at the breakfast table, enjoying his kippers. He wouldn't be rushed. I was anxious to get going; we had all those musicians hired, and it was costing. But for some reason, on this day he took his time.

I drove Oona and Charlie to Shepperton Studios in my second-hand Hillman Minx. Charlie sat next to me; Oona was in the back. We were now driving down a small country lane near Sunbury. A slight fog set in and, unknown to me, a thin layer of ice had settled on the ground. Suddenly, my car began to zig-zag and slide across the road. In the distance I saw a large bus. I was heading right towards it and couldn't stop. BANG! I hit it.

None of us was hurt, but we were all shaken. The front of my car looked like an accordion. But I was most concerned about Oona and Charlie. After checking that they were all right, I ran down the lane, spotted a gas station and rushed in. "Get me a limousine or something," I shouted. "I've got Charlie Chaplin and his wife down the road. We've just had an accident."

The young attendant must have thought I was crazy. But, seeing the maniacal look on my face, he did what I told him. A car soon drove Oona and Charlie to the studios; I stayed behind. The attendant advised me to drive back to London and get my car fixed there. "You can just about manage it," he said. But first I had to get to the studio.

KAY'S LAST STAGE APPEARANCE, IN *THE BRIGHT ONE*.

When I arrived, Matt Munro, the musicians and technicians all gathered round me. Charlie had told everyone about the accident. I was too embarrassed to talk. At the end of the day, I arranged for another car to bring Oona and Charlie back to London. As I went into my own car, Charlie said to me, "Oona and I are driving back with you." "You can't," I replied, "We may break down." But Charlie insisted that they were coming with me; he knew the accident had unnerved me, and he didn't want me to lose confidence. I was very touched. Oona and Charlie got into my tin lizzie and, very gingerly, we drove off.

As we cranked our way back to London, we passed Hammersmith roundabout. I saw a placard boldly blazing "CHARLIE CHAPLIN IN CAR CRASH". I died inside. We pressed onto the Savoy. At the front

entrance, there were photographers and reporters. On seeing them, Charlie, ever the showman, got out of the car and began limping slightly. I could have brained him. Later, Charlie insisted on paying for my car damage.

I was surprised when Rex Harrison called me. He wanted to present Kay on the West End stage, and asked if I'd assist him. He was to direct *The Bright One,* a whimsical comedy. The production was to tour Liverpool and Brighton, but because of *My Fair Lady* he couldn't travel with the show. I read the play and told Rex I thought he could find Kay a better vehicle. But Rex was set on this play. Kay had specifically requested me. So I accepted.

Kay had her own ideas about theater. She would only give a good performance if she knew she had friends in the audience. She'd say, very haughtily, "Who are these strangers? I don't know them. Why should I give my all to people I don't know?" So if there were no friends in the audience, I would have to sit there, and she'd play the show directly to me.

Backstage, I had noticed that she was taking large doses of cortisone. I was shocked, and told her the drug was very dangerous; "You only take that if you're seriously ill!" I said. Kay brushed it off: "I'm a little anaemic, sweetie, that's all." But I wondered who was the mad doctor who was prescribing such a powerful drug.

We rehearsed in London at the Winter Garden Theatre. Across the street was a Sainsbury's grocery shop. Kay looked at the store and told me that Jimmy Sainsbury, the multi-millionaire owner, was in love with her and wanted to marry her. "Who wants to be the wife of a *grocer?*" she said. "But he's a grocer with millions!" "Not interested," she replied.

The Bright One closed in London after twelve performances – Kay was suddenly taken gravely ill. As Rex was still tied up at night with *My Fair Lady,* I sat with her in her bedroom while she had blood transfusions. I didn't understand. She would wink at me, like a pixie: "I've too many white corpuscles, darling."

Then, one night, after his evening performance, Rex walked me to the gates of his house on Cheyne Walk. I saw tears in his eyes. "She has leukemia," he said. "They don't know when the end will be, but not very long." I couldn't believe my ears. Katie was larger than life and full of mischief; you'd never associate her with death. "I must keep her working. She must never know," Rex said.

After her transfusions, Kay was able to get back on her feet for short periods. She and I attended Rex's last Saturday performance of *My Fair Lady*. It was so moving. When he sang "I've Grown Accustomed to Her Face," he seemed to turn towards Kay.

I still don't know whether or not she knew she was dying. I sensed she did, but she didn't want Rex to know. I feel they were both playing games with each other. But no one could have been kinder to Kay in her last days than Rex. He devoted all his time and energy to her, trying to keep her cheerful and making plans for the future.

In September 1959, Rex called me. Kay hadn't long to live, he said. I rushed to the London Clinic. Rex was in the hallway. "She died ten minutes ago," he said. She was only thirty-two. Then he added: "Before she passed away, she looked up. I know she saw God." Afterwards I told this to Charlie. He was fascinated. Charlie was always intrigued by anything to do with death.

Recently, Kay's great friend Dirk Bogarde sent me a card informing me that Jimmy Sainsbury had just died, and had left his entire fortune of eighteen million pounds to a Kay Kendall Leukaemia lab. He added that Kay would have been so moved to know how much the "grocer" loved her.

In Vevey, Charlie was now hard at work on his autobiography. He would read me sections. "How can you remember in such detail all the events of your childhood?" I asked. "How could I forget?" he replied meaningfully. Oona told me that Truman Capote had been over to the house and didn't like the title that Charlie was giving his book: *My Autobiography*. Charlie flared up: "What's so good about *Breakfast at Tiffany's?*" he told Capote angrily, "That's the silliest title I ever heard!" The book was already a sensation.

Mr and Mrs Alexandrov were coming to dinner. Grigori Alexandrov, a tall, imposing man, was a prominent Soviet director, who had previously been Eisenstein's assistant. Alexandrov's wife, Lyubov Orlova, had starred in her husband's 1930s musicals. They were thrilled to be in Charlie's company.

All through dinner, Mrs Alexandrov kept looking at Charlie with stars in her eyes. "Oh, maestro!" she exclaimed in her thick accent, "You don't know how you are loved by the Russian people!" Charlie nodded modestly as she continued ecstatically. He didn't like gushing.

Top: Charlie reading his autobiography.

Bottom: Truman Capote with Charlie and Oona.

RIGHT: Eisenstein's assistant, Grigori Alexandrov, took this photo at the Manoir. Left to right: me, Mrs Alexandrov, Charlie and Oona. Shortly afterwards Charlie locked himself in his room and refused to see the Alexandrovs.

Below: Charlie with the European executives of United Artists. On the far right is Smadja. Poor Tooky had already died. On the wall is a photo of Arthur Krim, the president.
Below right: Charlie strangling Geraldine.

As we adjourned to the sitting-room, Mrs Alexandrov saw some of Charlie's music resting on the piano. "Oh, maestro!" she cried once again, "It would be such an honor if you could let me have a sheet of your music for the Moscow Museum." Charlie quickly took the music away and put it to one side. Then, as we walked further into the room, she noticed some loose pages from one of his scripts, with notations on the side. She picked one up and held it close to her bosom. "Oh, maestro!" she proclaimed emotionally, "If this could be presented to the Leningrad Museum, it would be preserved for ever!"

Suddenly Charlie stormed out of the room and signaled me to follow him. As he was going up the stairs, he said, "Get rid of those damned Communists. They're all the same. They'll take everything that's not nailed to the floor!" And this was from the man who Americans accused of Communist sympathies!! Poor Mr and Mrs Alexandrov. They didn't know what hit them. I had to drive them to the railway station and apologize that the "maestro" was suddenly taken ill.

Charles Smadja, the head of United Artists' European office, flew over from Paris to see the finished *Chaplin Revue* prior to its Paris opening. Smadja was a great enthusiast and a real Chaplin fan. You couldn't help liking him.

Smadja had a poodle called Tooky. Whenever he ran a new United Artists film in Paris, Tooky always sat next to him in the projection room. If Tooky barked, wagged his tail or began panting, Smadja would exclaim, "Tooky loves the film! It's going to be a big hit!" Tooky was his oracle. If, God forbid, Tooky fell asleep and snored, Smadja would moan, "We're in trouble. We've got a flop on our hands, a *big* flop." Thank God Tooky kept awake during *Limelight*. It became the biggest money-maker United Artists had up to that time.

Smadja was crazy about *The Chaplin Revue,* and he was anxious to take a print back to Paris to show it to Tooky and United Artists executives. We all held our breaths. Would Tooky like it? Unfortunately, during the screening, Tooky became ill and died shortly afterwards. To this day, we don't know what Tooky thought.

Oona and Charlie's children were growing up fast. The girls were now young teenagers, and becoming interested in boys. Charlie kept a watchful eye on them. Somehow Josephine managed to have dates

ABOVE LEFT: CHARLIE PRETENDING TO
SHOOT EUGENE.
ABOVE RIGHT: OONA AND CHARLIE ON THE
TERRACE AT THE HOUSE THEY RENTED IN
CAP FERRAT.
LEFT: SYD AND CHARLIE ON THE BALCONY
AT CAP FERRAT.
RIGHT: SYD WITH HIS NEW WIFE, THE
BALLERINA NOELLE ADAM.

without Charlie objecting; she knew how to handle him. But Victoria was kept under strict surveillance.

Vicky suddenly blossomed into a beauty, and Charlie wouldn't let her out of the house unless chaperoned. I was considered safe enough to accompany her into Vevey. Little did I know she was using me to take her to a certain restaurant because she had a crush on one of the waiters. When I discovered her ruse, I told her, "What if your father finds out?" Vicky grasped my arm firmly, and looked at me threateningly. "If you ever say a thing, I'll never talk to you again," she said. "Swear to me you'll never tell!" It was like a blood oath; I swore.

Then one day Charlie confronted me. "Did you know," he said, "that Vicky was going into Vevey to see a young man?" Timidly, I replied, "Yes." Charlie shouted, "Why didn't you tell us?" I replied, like a simpleton, "She made me swear!" Charlie somehow understood, and forgave me. But for the first time, Charlie was finding out what it was like to be the father of teenagers.

That summer, Oona and Charlie took a large villa in St Jean Cap Ferrat on the Mediterranean. I was invited. Charlie was looking forward to swimming in salt water. Unfortunately the Mediterranean was filthy. Charlie wouldn't go in and kept warning everyone to keep out as the sewage ran into it.

Most of the time, Oona, the children and I stayed in the house and played Monopoly. Charlie wouldn't have any part of us. Word got around that "Charlot" lived at the villa, and people always gathered outside – I often wondered what they thought went on inside. They couldn't have imagined we were all sitting around throwing dice at the Monopoly board.

Charlie soon had enough of the Mediterranean, and left for home. I went onto Paris, as brown as a berry from the sun, and stayed at the same hotel as Sydney and his bride Noelle Adam, the French ballet dancer. Paris was tense at the time. Algeria wanted its independence, and there were shootings and demonstrations throughout France. The police would shoot anyone suspected of terrorism. Every day, newspapers carried stories about innocents being shot.

It was late August, and Paris is deserted during the summer. I went out with my friend Jeff Davis. It was 2.30 in the morning when we said goodnight. There was not a soul in the street. As I made my way to my hotel through an eerie silence, I heard the click-click-clack of footsteps from behind. They were coming closer.

Instinctively, I turned. Standing beside me was a man with a gun. He pushed it into my ribs, grinning. He looked like a *clochard* (a tramp), and although he didn't ask me to put up my hands, I automatically did. I thought it was all a dream.

When I realized it wasn't, I tried to scream, but no sound came out of my mouth. I was paralyzed with fear. The *clochard* shoved me into the street. I heard more footsteps. I looked up; two more *clochards* were coming towards me with guns outstretched. I found my voice. "Help! Help!" I screamed; but I couldn't think of the French word for help (I'll never forget it now: *Au secours! Au secours!*).

I turned towards the buildings. All I saw were firmly barred shutters. No one heard my cries. I imagined myself in pools of blood. Just as the *clochards* began to converge on me, a doorman from the Hotel Tremoille shouted "American! American! He's American!"

The *clochards* grabbed and pulled me into the hotel lobby, and demanded to see my papers. I showed them my passport. They then broke into large smiles, and tried to shake my hand, but I wouldn't accept their apologies. I stood frozen to the spot. I was in a state of shock. They were the French secret police, disguised as tramps, looking for terrorists; with my suntan, I had been mistaken for an Algerian.

Trembling, I woke up Sydney, told him what had happened, and asked him to loan me some money to give to the doorman. "He saved my life," I said. Sydney, with his wry sense of humor, replied, "Don't overtip; you'll spoil it for all of us."

Later I told Charlie what happened. He roared with laughter. He saw the comic possibilities. One look at my face and he realized that I didn't think it was funny. He stopped laughing.

A phone call came from Eddie Constantine. He was filming in Berlin and asked me to join him for the weekend; he wanted me to meet some producers about the film I was writing for him. Stupidly I told Ella about it; I couldn't take a trip anywhere without Ella giving me a long list of things to bring back for her. This time I was to cross into East Berlin, to buy her a painting.

In those days, as an American, it was very dangerous to cross Checkpoint Charlie. But like a fool I did, making my way down Unter den Linden, then up dark side streets, where I found a little old bald-headed man waiting in a basement. He looked round furtively and quickly handed me the canvas. I gave him American dollars, and he disappeared. After getting her precious painting past the suspicious English Customs officials, Ella yelled at me, "You idiot, you brought back the wrong one!" I think she expected me to return.

Ella was incorrigible, and yet she could also be good-natured and generous. "Have you any money?" she would say to me, "Can I help in any way? Be sure to ask if you want a loan." And she always referred to me as her "darling Jerry".

In 1980, Don and Ella died within three days of each other. Several days earlier, someone had asked Don what he would put on Ella's tombstone. Don thought for a minute and then replied, "She was awful, but she was worth it." Their affection for each other went very deep.

Oona and Charlie had felt very close to Don and Ella: to me London seemed emptier without them.

Oona and Charlie vacationed every Easter in Ireland. They found the people, the weather and the landscape exhilarating. Just before a visit to Waterville, County Kerry, Charlie had a tiff with his son Michael. He'd been playing truant from school. Education was of prime importance to Charlie.

In Ireland, Charlie made an effort to reconcile things. He decided to teach Michael how to fish. Charlie had once landed a 162-pound swordfish off Catalina Island; so he was going to show Michael a thing or two about the art of fishing.

According to Michael, Charlie said to him as they stood on the bank of a stream, "The touch – you must have the touch." He threw back his rod. The line went into the air. He whipped the rod forward, and then tugged. He'd caught something large!

"Oh, this is a big one!" Charlie said. As he struggled, Michael looked round, and spotted that the hook had caught in Charlie's raincoat and was ripping its back out. Michael poked his father. "I think the hook's caught onto your coat, Dad," he said politely. As they walked home together, Charlie tried to hold together the two halves of his ripped coat.

Top: Charlie about to show Michael how to fish, in Ireland.

Bottom: Oona and Charlie walking through Chester Terrace in London. This is where I lived. I paid £7 a week for my flat – those were the days!

In London I phoned Eddie Constantine and told him that the comedy I was writing for him was almost finished. But he had had too many offers to play in Lemmy Caution-type films to consider my project for the moment. So I decided to turn it into a British film, *Follow That Man*. I took an apartment in Chester Terrace, overlooking Regent's Park – one of the original Nash houses. I paid seven pounds a week!! A week after I took the apartment, on December 3rd, 1959, Annie Emily Chaplin was born.

I worked away on the *Follow That Man* screenplay. It was going to be a crazy English comedy. I had read about a famous English legal case in the nineteenth century concerning the Tichborne inheritance. The eldest son of a baronet was lost at sea as a child, but his mother was convinced he still lived. Twenty years later, a conman learned about the case, and claimed to be the missing heir. In my version, Sydney Chaplin played the conman; he visits the mother with his girlfriend (Dawn Addams) moments before the heir's inheritance is to be distributed among relatives.

In the original Tichborne case, the mother took one look at the impostor and said "This is my son!" after rejecting scores of other "sons" through the years. Why would she take one quick look and proclaim this man her son? I asked. I felt there must have been a strong sexual attraction – some Freudian undercurrent. If he'd been a mug, I didn't think the mother would have accepted him. My film then turns into a cockeyed triangle. The mother eventually falls in love with her "son", can't understand the strange emotions she feels for her offspring, and wants to marry him. And the impostor begins to believe he really is her son. It was all mad. When I told Charlie the plot, he said "How I wish you had worked with me years ago! The Tramp could have played the impostor in one of my shorts! It's a marvelous premise."

Michael Chaplin had run away from home, and was living in London. Oona was going out of her mind, not knowing where he was. And the more distressed she became, the more it upset Charlie. Michael was finally found living with the family of a friend of Geraldine's from the Royal Ballet School, where she was now a student.

Christmas was coming. I was anxious to bring Michael home for a reconciliation. He was reluctant. Because of my insistence he finally agreed to come, but only after Christmas. The family had rented a chalet at a Swiss ski resort, Crans-sur-Sierra; most of the children were there with the nannies.

Back in Vevey, Charlie claimed there were strong smells in the house. He went into every room sniffing. He insisted the smells were poisoning him. No one in the family could smell anything strange except Charlie. Late at night, when I was visiting, I heard him prowling around and opening doors. Those smells again! All the lights went on. Finally he knocked on my door, and got me up. "Do you smell anything?" he asked. Yes, I did. Oona emerged from her bedroom. At last he had an ally. He was overjoyed: "Jerry can smell it too!"

Plumbers were called in – not for the first time. Everything around the garden and in the road was dug up. Trenches were made. The plumbers agreed they could smell *something,* but couldn't make out what or where it was. Charlie was going out of his mind. Finally, according to Michael, the plumbers discovered a little package. Someone in Ireland had given Charlie a gift; without opening it, he had Michael bring it back with him. Michael had put it in a cupboard. Inside, they discovered piles of rotten shrimps – months old. Everyone could now sleep in peace.

REMEMBERING CHARLIE

Right: Here I am directing Sydney in *Follow That Man*.

Below: Sydney with Elspeth March in *Follow That Man*; Syd kidding around, doing a "Charlie Chaplin".

Left: Waiting for the train *en route* for Crans-sur-Sierra, a winter resort. Left to right: Michael (he kept to himself), Vicky, Janine Hill (Geraldine's friend from the Royal Ballet), Geraldine and Josephine. *Center:* Inside the chalet in Crans; no one wanted to face the snow. Left to right: Michael, Janine, Geraldine, me and Vicky. *Bottom:* Charlie keeping warm in Crans. He would have preferred basking in the hot West Indies sun!

When Michael arrived, Charlie found it hard to talk to him because of the agony he had caused his mother. So Michael kept his distance. The atmosphere was frigid, outside and in. I think that was the last time Oona ever rented a chalet in the Alps. The reconciliation between Michael and his father came a few years later, when Michael married and began to have a family of his own.

I received a phone call: my father had been taken ill. From London I flew immediately to California. Luckily, my father improved. While in Los Angeles, I got a job on the *Alfred Hitchcock Presents* TV program. In those days Universal Studios had a family feeling to it. But the nicest thing were the people working on the Hitchcock Show: Joan Harrison, the producer; Norman Lloyd, the associate producer; Gordon Hessler, the story editor; and Bruce Lansbury, who supervised the Hitchcock show for CBS.

I had a great time. So many pictures and television shows were being filmed. Whenever we could, Gordon and I would wander onto the stages and watch Doris Day and Rock Hudson, or James Arness in *Gunsmoke,* or Marlon Brando filming *The Ugly American* (directed by my old Circle pal George Englund).

Charlie and Oona had just returned to Vevey from the Orient. The holiday rekindled Charlie's enthusiasm for a story he originally devised after a 1936 Far East trip. It concerned a handsome, young, wealthy man who was planning to run for President of the United States. In the story, he returns by sea from a fact-finding trip to the Orient, and discovers a beautiful stowaway – a White Russian Countess – hiding in his stateroom. He mustn't be seen with her; it could ruin his career. By coincidence, Kennedy had just been elected President. Here was another young, handsome, rich politician – and it made Charlie realize his 1936 screenplay was now topical.

A few months later, Oona wrote to me that Eddie Fisher had visited them in Vevey. Elizabeth Taylor, then his wife, was filming *Cleopatra,* and Fisher asked if Charlie would be interested in directing her in something. Charlie immediately thought of Taylor for his "stowaway" film. I wrote back that, although she was a fine actress, I couldn't see her doing comedy, and felt that Sophia Loren would be better casting. "She's got real excitement, vitality and a sense of fun," I wrote.

Most of my letter, though, was about *The Birds,* which Hitchcock was making at Universal. I gave Oona and Charlie a blow-by-blow description of what I saw:

Hitchcock walks around the lot like a medieval monarch. Whenever you go on stage, you see vicious crows casually strolling across the set, with several prop men quietly stalking them with their hands outstretched, trying to get them back into their cages. Hitchcock's new discovery is "Tippi" Hedren, whom he saw doing a television commercial. When I first saw her on the lot, she appeared serene, relaxed and gay. Several weeks into shooting, after working with those damned birds, her face is very tight, tense, and screwed up.

They've built the exterior of a house on the stage; on the roof are three dozen crows with their feet wired down. When Hitchcock is ready to start shooting, the assistant director throws a rock at them, and their wings begin fluttering.

The other day I saw Tippi put inside a glass cage with lots of birds. Only a few were live. The rest were dummies on the end of big sticks, held by prop men. When Hitchcock shouted 'Action!', the prop men, out of camera range, pressed their fingers together, making the beaks of the crows open. Then they thrust these phony birds into Tippi's face. Between the dummies and the lives ones, she looked hysterical. I don't think it was acting.

My time at Universal was up. I called Audrey Wood in New York; she advised me to get back there. I told her it was my dream to film *The Adding Machine.* She gave me Elmer Rice's phone number. Before leaving, my sister handed me a telegram that had arrived at her house: "Christopher James Chaplin," it read, "was born on July 8th, 1962. Signed, Oona and Charlie." Charlie was seventy-three years old at the time.

In New York, I immediately contacted Elmer Rice, and we arranged to meet.

I was living in a hotel when I ran into Rod Steiger. He insisted I move in with him in his brownstone house in Brooklyn Heights. I didn't want to ... the thought of moving back to Brooklyn depressed me. But Rod couldn't have been kinder, or more generous, so I moved in. I had met Rod originally through Claire Bloom, then his wife; she was filming in Europe, and he was about to make *The Pawnbroker.*

I had always heard about actors living their parts and taking their roles home with them at night. I was to witness the living proof. Rod would come back from the studio, still completely immersed in his emotional role. He'd mutter in a slow, almost inaudible voice: "Oh, Jerry, I had the most terrible scene to film today. I had to visualize my wife in a death camp." Then he'd scare the living daylights out of me by baying like a wolf at night and pounding his fist against the wall. I decided to move.

Elmer Rice and I met for lunch at the Museum of Modern Art. After assuring him that the film would retain the play's spirit, he gave me the rights. He asked me, "Do you think Chaplin would consider playing Mr Zero?" "I think he would be very flattered, but he only appears in his own vehicles," I replied. But I still had to pay Rice a sizeable sum for the rights. I needed to find a job.

Through a friend, Joel Glickman, I worked with Garson Kanin on *Mr Broadway,* a TV comedy pilot made under the auspices of David Susskind's Talent Associates. As we were shooting, President Kennedy was assassinated. The pilot was quickly wrapped up. Susskind kindly allowed me to stay on in my office. There, I began writing the first draft of *The Adding Machine.* But I was always nervous that David was going to ask me to leave, so I kept out of sight.

David was always coming up with new concepts for plays, films, or TV shows. Now he was conducting a call-in radio program. Before it went on the air, everyone at Talent Associates, including me, was given pre-arranged questions to ask him over the phone. This guaranteed that the show would be lively and David – with his prepared answers – would come off brilliantly.

That evening, I phoned in at the prescribed hour. Over the radio I could hear David answering a previous caller. He was attacking expatriate Americans, and Europeans in general. Suddenly I was on the

OONA, CHARLIE AND THE CHILDREN READING VARIOUS TRANSLATIONS OF CHARLIE'S AUTOBIOGRAPHY. THEY USED THIS PHOTO FOR THEIR 1964 CHRISTMAS CARD.

air – but I was so incensed by what he had said that I lost my head, and instead of asking my question I yelled at him for saying such stupid things. Next day – and every day after that – whenever he saw me, David began apologizing for what he said. He was so embarrassed that my stay in the office was now secured.

In New York I ran into Kay Kendall's sister Kim. She was, if possible, even more beautiful than Kay. She had married a banker and was now living on Park Avenue. We had something in common: our love for Kay.

The first draft of *The Adding Machine* was finished. I sent the script to Martin Balsam and Eli Wallach. I even called Rex Harrison, on the movie set of *My Fair Lady,* to see if he'd play a small role. Then from out of the blue I was given three plays to direct: first, *The Wayward Stork,* followed by Jack Perry's hilarious *Easy Does It,* with Louise Lasser, Tom Poston and Reneé Taylor. Then through Philip Langner and the Theatre Guild, I directed George Bernard Shaw's *The Millionairess,* starring Carol Channing and Gene Wilder. It was a big hit. Carol was delightful. Audiences adored her, and she could do no wrong. As Charlie always said, "There's nothing like personality!" And she had it in abundance. As a result of the production, Gower Champion gave Carol the lead in *Hello Dolly.*

The Adding Machine had political overtones that some people were afraid of. I couldn't understand their reaction. But no one could kill my enthusiasm. I was surprised to hear from Oona that Charlie was interested in directing the film if I had a script. He loved the play as much as I. I pressed ahead with the project: Elliott Hyman of Seven Arts was particularly encouraging.

Auditions were announced for the musical *Funny Girl* – based on the life of our old Circle supporter Fanny Brice; it was to star an unknown Barbra Streisand. Sydney landed the leading man's role of

Nicky Arnstein, Fanny's gambler husband. But the show was beset with problems and feuds between Sydney, Barbra and the producers. There were changes of director, forty different endings, and the choice of songs varied daily. But when the show finally opened, Streisand reigned over Broadway.

Charlie's autobiography was published in September 1964, and quickly became a best-seller. Joel Grey, Anthony Newley, and Tommy Steele kept writing for the movie rights. Charlie never wanted his life story filmed. He always said, "I can see the big scene in the movie, when I come home to my poor mother and say, 'Mama, I've made it! Ugh!' He was thinking of Al Jolson in *The Jazz Singer.*

Max Reinhardt, Charlie's publisher at Bodley Head, arranged for Charlie to make a Scandinavian tour for the publication of the book. Oona, Vicky and Josie accompanied him. This was the first time Charlie had ever been to Scandinavia. It was like a royal visit. In Oslo, late at night, an entire boulevard became a river of light as people held torches parading past Oona and Charlie on the balcony of their hotel. Vicky and Josie had heard stories about the receptions Charlie had received in the early days, but now they were witnessing one themselves. Charlie turned to them and said jokingly, "You didn't know your father was such an important guy, did you?"

In Sweden, he met Ingmar Bergman – another master of cinema. They were both overwhelmed at each other's presence. Neither of them could speak the language, but it didn't matter; they knew exactly how they felt about each other.

Syd was miserable in *Funny Girl.* He and Barbra Streisand were not getting along. When the show was on the road, they had been very close; now they were not talking. Barbra threatened to leave when her contract was up unless Sydney was out; and Sydney was not leaving. The tension onstage and off was unbearable. Eventually a settlement was reached with Syd. He was happy to go, especially since he had heard his father was writing a part for him in a new film.

I continued my quest to film *The Adding Machine.* So many meetings and lunches, false hopes and rejections. But I never lost faith.

A letter arrived for me at Susskind's office. It was from Oona. Charlie and she were in Jamaica with their younger children, and she asked me to join them. There was something Charlie wanted to speak to me about . . .

A COUNTESS 7 FROM HONG KONG

Jamaica was paradise. Oona and Charlie were staying in a hotel on the beach in Ocho Rios. Charlie was lapping up the sun. How he loved his early morning swims in that crystal-clear blue water.

Charlie was anxious to get his "stowaway" story into production. A man called Pierre Rouve had recently introduced him to Sophia Loren – she'd been making *Lady L* in Switzerland – and Charlie thought she'd be excellent as the Russian Countess; he'd seen her in de Sica's *Yesterday, Today and Tomorrow* and raved about her performance.

He handed me the script to read. I took it on the beach so I could be alone and concentrate. As I was reading, I saw Charlie hovering nervously behind me, trying to gauge my reactions. The moment I gave the slightest titter, he rushed over anxious to know what had amused me. When I told him, he began bubbling over with laughter.

Because of similarities between Charlie's character, Ogden Mears, and President Kennedy, Charlie felt it would be in bad taste, now that Kennedy had been assassinated, to make a comedy that people would think was based the former President. He was especially concerned about the feelings of Kennedy's widow. So he changed the Ogden Mears role into a man hoping to become an Ambassador. Several years later I met Pierre Salinger, Kennedy's press secretary. He said that Jack Kennedy had planned to do something about Chaplin's exile – Salinger was supposed to visit him to invite him back to the United States. But of course in the meantime Kennedy had been killed. Salinger also mentioned that he'd seen *A Countess from Hong Kong*. "I know who that picture was based on," he told me; "Mr Chaplin captured it very accurately." So I guess we didn't disguise the Kennedy aspect too well.

Charlie had written hilarious comedy sequences, but he wanted, above all, to make a romantic film. He often said "A good love story will never go out of fashion." With my long experience of Charlie's way of working, I could visualize the elements that were merely implied in his scenarios. So many of Charlie's screenplays depended on his interpretation and direction. Could you imagine anyone but Chaplin making *Modern Times, City Lights* or *The Gold Rush?* I felt the script had all the necessary Chaplin ingredients: sympathetic lead characters, a strong premise, and five set pieces. It was funny, charming and above all romantic.

While we were basking in the sun, I mentioned to Charlie an idea I had for a movie. It dealt with an upstanding judge, a strong advocate of law and order, but little did he know that his two obstreperous sons were causing all the havoc in town.

Charlie got very excited. "I could play the judge. It would make a marvelous vehicle for me. My big scene would be where they convert me into a hippie." "The idea is yours," I said. "Take it."

For a while he thought of abandoning the *Countess*, but the thought of writing a new screenplay seemed daunting. And he was anxious to get started on a new project. So back we went to the *Countess*.

Charlie wanted Noel Coward for the part of Ogden Mears's valet. Noel said he would be more than happy to play in the film, but he was only available until the end of the year. The panic was on. We had to start shooting by September, or at the latest, October. Charlie wanted me to secure the financing immediately.

"Get me a deal," he said. I assured him that, with himself directing and Sophia starring, there would be no problem; "And Sophia," I added, "is very bankable." He had never heard the expression before. I explained that it was a new Hollywood term to describe stars on whose names the studios would finance the film. Charlie roared with laughter. "Do you think I'm 'bankable'?" he asked. "Absolutely!" I replied. He liked that. "Trust the Americans," he said, "They think up the most wonderful expressions. Bankable, bankable . . ." He kept savoring the word.

We were all leaving Jamaica – I to New York to work on a deal, Oona and Charlie to Switzerland. The quickest way for them to return to Europe was by making a stop-over and changing planes in New York. This would be the first time Charlie would set foot on American soil since his re-entry permit was revoked. He was a little apprehensive. Would they keep him for questioning? Was he re-entering the country illegally? He was assured that it was perfectly alright to stop in transit, and that nothing could happen. But he was still concerned.

At Kennedy airport, he showed his passport to the Immigration Officer, who looked at it hard. He couldn't believe his eyes: Charlie Chaplin was standing right in front of him. The official thumbed through a list, presumably to see if Charlie's name was on it. We held our breath. After a moment, he waved Charlie through. Phew!

In New York I began contacting the major studios. First I went to my friend Elliott Hyman of Seven Arts, then to Columbia, MGM and Joe Levene.

Levene, who had distributed many of Sophia's foreign films, was a strange man to do business with. He was short and rotund, with a high speaking voice that became even higher if he thought he was being swindled. It was usually the other way round.

In his office, with his associate Leonard Lightstone present, he proposed a deal for the film, and wrote down the figures on a piece of paper. I took it away and conveyed the figures to Charlie. He liked what he heard and told me to make the deal.

I went back to Levene and told him excitedly, "You can have the Chaplin/Loren film." I reiterated his figures. Joe was stunned. "I never gave you those figures," he said. I showed him the paper, in his own handwriting. He claimed it wasn't his writing. "Let's call in an unbiased person," he said. He then rang for Leonard Lightstone and asked him,

"Did I ever mention these figures?" "No, Joe," he replied. Levene looked at me and said, "You see – and Lennie's unbiased!" That was the end of our deal with Joe Levene.

I flew back to London and met with Charlie. We began making a budget. Carlo Ponti, Sophia's husband, had produced many of her films, including *Marriage, Italian Style*. The very "bankable" Sophia was now his biggest asset. Ponti thought we should bring the picture to MGM. He and Sophia were on very good terms with Jim Aubrey, head of the company. "All I have to do," Carlo said, "is to bring Sophia into Jim's office, and we'll have a deal." But Charlie wanted me to feel out the market.

My cousin Irving, whom I grew up with in Brooklyn, had a small dry goods store in a side street in Flatbush. It was so crowded with merchandise – linens, sheets, towels, men's shirts – that you could hardly move. I needed someone to talk to. Charlie was four thousand miles away, and no lawyers or agents were involved. I could trust Irving, and he served as the perfect sounding board. So, among all the linens, Irving and I mapped out the campaign for setting up a multi-million dollar movie production.

I made appointments with all the interested studios, and told them they had seven days to make up their minds. Norman Lloyd, whom I'd seen in New York and was still working at Universal, mentioned the film to Jay Kanter, a studio executive. I was now being courted. I liked the idea of Jay Kanter: when Elliott Kastner was a rising agent at MCA, he always bandied around the name of Jay Kanter. I felt I knew him.

While Irving and I were having a bite in a luncheonette near his store, his stock clerk came running over: there was a Mr Kanter, he said, on the phone from Hollywood. "Did you make a deal on the *Countess* yet?" he asked as soon as I reached the phone. "Not quite," I replied. "My mouth is watering," Mr Kanter said, "how do I get the picture?" I told him I'd be returning to London in two days, so he'd have to come to New York immediately. "Don't make a deal with anyone till I get there," he said. "I'll be in New York in the morning." I liked the way he talked.

Kanter had started in the mail room at MCA, then the largest theatrical agents. When Marlon Brando arrived in Hollywood for his first film, Jay picked him up at the train station; and through Marlon, his career took a big step forward. He was now a movie executive.

Kanter flew in the following morning and we began negotiations. I had to return to London to discuss the film with Charlie. But Jay wasn't letting me out of his sight; he came along.

Jay expected his London trip to be brief. But negotiations between Charlie, Jay and myself seemed to go on for ever, so Jay decided to send for his wife and children. Still the negotiations went on. So he enrolled the kids in an English school and started looking for a house. Whenever we were nearing a deal, Ponti would call me: "Go to MGM, I'll get you everything you want."

Now that Charlie was embarking on a new film, he was anxious to see the latest box-office successes. The big money-maker playing in London was *The Sound of Music*. It was breaking all records. Charlie wanted to see why. So with Oona, Vicky, Josie and myself, we trotted off to the Dominion Theatre. The place was packed. We had to sit in the second balcony. The film started with Julie Andrews bursting into song: "The hills are alive with the sound of music ..." After ten minutes, Charlie exclaimed "This is the most disgusting film I've ever seen. I'm not sitting through this!" So he and Oona left, leaving Vicky, Josie and myself. The girls, who had been schooled in a convent, were not too keen either.

We needed a leading man to play opposite Sophia. We heard Cary Grant was interested. As we sat in Charlie's Savoy suite, mulling over casting possibilities, the most amazing sound came from the suite above. It was Maria Callas, rehearsing for Franco Zeffirelli's production of *Tosca* at Covent Garden. When Josie and Vicky entered, Charlie shushed them immediately. We all had to whisper and walk on tiptoe, so that everyone could listen to her glorious voice. To hell with the casting!

Jay came in to see how things were going. Off-handedly, he suggested Marlon Brando. Charlie sat up. He couldn't believe his ears: "Do you think he would do it?" "All I can do is phone him and find out," Jay replied. We left for his apartment, where he placed a call, using Marlon's nom de plume. (Marlon, afraid that operators would listen in, had invented a code name.)

"Hold your breath," Jay told Marlon over the phone. "Charlie Chaplin wants you for his new picture." Marlon was overwhelmed. "You can't see the script. He'll speak to you himself. If you're interested, be here by the weekend."

Before Marlon arrived, we ran *A Streetcar Named Desire*. Oona and

Charlie had forgotten how brilliant Marlon was. They awaited his arrival with bated breath.

The meeting between Marlon and Charlie was held at the Savoy. Brando was like a schoolboy in front of Charlie. He loved his films, especially *City Lights*. Charlie thanked him for flying over, then acted out highlights of *A Countess from Hong Kong*. Marlon roared with laughter and was amazed at Charlie's agility. Afterwards, he agreed to do the film without reading the script – just for the privilege of working with Charlie. I said we'd be getting in touch with his agent. Then Charlie told him he had to lose weight before shooting. Marlon assured him he would.

That evening Oona and Charlie, along with Vicky, Josie and me, went out to Trader Vic's at the Hilton Hotel to celebrate. Charlie loved their navy grogs, spare ribs and fried shrimps. Usually on their first night in town, that's where Oona and Charlie would head. After Trader Vic's, it would be the White Elephant, or Simpson's on the Strand.

Charlie was in an expansive mood. The meeting with Marlon had gone well, and after his navy grog he felt the world was his oyster. Perhaps we were laughing and making more noise than Trader Vic's is used to.

From across the aisle, a tipsy American matron's voice boomed out at Charlie: "I've got more money than you!" Uh uh, I thought. This could turn ugly. I intervened: "Would you please leave us alone?" She sniped at Charlie again: *"I'VE GOT MORE MONEY THAN YOU!"* Charlie now entered the fray: "So that's the kind of person you are," he said. "That's right," she yelled back, "I'M RICHER – MUCH RICHER THAN YOU'LL EVER BE!" With that, her weaving escort yanked her gently by the arm: "C'mon honey," he said, "it's time we turned in."

Marlon's agent George Chasen flew in to see me. The money and percentages were settled at once. There was only one thing that Chasen demanded: Brando gets top billing in every country in the world. I agreed. Marlon, to me, *is, was,* and *will always be* a giant. Before leaving, Chasen added, "Has Ponti pulled the billing trick on you yet?" I said "No"; I didn't know what he was talking about. "He will," Chasen said. "He always comes up with that at the last minute."

How right he was. I thought Carlo was going to have heart failure when he heard Marlon was having top billing over Sophia. "You can't do this to Sophia. She's at home weeping!" (I had visions of her in her

Roman palazzo, sobbing beneath the water fountains.) Carlo continued: "Marlon *nutting* in Japan, Sophia *BEEG!* Marlon *nutting* in Italy, Sophia *BEEG, BEEG* star! Marlon *finished* in America, Sophia *TREMENDOUS!* At least let them split the world 50–50! In some countries, Sophia come first, in other countries, Marlon!" I said no: "I made a deal with Chasen, and that's that!"

Carlo appealed to Charlie, and warned him that if he used Marlon, the picture would go over budget. "Contact Lewis Milestone," he said; "The trouble he gave him on *Mutiny on the Bounty!* He was always late; he never knew his lines. Sometimes he never even showed up! At least he can give her Italy – her own country!"

Carlo was getting Charlie worked up, especially since he agreed to pay the overage on the film if it went over schedule. In a fury, Charlie called Jay Kanter on the phone: "If Marlon doesn't give her a few countries, you're not getting this picture." Jay was completely flummoxed. Here we were, close to a deal – and the deal was not predicated on Marlon's involvement. Jay had merely suggested him to help Charlie out. Now the whole deal was blowing up in his face. Carlo saw his opportunity again: "Go to MGM," he implored.

That night, Charlie, Oona and I dined in a small Chinese restaurant near Covent Garden. It was a hot summer's night. Everyone was on the streets. Charlie was still preoccupied with the billing, and wanted to take a walk. There were crowds outside the Opera House – the Queen, Prince Philip and the Queen Mother were expected any minute for the gala opening of *Tosca*. This was to be Callas's final operatic role.

Oona wanted to join the crowds and watch. But Charlie wouldn't have any part of it. Perhaps he was remembering the gala opening of *City Lights* in Los Angeles years before, when Charlie and his guest, Albert Einstein, had been jostled by a frantic mob of twenty-five thousand spectators. "I have visited the world's famous laboratories," the professor said afterwards, "I have looked through the greatest telescopes. I have seen science's wonders. But *never* have I seen anything like that. And I hope I never shall again!"

So Charlie continued walking through Convent Garden, while Oona and I behaved like two fans at a Hollywood opening. Afterwards, we caught up with Charlie and told him we had seen the Queen, Ava Gardner, and … But Charlie turned a deaf ear. His mind was on the *Countess*.

The billing problem had not subsided. From the coast we heard that Marlon had finally agreed that Sophia could have her name first in two countries – Iceland and Pogoland. Carlo was furious. Now Charlie was getting fed up with all this nonsense. I think he was beginning to feel left out. "Who the hell are they?" he cried, *"I'm* Charlie Chaplin!" He refused to go on with any further negotiations until the billing was resolved. He told me to meet with Ponti and gave me precise instructions about what to say.

I was looking forward to my meeting with Carlo at the Caprice restaurant in London. Carlo was in a happy mood. I wondered why. Had he figured out the billing problem? He had. "It's all so simple!" he said – "I should have thought of it before!"

Out of his pocket he fetched a drawing of a small wheel: Marlon and Sophia's names would appear in all the advertisements in a circle, so you couldn't tell whose name came first. The only trouble was, you couldn't tell who was in the picture either; it made you dizzy to look at it. I laughed. He put it away, slightly affronted.

Then, following Charlie's instructions, I pulled the *pièce de résistance*: "Either Sophia accepts second billing, or we're making the film with Elizabeth Taylor!" Carlo sat there frozen – dumbstruck. The blood drained from his face. When he came to, there was no more talk about billing.

The contracts were now ready for signing. Charlie's clever lawyer Keith Allison, along with Universal's, had already left for Switzerland. Jay and I were preparing to take a later flight. I was about to head for the airport when my phone rang. It was Oona.

"Don't have the lawyers come!" she insisted. I couldn't understand why. "Charlie read his horoscope in the *Daily Express*. It said 'Don't sign any papers today'." But it was too late to stop the lawyers. Jay and I took off for the Manoir, hoping we could save the situation. We frantically looked for horoscopes saying "Sign!" But it was futile. Charlie was a charming host – escorting all the lawyers around the grounds. But there was no question of him signing any contract.

I don't think Charlie really believed in horoscopes, but I felt this was a perfect excuse for him not to sign. The act of putting his name to a contract was like signing a death warrant.

That evening in Les Ambassadeurs, Jay and I wept into our beers. "Let's not do anything," I told him. Something may happen."

It did. Several days later, Charlie called. There was just one small item that needed clarifying in the contract, and he was now ready to sign. Before Universal booked the film, anywhere in the world, he wanted to okay every contract, including second and third runs.

Lew Wasserman blew his stack: he had never heard of such a thing. But a compromise was reached. Charlie could okay the contracts in fifty international cities. Oh what fun we had going through our atlas and selecting the fifty . . . Brussels, Hamburg, Rome, Berlin, Paris, London, New York, Philadephia, Miami, Albany, Bangkok, Hong Kong, Liverpool, Blackpool . . . fourteen down, thirty-six to go . . .

The contracts were now ready for signing again. Jay and I flew to Vevey. Would there be another last-minute hitch? Would he sign? It was an anti-climax when Charlie finally put pen to paper. Oona couldn't believe her eyes, and to make sure she wasn't seeing things, took photographs to commemorate the occasion. When it was signed, Jay said, "After this, negotiating peace in Vietnam would be a cinch!"

There was so much to do before shooting could start: working out budgets, selecting the technical staff. We were elated with both Arthur Ibbetson, the cameraman, and Don Ashton, the production designer. Now we had to concentrate on casting.

Sydney had left *Funny Girl* and was due in Europe shortly. Charlie was hoping that the part of Ogden Mears's friend and press agent would help his career as a young leading man in films. He wanted Syd to emerge as a star.

When the film was postponed, we had lost Noel Coward. Charlie still felt the part of Marlon's valet was crucial to the film. But we couldn't find anyone. The producer Sandy Lieberson, then Peter Sellers's agent, told me Sellers would love to do it. At first Charlie was excited, then he changed his mind: "This picture is getting too overloaded with stars. I don't want any more."

In the script there was a small role for an old woman laid up with seasickness, whose room is confused with Sophia's by the Captain and a passenger on the make. Though the part consisted of four lines and a couple of reactions, it was very amusing. I suggested Margaret Rutherford. Charlie turned on me: "You only want stars!" "That's not true," I replied, "I just think Margaret Rutherford could make that little scene. She's so outrageous." But he wouldn't hear of it. Finally, he snapped at me: "Alright, get her over here. I'll see her."

TOP: WATCHING NERVOUSLY TO SEE IF CHARLIE WILL SIGN.
BOTTOM: OONA TOOK THIS HISTORIC PICTURE OF CHARLIE AND JAY KANTER PUTTING THEIR SIGNATURES TO THE UNIVERSAL CONTRACT. THE *COUNTESS* WAS ABOUT TO BEGIN. I'M MUNCHING AN APPLE – NERVES!

Dear Margaret Rutherford wobbled towards Charlie's suite with her husband Stringer Davis. Charlie, at his most charming, greeted her with open arms. "How nice of you to come. Would you consider playing such a small part for me? It would be such a privilege to have you." Rutherford was completely bowled over: "It would be a privilege for me to work with you," she said.

London in the mid 1960s was the place to make films. Studios were bulging. Stage space was at a premium. Pinewood was busy with *To Sir, With Love,* with Sidney Poitier, the new Bond film *You Only Live Twice,* Truffaut's *Fahrenheit 451, Kaleidoscope,* with Warren Beatty, Peter Brook's *The Marat/Sade,* and others. *Time* magazine had just run an article referring to "Swinging London". London had come alive; everything was happening there, from the Beatles and Twiggy to the new Chaplin film. Miniskirts and discos were the rage; Tramps on Jermyn Street was a popular hang-out; the Rolling Stones had just

released "Satisfaction"; Carnaby Street was in bloom . . .

I found a charming maisonette in Shepherd's Market, just off Curzon Street in Mayfair. The Market, hidden away in the heart of the West End, is like an eighteenth-century village, with cobbled streets strewn with antique and book shops. But little did I know that it was also the heart of London's red light district. Most doors carried illuminated name plates with the names of various tenants – *Miss Doreen Lovelace, Brenda Backlash,* etc. The girls kept their distance from the Market residents; we had just a nodding acquaintance. Sometimes I would see a cop approaching and tip them off; they would then scatter in all directions.

At night the Market was a hive of activity. So was my apartment. Since it was also near the fashionable White Elephant restaurant, every friend and acquaintance came to see me after dinner – though I think they were more intrigued by the location.

CHARLIE ANNOUNCES TO THE WORLD PRESS THAT HE IS TO MAKE A NEW FILM.

One evening, Warren Beatty and Geraldine Chaplin turned up. Warren peeked out of my upstairs window and looked across the alleyway, where a pretty girl waited for a customer. For a joke, Geraldine stuck her head out of the window and began to flirt with two young men down below. A moment later there was a knock on the door. The two young men came upstairs. Warren immediately took over and began the negotiations. I was dying with embarrassment. Warren concluded a good deal, and for a while Geraldine fell in with the ruse. But when the men wanted to take her upstairs she suddenly hid in the kitchen. The young men were completely perplexed, and departed. Luckily, they never realized who the pranksters were.

Some nights it was impossible to sleep. Potential customers and drunks would get confused and ring my doorbell by mistake. I was told by my landlords that Garbo had once rented this apartment. I wondered if she went through what went I went through.

Oona and Charlie were leaving for Vevey. Before he left, Charlie asked me what credit I wanted. I said "associate producer". "Fine," he said, "but you'll share that credit with Pierre Rouve." I was taken aback: "I've been doing all the work, and just because he introduced you to Sophia Loren, I'm to share the credit with him?" I told him I was going back to New York. Charlie said he'd think about my credit. When he and Oona returned from Vevey, he announced I was to be the full producer on the film. I felt Oona's hand once again.

On Monday November 4th, a placard outside the River Room at the Savoy Hotel read: "C. CHAPLIN WILL BE HOLDING A PRESS CONFERENCE THIS MORNING TO MARK HIS NEW FILM." (I loved that "C. Chaplin" – so English!) Present were Charlie and Sophia. I don't think there was ever a press conference to announce a film so jammed. There was no place to walk or move. It was packed with reporters and photographers.

Bottom left: Vicky turning into a beauty.

Opposite: Relaxing on our "luxury liner" – Charlie, Sophia, me and Syd.

First came the photo call; afterwards, Charlie answered questions. In another room Sophia held court. But surrounding the glamorous Sophia, bejeweled in her expensive emeralds, were just a handful of reporters; around Charlie, there were scores. "Now I know what a real star is," Sophia commented.

Charlie was concerned about Sophia's costume. She only had one dress to wear for about 99 per cent of the film, and it had to be right. Charlie was going to give her dress the same care and attention he had given Paulette Goddard's costume as the gamine in *Modern Times*. He scouted around the London stores, and picked up an eighteen-dollar dress that he thought would be perfect. When he showed it to Sophia, I thought she was going to break out in hives. He explained that her character was supposed to be penniless. But to Sophia, this was going to be a glamorous, expensive film. She left London and called to tell me she was having her dress designed by Christian Dior. And that was that!

Vicky Chaplin, who was now fourteen, came with me to a press conference held by Albert Finney for his recently completed film *Charlie Bubbles*. At the end, Albert looked at lovely Vicky and called her "Alice in Wonderland". And he was right. With her large blue eyes and sandy-colored hair, she would have been the perfect "Alice".

Afterwards, we dined at the White Elephant with Oskar Werner, Michael Medwin, David Puttnam (then working in advertising), and Geraldine. Vicky was enjoying herself, but I was getting nervous about the time. I didn't realize that it was nearly twelve o'clock when we reached the Savoy. I quickly put her in the elevator and said goodnight. The next day, Charlie was furious. "How could he keep a child of fourteen up till twelve o'clock?" He was even more annoyed that I hadn't escorted her to the door.

It was three weeks before shooting was due to start, and because of this incident Charlie sent a message to me that he was calling off the picture. Vicky and Josie were hurtled back to Switzerland. Charlie locked himself in his suite and wouldn't accept my calls. Everything was in limbo.

Sophia would call me. Marlon would call. Don Ashton and Arthur Ibbetson would call. I had to put them off; I didn't know what to say. I told Jay Kanter what had happened: "Oh my God," he moaned, biting his nails and twisting his ring. Oona called me in secret, and said there was nothing she could do – I'd just have to wait and see what happened. Four days later, Oona called again; Charlie wanted to see me.

At the Savoy, he pounced at me, practically throwing me into a chair. "Do you want to make this picture or not?" he demanded to know. I replied, "You called it off, I didn't." I shouldn't have said that, but I couldn't help myself. He was getting angrier, and I was getting more and more flustered. I really think he felt I was having too good a time in Swinging London.

Charlie then realized that I was feeling terrible, and we resolved our differences. The sun was shining again. The picture was on. Now we were awaiting the arrival of our two stars, Sophia and Marlon – oops, Marlon and Sophia! There couldn't be any more problems. . .

Oona and Charlie took a beautiful house in the country, and a week before shooting, Charlie invited Marlon, Sophia, Sydney and me to the house to discuss the film. The first thing Charlie told Marlon was that he had to lose more weight. Again, Marlon promised that he would.

Then Charlie explained what he felt was the underlying meaning of the film. Although it was a romance, it had to do with power and control – the essence of the battle of the sexes. He explained Ogden Mears's character to Marlon: "Rich men with inherited wealth, like Ogden, have nothing to sell. They're very modest about their

possessions. He mustn't ever give the impression of being wealthy. He must always be disarming and self-effacing."

Marlon began asking pointed questions. At times, Charlie had difficulty articulating his ideas, and Marlon seemed to be putting him on the spot. A certain tension was developing. Afterwards, when Sophia, Sydney and I returned to London in the same car, Sophia was livid. "Did you see how he was trying to embarrass Charlie?" Were the seeds of future trouble being sown?

The picture was finally on its way. We were to start shooting on Monday, January 24th. I couldn't sleep the night before. Nerves. I woke up very early to get to the studio in preparation for Charlie's arrival. As I was about to leave, the phone rang. It was Marlon. His voice was weak, hardly audible: "I'm sick, I can't work today." I couldn't believe my ears. I advised him to stay in bed, and said I'd send for a doctor. I tried to reach Charlie but there was no reply. I dashed to Pinewood.

There was Charlie, on the set explaining the first set-up to Arthur Ibbetson. He was raring to go. He wore a bright red cashmere sweater, with his hat tilted to one side. I stood behind him and tapped him gently on the shoulder. He looked at me annoyed and went back to the camera. I tapped again. This time he stopped, sensing something.

I told him the news. No Marlon. He gave no outward reaction. Oona, Charlie and I walked to his dressing-room. "I thought you'd be furious," I said. "I'm not God," he replied, "if he's sick, he's sick."

We filmed without Marlon, shooting most of Sophia and Sydney's scenes; but after three days we needed him. We were scheduled to move onto another sound stage to film the ballroom sequence, and it had to be completed in two days; after that, another film was booked.

We were advised that Marlon would be on the set for the sequence. No need to panic. Two hundred extras were hired. Charlie and Sophia were there at eight-thirty in the morning, ready for rehearsals. Two hours went by. No Marlon. Charlie was fit to be tied. It's so demoralizing having two hundred people hanging around, drinking tea,

RIGHT: CHARLIE AND SOPHIA BETWEEN TAKES. ALL THE FURNITURE IS NOW PART OF MY LIVING-ROOM.

OPPOSITE: SOPHIA EXUDED SUCH WARMTH AND ENTHUSIASM; SHE WAS A PLEASURE TO WORK WITH.

eating cheese sandwiches and playing cards as their make-up disintegrates. Sophia, Charlie and I sat at one of the dining tables on the set waiting for our male star to arrive.

Word came to us that Marlon had left his house and was on his way. Charlie paced like a caged animal, then he sat and nervously tapped his fingers on the table (he gave that bit of business to Marlon in one scene). The tapping was a sure sign that the kettle was about to blow its fuse. Sophia was no help. "When he gets here, you must tell him off. You mustn't let him get away with this behavior," she said to Charlie. She seemed to be winding him up. I snapped at her: "Sophia, keep out of this. It's between Marlon and Charlie." I didn't want any fights on the set in front of all those extras. Whatever Charlie had to say to Marlon should be said privately.

Suddenly, we got word from the gateman; Marlon had arrived. He was now in his dressing-room putting on his tuxedo. All at once Marlon came on the set like an innocent little boy. Charlie stormed towards him like a tornado. I tried to hold him back but it was futile. He grabbed Marlon by the arm: "Listen, you son-of-a-bitch, you're working for Charlie Chaplin now. If you think you're slumming, take the next plane back to Hollywood. We don't need you."

Sophia was sitting at the table with a Mona Lisa smile. Revenge for the billing? But Marlon was like a small child in front of Big Daddy; sweet and apologetic. "Gee, Charlie, I was sick and . . ."

Charlie continued: "Listen – I'm an old man and I manage to be here on time. Now you're to be on the set every day, ready to shoot by eight-thirty, just like me." Marlon, the little boy, nodded, wide-eyed: "Yes, Charlie."

Thereafter, even if he had been up until dawn, Marlon would dress in his limousine as it sped down the motorway towards the studio. Then he'd rush onto the set. Eight-thirty. He'd made it! Once Charlie arrived five minutes late. Marlon smiled at him wickedly: "I've been waiting for you, Charlie. I'm ready to go. Where were *you?*" But Charlie wasn't interested in playing games. There was a film to make.

There was so much laughter on the set. Both Marlon and Sophia watched Charlie act out their roles with delight, and marveled at his sprightliness. Sophia was a dream to work with: co-operative, funny, and natural. She was the first one on the set every morning, fifteen minutes before Charlie and Marlon, checking all the lighting and

BELOW: MARLON AND ME. THEY DON'T COME NICER THAN M.B.

RIGHT: CHARLIE INSTRUCTING MARLON AND SOPHIA. CHARLIE IS TIRELESS; THEY ARE BEGINNING TO WILT.

OPPOSITE, FAR RIGHT: CHARLIE POSITIONING MARLON, SHOWING HIM EXACTLY WHERE TO STAND.

set-ups. As she walked on the set, she looked like a nice, simple girl. But the moment she was in front of the camera, a transformation took place: she became the dazzling Sophia Loren, superstar. She knew just how to hold her head at the right angle. And her eyes, as if by magic or muscle control, seemed to become more almond-shaped.

Charlie told Marlon where to stand, how many steps to take, and how many beats to count before turning. Marlon kept saying, "This is the easiest picture I've ever made. I don't have to do anything. Charlie's doing it all!" Marlon took Charlie's direction in his stride, although he came from a different school of acting.

The set was always jam-packed with reporters and cameramen from *Life, Look, Newsweek,* and other prestige papers. When he financed his own films, Charlie wouldn't allow journalists on the set. He felt pre-publicity was a waste. But since *Countess* was financed by Universal, he agreed, against his better judgment, to accommodate the press. Photographers were crawling all over the place, much to Charlie's annoyance. They were given strict orders to keep out of his sight.

But Sophia loved them, and co-operated with each and every one. As a result, her photo made almost every magazine cover in the world. Marlon had given instructions that he wanted no publicity and would give no interviews. But the sight of Sophia's picture wherever he looked began to rattle him. "She's getting all the attention!" he complained to Dave Golding, the London head of Universal publicity.

Left: Sophia pretends to get Charlie into focus. It was this scene that Sophia objected to — we shot her on her "wrong" side.

Opposite: Everyone fell for Margaret Rutherford. Sophia wasn't needed that day, but she still wanted to be on the set with her.

At the beginning of shooting, Sophia was in her dressing-room when Charlie entered and saw her applying her extraordinary eye make-up. "Go wash your face," he demanded, "I don't like all that goo." She did so, then walked on the set, brooding. "I feel so naked!" she said. But – just like Dawn Addams's vaselined lips – little by little the eye make-up came back, until one day she was in full regalia again. Charlie was too busy to notice.

Charlie would muss up her hair a little before a scene. He didn't like the perfect look. Sophia even helped him. "Is this the way you want it?" she would ask. Charlie nodded. But the minute he walked away, she'd rush to a portable dressing table and brush it back the way she liked it – *perfect*.

Sophia was convinced that the right side of her nose wasn't as attractive as the left. She had a theory that her left profile was more suited to comedy, and the right side to drama. So for this film she had to be photographed either full face or with her left profile.

In the completed film there was just one scene that showed her right profile for the briefest moment. Sophia was so upset that she tried to make us reshoot the sequence. Charlie considered it, but the scene involved back projection, which takes ages to set up. He finally couldn't be bothered – just for the sake of her nose. I think Sophia is still upset.

It was now time to shoot Margaret Rutherford's scene. Charlie was embarrassed that her part as the seasick passenger was so small, so he improvised more business. He placed a multitude of colored ribbons on her bed, and everytime she looked at the yellow or green ribbons, she'd feel faint and want to retch. She was so funny, she had the whole crew laughing. Poor thing, she *was* ill at the time, and was delighted that the scene required her to be in bed.

MELANIE GRIFFITH, TIPPI HEDREN'S DAUGHTER, READING ON THE SET. WHO WOULD HAVE THOUGHT THAT QUIET LITTLE GIRL WOULD BECOME A VOLUPTUOUS PIN-UP.

Oona was always present when we ran Margaret Rutherford's rushes. No matter how often she saw them, she always laughed hysterically. The scene brought the house down in the movie theaters too. And Charlie was most pleased.

Tippi Hedren played a cameo part as Marlon's estranged wife. We were sorry the part wasn't larger. She and her husband Noel Marshall approached Charlie about giving Tippi extra scenes. He tried, but it would have spoiled the film's construction.

Tippi kept to herself and didn't get involved in any of the antics that went on. She brought her quiet young daughter with her to the studio – Melanie Griffith. Tippi was completely professional – poised, and with a genuine sweetness. I loved her speaking voice – throaty, sensual and musical. Charlie found her so easy to direct. She had that quality he liked in American actresses – very relaxed.

We were now shooting the first kiss between Marlon and Sophia. Kisses are sometimes very difficult to film. Actors feel a certain embarrassment, and it's especially difficult if there is an antagonism between the stars. Sophia still had not forgiven Marlon over the billing. In the scene, Marlon had to taunt and insult Sophia. Then out of his rage grew passion; he grabs and kisses her.

TAKE ONE: We shot the scene. Sophia stormed off the set and announced to everyone, "Do you know what he just whispered to me

… that I've got long hairs growing out of my nose?" She gesticulated wildly like a true Italian. "How can you play a love scene with him?"

TAKE TWO: Charlie didn't like it. He wanted more passion from Marlon.

TAKE THREE: Marlon grabbed Sophia roughly. Again she stormed off the set. "He bit my lip. Look, it's bleeding! Doesn't that method actor know how to fake passion?" We stopped the bleeding.

TAKE FOUR: Perfect. When it was over, the two "lovebirds" parted in opposite directions.

In the evenings, Sophia would watch the previous day's rushes in private, with her secretary and companion Inez. Sophia liked to study how she photographed without anyone present. One morning she said to me, "Marlon's close-ups are larger than mine!" "It's impossible, Sophia," I replied – "the camera is the same distance for you and Marlon. It's been measured precisely." "Yes," she replied, "but his head is bigger than mine – so for me, you should push the camera in closer!" Someone muttered in the background: "But your hairstyle's about three inches higher than his – so that makes it even-stephen!"

To our surprise, Sean Connery was our neighbor. At Pinewood there was a long corridor. On either side were suites for the stars. Oona and Charlie had one; my office was directly opposite theirs. A hundred feet away was Sean Connery's dressing-room.

We had once considered him for the role of Odgen Mears; he had come to the Savoy to see Charlie, fresh from the South of France, looking very tanned and handsome. But we had already chosen Brando. Now he was filming *You Only Live Twice* on the next stage. Oona, Charlie and I became very friendly with him, and the friendship was to continue years after *Countess* was completed.

Josie and Victoria, the two lovely teenagers, visited the Pinewood set many times, and Josie developed a crush on Sean. Sean was aware of her feelings, and liked her very much. Whenever the girls came to London, the first thing they said was, "Let's eat at the White Elephant tonight. Maybe Sean Connery will be there!" They were starry-eyed.

Josie also hero-worshipped Maria Callas. She wrote her fan letters, and in London wherever Callas walked, Josie was not far behind. She even wanted to become an opera singer, and took lessons; eventually she and Callas became close friends. But now she was in a dilemma: she was also beginning to like Marlon Brando.

Right: Charlie and Tippi Hedren.

Far right: Sophia about to jump off our ocean liner.

Below: Charlie playing Sophia's part, showing Marlon how to do the love scene.

Below right: Charlie trying to get some passion into Marlon and Sophia's love scene.

SOPHIA BEING KISSED BY OONA AND CHARLIE'S YOUNGEST SON, CHRISTOPHER, WATCHED BY THEIR DAUGHTER JANE AND KAY-KAY, THEIR NANNY. AT THE TIME SOPHIA DESPERATELY WANTED CHILDREN.

I was always eating apples on the set. Just before we were about to shoot a scene, Sophia spotted one in my hand and came over. "What's with the apples?" she asked. "Sophia, get on the set," I said tensely – "Charlie's ready to shoot. I'll tell you afterwards." The moment the scene was finished, Sophia came rushing over: "So what's with the apples?" "It's supposed to be a breast substitute," I said. "You'll never substitute an apple for this!" she exclaimed, looking down at her ample bosom.

Just as he was at the Circle, Charlie was patient with all the other actors except Syd. In films, you have to come on the set prepared, but Syd needed time to digest his directions. Charlie was impatient. "For Chrissakes, come on Syd!" Charlie would say irritated. "Get some feeling into the lines. You're trying to make Sophia feel better. Show a little warmth!" When Syd didn't respond immediately, Charlie became more agitated. "For Chrissakes, what's wrong with you? Get the lead out of your pants!"

Marlon, watching from the sidelines, became worked up as he saw Charlie hammering away at Syd. He took me to one side: "How can he humiliate his son like that in front of all these people?" "Marlon," I replied, "Syd knows Charlie is doing it for his own good. He adores his father. So keep out of it – it's between father and son."

But Marlon's anger didn't subside. From that moment on, Marlon, the champion of the underdog, refused to take Charlie's directions. Just two weeks earlier, Marlon had said this was the easiest film he'd ever worked on. Now, whatever Charlie wanted to say to him had to be relayed through me. Charlie wouldn't get intimidated by Marlon's behavior; nothing was going to kill his enthusiasm for the task at hand.

Charlie was now to play a cameo scene as a seasick steward with Marlon. Marlon still felt frosty towards Charlie. But the moment Charlie started acting, Brando melted. He marveled at how Charlie could shift from soberness to seasickness in a flash. He beamed at Charlie with great warmth; all his hostility vanished. Talent triumphed. They were friends again.

The following day, Charlie became feverish. He asked me to finish shooting a scene with Sophia and Marlon. The minute he left the set, all hell broke loose. To Marlon and Sophia I was the substitute teacher. Every time I said "Action!", they'd each come in and out of different doors laughing and giggling. Everyone had a good time except me. I was

LEFT: CHARLIE, SOPHIA AND ME, WAITING
FOR THE NEXT SET-UP.

BELOW: FATHER AND SON. CHARLIE AND
SYD REHEARSING.

terrified. What if Charlie came back and saw the mayhem that was going on! I finally got the scene, and sent the "stars" home.

Patrick Cargill was given a big break when Charlie cast him in the main featured role alongside Brando and Loren. He played Marlon's valet – the part originally written for Noel Coward. Cargill was grateful for the opportunity. In one scene, Charlie wanted Cargill to ogle Sophia seductively and raise his eyebrows simultaneously. Cargill turned to Charlie and said, "I'm not that sort of actor. What is my motivation for raising my eyebrows?" Charlie was speechless. I tried to explain to Cargill that it was to punctuate the moment. But Cargill wasn't buying it – he had to know his motivation. Marlon's influence was spreading. Pretty soon the extras would want to know their motivations for dancing in the background.

I never enjoyed acting. To me it was nerve-racking. From *Limelight* onwards I used to read Charlie's scripts out loud to him and throw myself into the characterizations. Charlie would listen intrigued: he begged me to play the role of the television announcer in *A King in New York* – he liked my staccato Walter Winchell-like readings. But I refused. Acting in front of the camera was something else. There were plenty of actors around for that.

Marlon and Sophia were sitting in the ship's bar, waiting to start the scene. I told Charlie, "We still haven't cast the bartender." "Yes, we have," he replied, "you're doing it." My heart sank. I offered an excuse, but he stopped me short: "There's no time for that nonsense. Get into this outfit!" I lost my sense of orientation and began walking in a circle. Charlie told me to enter on the right and exit on the left – but I was too nervous to absorb what he was saying. I came in from the wrong direction. I was quivering like a mass of jelly.

Marlon then took me aside, put his arm around my shoulder, and whispered into my ear, "Do you know your motivation when you serve the drinks? Do you know who your father and mother were? What problems did you have on your way to work this morning?" I shouted, "Get the hell out of here, Marlon! Stop this Method shit! Leave me alone!"

Charlie was ready for a take. I entered the scene, and tried to ask Marlon and Sophia what they wanted to drink. But my line came out garbled. Marlon and Sophia burst out laughing. So did Charlie; so did the entire crew. Talk about humiliation. "Let's try it again," he said.

LEFT: CHARLIE ABOUT TO IMPRESS
MARLON WITH HIS CAMEO AS THE SEASICK
STEWARD.
BOTTOM LEFT: CHARLIE DEMONSTRATING
TO SOPHIA, PATRICK CARGILL AND SYD
HOW TO PLAY A SCENE.

BOTTOM RIGHT: ABOUT TO DO MY BIG SCENE
AS THE BARTENDER. I'M HIDING BEHIND A
WALL. SEATED AT THE BAR: MARLON AND
SOPHIA; CHARLIE IN THE FOREGROUND.

Marlon was about to come over with more advice, but I shoved him aside. I did my scene; Charlie, Marlon and Sophia were still wiping tears from their eyes when I angrily walked off the set. I have never performed since. At least I retired from the silver screen having played with Brando, Loren and Chaplin.

Countess was winding down. Celebrities had filled the set every day: John Huston, Ruth and Milton Berle, Truffaut, Tom Wolfe, Maximilian Schell, Patricia Neal, Sammy Davis Jr. Harold Clurman, the well-known director, founder of the Group Theater and a long-time friend of Charlie, also visited. He asked me if I could persuade Charlie to do an interview with him for *Playboy* magazine. "They do very intelligent ones," he said.

Charlie was outraged. He loathed the magazine and the way they displayed teenage girls in the nude, then wrote that they were well-bred and university graduates. Charlie now had teenage daughters of his own, and wouldn't even discuss the matter with his friend.

Gloria Swanson arrived, accompanied by the film historian Kevin Brownlow. But it wasn't like the scene in *Sunset Boulevard;* no one stopped working. Charlie was very cordial, yet there was no mention of the old days. After a brief conversation, he excused himself and went back to the set.

Left: Sophia waiting for my entrance as the bartender.

Right: Charlie and Arthur Ibbetson, our cameraman, laughing at my performance. Never again!

Below: An alleyway at Pinewood Studios in England. It's supposed to be Hawaii — thank God the sun shone that day! Here's Sophia on a truck, with Charlie directing her, and in the background Jane Chaplin and Syd.

REMEMBERING CHARLIE

Top: John Huston visiting the set.
Bottom: This was going to be the last shot of the film, but we cut it.

The shooting was completed. The actors were no longer needed. Marlon was the first to leave. I was sad to see him go. He was a genuinely decent person, with no humbug. I would also miss Sophia's gaiety and infectious laughter. No matter what age she reaches, she will always remain beautiful.

Oona had been on the set every day, seeing that Charlie was relaxed and well looked after. Whenever he finished a take he would always seek her approval. Oona was the rock behind the production. Sophia was especially fond of her. It was sad when everyone began to leave.

Oona and Charlie then took a week's holiday at Paul Louis Weiller's villa. I prepared the rushes in sequence, so Charlie could begin editing on his return. The cutting went smoothly, and we were delighted as sequence after sequence began to take shape. Charlie now began composing the music.

On one hot summer's night, England played West Germany in the World Cup Final. Oona, Charlie and I decided to take a ride around London. We listened to the match on my car radio. After playing overtime, England put in the winning goal. There was pandemonium in the streets. That evening, all London ran wild.

There, in my car, the three of us were weeping with joy. England victorious over Germany. It seemed like the end of the Second World War! For Charlie, football was the working man's sport; he was always thrilled by the enormous crowds that went to soccer games. "There's no audience like them in the world," he said. He loved the way they sang, cheered and waved their banners. We never forgot the thrill of that evening – July 30th, 1966 – when England won the coveted Cup!

On an October afternoon, outside Pinewood, while Charlie and I were walking, he suddenly slipped on a cracked pavement and broke his ankle. I rushed him to the Slough Hospital. While his leg was put in a cast I said, "Let's call up Oona and tell her what's happened." But he told me not to – he didn't want to worry her.

When we arrived back at the Savoy, there were photographers waiting outside. For fifty years in movies and Karno's music-hall, Charlie had executed intricate back flips, somersaults and cartwheels. And now, because of a tiny piece of uneven pavement, he had had his first serious fall.

Oona was semi-hysterical. "Why didn't you phone me?" she cried when we reached their suite. The press had been calling non-stop, and she had feared the worst. Charlie was her life – wholly and completely. I think the accident had a worse effect on her than it did on Charlie.

For seven long weeks, as we dubbed and scored the film, Charlie's leg was in a cast, and he walked on crutches. It was beginning to get him down. But the picture had to be completed, and he never shirked his responsibility. He never missed a session at the studio.

This letter arrived in the post from an old-age pensioner.

Dear Mr Chaplin,

Seeing your photo in the *Daily Telegraph*, I wondered if you'd care to have this toe cap to keep your toes warm. If it is too small I could always make you another one . . . it can be very cold, even in June.

The cast came off towards the end of November. It was the best present Charlie could have received. He was moving again with his old speed. It was hard to keep up with him. Now all that remained were the film titles, and grading the color.

The title people prepared samples of various sizes and types of lettering. For illustrations, they used the names of Charlie, Sophia, Marlon and myself. Stupidly, I never ran the tests, and saw them for the first time with Charlie in Pinewood's huge new projection theater. Marlon and Sophia's name flashed on the screen in smallish type. Then Charlie's name flashed on in somewhat larger type. Finally, my name burst upon the screen, in gargantuan-sized lettering. No one's credit, but no one's, in the history of movies was ever this large: my name stretched across the Panavision screen like the Golden Gate Bridge!

I sank in my seat. Charlie was furious. I think he thought I was taking the credit for the whole picture. I tried to explain that these were simply samples to judge sizes, and they had used my name for the largest – I didn't tell them to do it. But Charlie wasn't buying my explanation. He was certain the film had gone to my head.

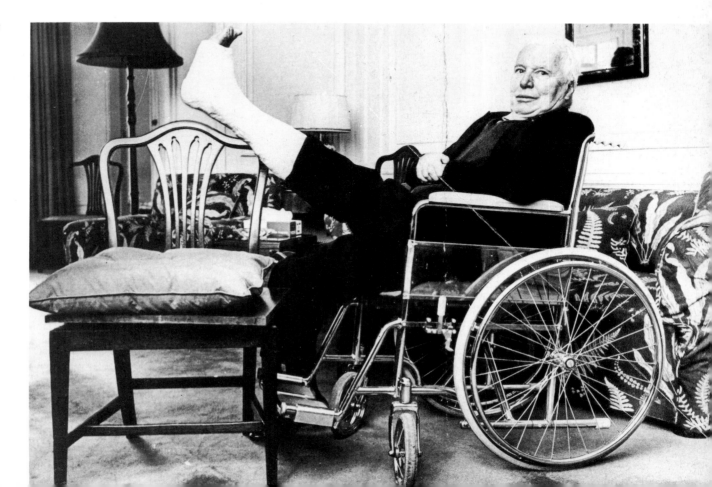

CHARLIE MADE THE FRONT PAGE OF EVERY PAPER WHEN HE BROKE HIS ANKLE.

Oona and Charlie were due to leave for Vevey. The night before, we went out with Edie and Lew Wasserman and Vicky and Josie to Annabel's, a fashionable club. A young girl stopped us in the street. It was the singer Alma Cogan; she was standing with a young man. Charlie thought they wanted an autograph, and he was always obliging.

But they didn't want his signature. "Mr Chaplin," she said, "do you mind if I introduce you to someone – he's dying to meet you." It was Ringo Starr. Charlie and Oona were charmed by his Liverpudlian accent, and the children were thrilled. Ringo said, "Mr Chaplin, how would you like to direct a movie for us?" "I'm sorry," Charlie replied, "but I've never seen any of your films." "I can't say the same about yours," Ringo said. Charlie laughed. Then he went on about how proud he was of *Countess*. Ringo said, "Well, if it isn't a hit, you can always run it as a home movie."

The Royal Première of *A Countess from Hong Kong* was to be held at the Carlton Theatre in London on January 5th, 1967. In the weeks before, I flew to Vevey every few days for Charlie to check on the color grading. He was very particular. Sometimes the colors had to be muted; at others, brightened.

With the opening coming up, I was in a state of nervous euphoria. I was happy to spend a quiet Christmas. I bought a large cooked turkey and a few other things, just in case anyone dropped in. As I was watching television, the doorbell rang. One by one, the apartment began to fill with lonely Americans whom I didn't know. In the States, everything jumps on Christmas Day; in England everything dies.

First, in walked a group called the Limelighters. Shortly afterwards, Adam West (Batman) arrived, along with the producer Allan Carr and Roger Smith (Ann-Margret's husband). The bell rang again. In walked Bobby Darin, followed by Liza Minnelli, Michael Medwin and a group of friends. Sitting on the floor, Liza Minnelli began to sing, accompanied by Bobby Darin at the piano. Then he sang; then we all sang. An American Christmas had come to London!

Liza's singing knocked me out. She had just finished making her first film, *Charlie Bubbles,* with Albert Finney, and she was not widely known. I adored her, and was determined to help her career along. Plans were being made for a gala party at the Savoy after the première; and I persuaded Liza to entertain with a medley of Charlie's songs. I felt it could help her career. Liza was excited, but Universal nixed the idea. She wasn't a name yet.

Marlon would be at the première, but Sophia declined. Before Marlon's arrival, he called Jay Kanter from California, enquiring whether or not I had a percentage in the film. Jay told him I didn't. He then said that he knew what my contribution was, and that I should have a percentage. He was going to contact Universal and Charlie. I told Jay that he shouldn't make waves – I was happy with my deal. Then Marlon said if that was the case, he was going to give me part of his percentage. Of course I would never have accepted it. But it illustrates how generous, kind and thoughtful Marlon is.

On the morning of January 5th, the film was to be shown for the press at the Empire Theatre. *Dr Zhivago* was playing in the afternoons. The previous day, I ran the film, checked the volumes, the projection, and the quality of the print. Everything was in good shape for the press preview.

At ten o'clock the next morning, the Empire was packed to the rafters with every prominent critic, film producer and agent. This was the first screening of the film. Charlie and I stood in the aisle in the Dress Circle. During the projection, I noticed that the color seemed different. Charlie and I looked at each other askance. The print had a faded, washed-out look. The sound suddenly started crackling. The film then flickered, sputtered, and stopped. Charlie and I were frantic. I was about to run up the hundred steps to the projection booth when the film started again. Once again the screen looked fuzzy and washed-out; then it stopped, started, and stopped again.

It was a living nightmare. I rushed into the projection booth. I noticed it was a new projectionist. "What the hell's happening!!!" I shouted. It didn't seem to matter to him. He was cool, calm and collected. He was simply paid to run the film; whatever the fault, it had nothing to do with him. In the meantime, our baby was being mutilated.

Then we discovered that the projection machine had a special lens for the afternoon performances of *Dr Zhivago*; it hadn't been removed, and this nincompoop didn't know how to remove it. So our picture was shown with all the sputters, jerks and stops to the very end.

Charlie and I couldn't watch. We went into the lobby, and paced up and down. There was no laughter; we only sensed discomfort. When the picture was over, the first person we noticed exiting was Ken Tynan, the critic. He looked at us both with hostility. Our fate was being sealed.

Top: The wonderful Liza Minnelli and me at the lavish Savoy party for the *Countess*.

Bottom: Also at the party – Kit and Jay Kanter. Jay had the patience of a saint with Charlie.

The critics were going to have a field day.

As we walked back to the Savoy, we passed a placard next to a news stand. It was from the *Evening News*: "CHAPLIN'S NEW FILM – A DISASTER".

The body was still warm, and they were already dancing on its grave. Charlie and I entered the hotel in a daze. Oona greeted us excitedly. "How did it go?" she asked with a large warm smile. "A disaster," I replied. She couldn't believe her ears. We had all had such high hopes; but because of that terrible projection, we weren't even given a fighting chance. And once a major critic pans a film, it takes a very brave soul to go against the tide. Each review was similar in content; in fact some even used the very same words.

Oona, Charlie and I went for lunch at the Savoy Grill. We sat in silence. But we had to prepare for the première in the evening.

The opening was televised. Crowds stood outside gazing at Princess Alexandra, Marlon, Lord Mountbatten, Noel Coward, Douglas Fairbanks Jr, Liza Minnelli, and Zero Mostel as they entered. Then Oona and Charlie arrived with six of their children. How Charlie managed to behave like the conquering hero, waving to the crowds outside the theater, I shall never understand. There was no sign of the gloom that had descended on us hours before.

The première went well. The audience was responsive; at the Savoy party afterwards, Charlie went from table to table speaking to the various guests. He and Marlon embraced. When the band went home, my friend Jeff Davis went to the piano and played all the old favorites. Charlie and Marlon stood behind him singing along with the others.

At two in the morning, Marlon, Noël Coward, Syd, myself, and a slew of others continued the festivities at the Pair of Shoes club on Curzon Street. Marlon suddenly had the urge to speak to Sophia. He woke her up in Rome and told her how great she was in the picture. He meant it, too. Sophia was genuinely touched by his consideration.

The next day, the notices were devastating. Some critics even had the audacity to say that the technical side of the picture was very bad, since the film kept breaking down. Those cretins – didn't they realize it had nothing to do with us?

Charlie was furious. He swore he would never première a picture in London again. He felt all London was swinging drunk. The critics called him "out of fashion". "What is fashion?" he retorted. "It's only

something facile that everyone copies." He saw part of a Beatles film where they used the old bubble bath gag. "We did all that stop action business in 1914," he told the critic Francis Wyndham, "it was very dull then, and it's just as dull now."

What hurt Charlie most was that the reviews read like personal attacks. The critics seemed delighted that Chaplin had a flop. He felt *they* were terrified of being called old-fashioned. In ten years' time, he said, the Beatles films would be called old-fashioned, whereas *Countess* would be finally appreciated.

This was the case with so many of his films. On release, each one was criticized as being inferior to the one before. When he made *The Great Dictator*, critics said it wasn't as good as *Modern Times*. When he made *Modern Times,* they complained it wasn't as funny as *City Lights*. Yet when these pictures originally came out, they didn't give them good notices.

The following night, Charlie and I stood in the back of the Carlton and watched the film with a paying audience. After reading the reviews, Charlie had felt that perhaps something *was* amiss with the film. But viewing it with the public, he regained his confidence. The audience were lapping it up. Yet he still decided to make a few trims before the Paris opening.

Mail flooded in from all over the country protesting against the notices. There was one from John Betjeman, the poet:

Dear Mr Charlie Chaplin,

I have spent a most enjoyable afternoon watching your new film . . . I enjoyed every minute . . . and the lovely girls . . . I think the critics need a cruise in your ship to get some fresh sea air in their brains . . . Hurry up and make another film.

Another one:

Dear Mr Chaplin,

I wish I were a film critic again, as I was in the early thirties for the Evening Standard, so as to acclaim *A Countess from Hong Kong* . . .

This letter appeared in *Punch* magazine:

Sir,

Your film critic followed the party line over *A Countess from Hong Kong*. Clearly he was insensitive to its overall beauty and sincerity . . . Only Ingmar Bergman and Peter Brook have done anything comparable in this way . . . critics notwithstanding.

Because of the disaster I was put into a very tiny office at Universal, with barely room to move. My status had quickly changed. One day Albert Finney visited. He had taken his son to see the film and came to tell me how much they enjoyed it. The letters and personal comments lifted our spirits.

Sophia and Carlo remained loyal to the film to the very end. So many actors have a close relationship with their director when they are making a film. But if the picture isn't a hit, the honeymoon is quickly over. They rarely see each other afterwards. But not Sophia. In spite of the film's reviews, her devotion to Charlie never wavered. She was just as enthusiastic as she was at the beginning: "I would work again with Mr Chaplin at a minute's notice, any time, any place!"

Charlie had to return to Vevey because of English tax laws. It was left to me to prepare the film for the French opening. Because we had cut six minutes, most of the reels needed to be redubbed. We no longer had cutting rooms at Pinewood. So in mid-winter I was put into a trailer in a lonely field, and Charlie and I worked out the cuts via the long-distance telephone.

The Paris première took place at the Opera House five days after the English opening. A select corps of the French army stood on the Grand Staircase as Charlie and Oona arrived. The opening was brilliant: all Paris was present. My problem was to get the French subtitles put onto the new reels in time. On the night of the gala, they were still being prepared in a small upstairs room in Montmartre. As the army saluted and the trumpets blared, I ran from Montmartre to the Opera House with the first subtitled reel, dashed back to Montmartre to collect reels Two and Three, raced to the Opera House and threw them at the projectionist, then ran back to Montmartre again to pick up the remainder. I was far too exhausted to enjoy the party afterwards.

We received five rave reviews and two negative ones. Things were looking up. The trims we made were helping, and the French critics attacked the English press for being so cruel. Charlie decided to make additional trims for the New York première. He refused to give up.

I went to New York to prepare for the March 15th opening at the Sutton Theater. Lew Wasserman, head of MCA-Universal, laid down an edict that all the New York film critics had to see the picture at the première. There would be no special screenings. Universal had a lot of money invested in the picture, and they wanted the critics to see it with an audience and hear the laughs for themselves.

The day before the opening, I received an anonymous call at my hotel. It was from someone on the *New York Times*. He wouldn't give his name, but he told me we had met years before, and he was calling to tip me off . . . the eminent *Times* critic Bosley Crowther, who could make or break a film, was gunning for our picture. Crowther was furious that he couldn't see the film privately, and unless a private screening was arranged, we would be in for it. He advised me to do everything I could.

I phoned Lew and told him about the call. He was very firm: "We're not changing our policy for *anyone*." Crowther had to see the film with the audience.

During the production of *Countess,* Crowther had wanted to interview Charlie at his house. The only day Crowther could make was Sunday – Charlie's only day of rest. Charlie apologized: he was still shooting, needed to relax, and just couldn't see him. Charlie had given him an exclusive interview in Vevey years before, but now it was impossible. Crowther wasn't used to being turned down. He now had two things against the picture: no private interview, and no private screening.

A blizzard hit New York on the night of March 15th. Traffic was paralyzed. I stood outside the Sutton Theater on East Fifty-Seventh Street, watching limousines pull up. New York society was gathering for the charity performance. Then in the distance I saw Bosley Crowther edging down Fifty-Seventh Street with his wife, with gusts of snow hitting his face. He looked like the Abominable Snowman. His lips were hard set, his face blue and bitter. Oh, why did we have to open on the Ides of March? I had met Crowther years before when I directed his son in a play; I took my chance and greeted him with a smile. But he dismissed me. I guess all we could do was grin and bear it.

During the screening, I paced in the lobby. Noticing my anxiety, Lew Wasserman came over and patted me on the shoulder. "Don't worry, Jerry," he said, "it'll be alright. Just calm down." People think of Wasserman as a reserved, austere man, but I shall always remember his warmth on that cold night.

In the following day's *New York Times,* and ten days later, in the Sunday edition, Bosley Crowther massacred the film. He must have written the most stinging and vitriolic review that any great artist ever received. Again, it seemed to be a personal attack on Chaplin. Everyone and everything was lambasted – the actors, the music, even the color.

Crowther's first review was bad enough, but his Sunday follow-up was the cruellest thing I have ever read. Even if he disliked it, there is a way to criticize with tact. Out of pettiness, he seemed to want to destroy the man who helped create the American film industry. How they like to see giants fall! Among other things, Crowther wrote that at Chaplin's age he should never have tried to make another film. If Bach, Haydn, Verdi, Graham Greene, Shaw had retired through old age, what masterpieces the world would have been denied.

After the L.A. première, I flew to Switzerland. Charlie was anxious to hear all the reviews. I held back what Crowther had written; I never liked being the bearer of bad news. But he insisted I read him Crowther's notice *out loud*. He must have heard about it.

He sat on the sofa opposite. I could barely get the words out. He listened stoically with his arms folded on his chest – his expression never changed. He made no comment. When I finished, he left the room.

I was beside myself after the Crowther notice. I wanted revenge. I sent a letter to the Editor of the *Times,* reminding him how in 1947 Mr Crowther had blasted Charlie's masterpiece *Monsieur Verdoux.*

"Unfortunately," Crowther wrote in his notice. "Mr Chaplin has not managed his film with great success. It is slow – tediously slow . . . and thus monotonous. The bursts of comic invention fit uncomfortably into the grim fabric, and the clarity of the philosophy does not begin to emerge until the end. By that time – almost two hours – Mr Chaplin has repeated much and has possibly left his audience in an exhausted state . . ."

Yet when *Monsieur Verdoux* was re-released in 1964, Crowther saw the picture in a new light. He wrote: "So few people had the pleasure or the experience of seeing the film when it was briefly shown in this

WEATHER COLD...PICTURE HOT

Chaplin's "Countess" Captures New York!

*3 P.M.
Temp. 27°

Sunday, March 19

UNIVERSAL presents

MARLON BRANDO **SOPHIA LOREN**

in

"A Countess from HONG KONG"
TECHNICOLOR®

WRITTEN, DIRECTED and MUSIC by

CHARLES CHAPLIN

also starring

SYDNEY CHAPLIN and TIPPI HEDREN with PATRICK CARGILL

and MARGARET RUTHERFORD   PRODUCED by JEROME EPSTEIN

*8 P.M.
Temp. 15°

Saturday, March 18

CHARLIE STILL HAD A FAITHFUL
FOLLOWING IN NEW YORK.

*OPPOSITE: CHARLIE CELEBRATES HIS
SEVENTY-SEVENTH BIRTHDAY WITH
MELANIE GRIFFITH AND SOPHIA.*

country seventeen years ago [possibly due to your review, Mr Crowther] . . . No one should miss it . . . it is an extraordinary picture . . . a splendid film . . ."

"Ten or fifteen years from now," I wrote in my letter, "when *A Countess from Hong Kong* is revived, your reviewer will be saying: "No one should miss it . . . it is an extraordinary film . . . a splendid film."

The Editor of the *New York Times* contacted Universal and told them my letter was going to be published. Crowther, enraged, notified both Universal and myself that if it was published, he would reply with an even more stinging attack.

I didn't care. I was determined that the letter be printed. But the nervous Universal publicists pleaded with me to stop publication: Crowther was *the* major critic, and they could not afford to offend him. They had so many big films soon to be released. I resisted. But they made me feel as though I were a traitor.

After much badgering back and forth, and calls through the night making me feel guilty, I told them to notify the Editor to forget my letter. Six months later, Crowther retired, leaving much damage in his wake.

Charlie would often say, "Critics in my day made you laugh when they didn't like something. They weren't vindictive. They were fun to read, even if they lambasted your film." Luckily, the policy at the *New York Times* today has changed.

The *Countess* saga was over. But I shall never forget the pain and horror when I had to read Charlie that Sunday review.

THE 8 FREAK

It was time for me to start a new project. Charlie, too, was determined to make a new film. Ideas were buzzing around in his head. He thought of playing a dual role – a mad Roman Emperor (shades of *Caligula?*) and also his slave.

Then he thought of making a film about the early history of motion pictures. He devised a marvelous opening sequence illustrating the patents war, in which rival entrepreneurs hit one another over the head, running off with each other's cans of film. But the project never developed beyond that opening scene.

Another idea was for Sydney to play a sympathetic convict. The picture would start with him getting ready for his execution by tidying up his cell. The convict had been double-crossed by his partner, who married his wife while he was in jail. Just as he is about to be executed, someone yells "FIRE!", and he escapes. Charlie also abandoned this idea.

After months of negotiating with Universal, I finally received the go-ahead to film *The Adding Machine*. Now I had to satisfy the powers that be on casting. Walter Matthau badly wanted to play Mr Zero and he was my first choice, but it would be a year before he was available. (He had just signed to star in *Hello Dolly*.) Zero Mostel, whom I now wanted, was turned down by Universal. Then I had my heart set on Art Carney: he agreed, and was accepted. The next question was, who should play Mrs Zero?

Universal had the comedienne Phyllis Diller under contract, and they needed to find a film for her by a certain date or pay her off. So I cast her in this very difficult part. I had found that music-hall artists usually had great timing and could act if given the opportunity. Phyllis proved my instincts were right: she gave an outstanding performance.

But it was the billing battle all over again. Phyllis's agent insisted she have top billing over Art Carney. Carney's agent wouldn't accept this, so he dropped out. After seeing Joseph Strick's *Ulysses*, I cast Milo O'Shea. What a performer!

While preparing the film, I visited Oona and Charlie. I read Charlie my screenplay. In the film's second half, Mr Zero dies and is sent to the Elysian Fields. I became very excited by Charlie's concept of Heaven. "You don't want people floating on clouds, carrying harps around in a beautiful park. It's so boring – if that's what Heaven is like I'd cut my throat. Why don't you make it like a huge fairground, with amusements, gambling, fun houses, hot dogs and ice cream? That's Heaven!" I remembered years ago Charlie telling me how much he enjoyed Marc Connelly's play *The Green Pastures* – which also had a fun Heaven.

LEFT: The good-natured Phyllis Diller as Mrs Zero in *The Adding Machine*.

TOP RIGHT: Sydney Chaplin as Lieutenant Charles in *The Adding Machine*.

BOTTOM RIGHT: Charlie's idea of Heaven – as a fun-fair. Milo O'Shea (lower right) entering the Pearly Gates.

OPPOSITE: The family Christmas card: Charlie, Oona and all eight children.

Then he suggested some marvelous gags. "When you first show dead people arriving at the Pearly Gates, have one person come in a bathing suit spouting water out of his mouth, wondering where the hell he is." Obviously he has just drowned. "Then another person arrives, on fire, trying to put out the flames. Someone else arrives with an arrow in his heart . . ." Charlie was giggling as he improvised the dead arriving. He certainly sold me on his idea of Heaven.

The filming of *The Adding Machine* went smoothly. Walter Lassally, the very fine cameraman who photographed *Zorba the Greek*, excelled himself. Sydney Chaplin played his old Circle role of Lieutenant Charles, the guardian in Heaven. I think it's one of the best thing he's done in films. My friendship with Sean Connery had by now blossomed. He was anxious to see the rushes. After viewing the Heaven sequences he commented, "You're copying Ingmar Bergman." I thought it was a great compliment.

Charlie was in London. After taking one of our ritual drives we stopped at the Royal Festival Hall restaurant for coffee. The picture was finished, but I wasn't sure of the title music. There, overlooking the Thames, Charlie improvised how it should sound.

"Start out with some Gershwin to capture New York" – and he sang the opening bars of *Rhapsody in Blue*, pantomiming a trombone's wah wah wah wah wah – "then, as you show scenes of people operating adding machines, get the feeling of automation and regimentation." He began rapping his fingers on the table, like a tom-tom. Over this he intoned "Da da da da/da da da da," and his beating increased in intensity. I remembered everything he sang, and passed it on to our arranger. The opening title music on *The Adding Machine* is all by Chaplin.

The first time Charlie saw the film, I was sitting behind him in the theater; he had his handkerchief in his hand and he was weeping. He loved the picture. Several weeks later, when he was back in London, he asked me to show him the film again. Charlie was such an enthusiastic audience when he liked something. And I knew Charlie well enough to know he wasn't simply being nice. If he didn't approve, you could read it in his face.

More problems. The top executives at Universal didn't know what to do with the picture. In those days, if you gave them Doris Day and

A PAGE OF SEAN CONNERY'S VERSION OF
MACBETH, WITH SKETCHES OF OUR THREE
WITCHES AND THE FIRST BATTLE SCENE.

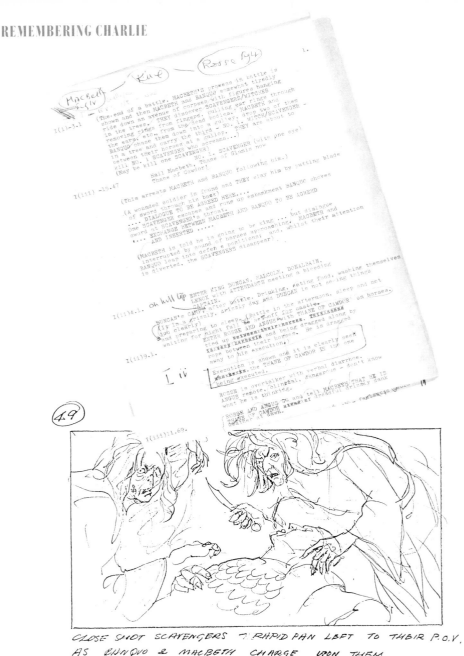

CLOSE SHOT SCAVENGERS - RAPID PAN LEFT TO THEIR P.O.V.
AS BANQUO & MACBETH CHARGE UPON THEM

Rock Hudson, you were home and dry, but anything unusual and different made them suspicious. But I had one great ally at Universal, Art Murphy. He was originally a film reviewer for *Variety*, then Universal hired him for a short time to assess their films – how best to release them and prognosticate their future. He liked and understood *The Adding Machine* and felt that with special handling it would do well.

Lew Wasserman also supported me – against the advice of his executives. He was sympathetic and a good listener. Lew was an amazing man. He had all the daily grosses of every picture playing in New York at his fingertips, and as he rattled them out, his fingers became like tabulators on an adding machine. (A good omen?).

But Art Murphy's advice went unheeded, and the film was dumped on the market with meaningless ads. It opened in a small theater in New York that no one had heard of – the Kips Bay Thirty-Fourth Street Theater. Or, rather, it opened and closed. But the film did receive some excellent notices, both in New York and London.

"Lyrical, funny, meaningful, intelligently conceived … ingredients which could well make the picture outlive cinematic trends. I found it quite enthralling."

(William Wolf, *Cue*.)

While trying to find an idea for a new film, Charlie decided to put music to his silent film *The Circus*. In no time he wrote a seventy-minute score. The topper was the opening credit sequence, where Charlie sang his own song "Swing Little Girl" in a voice that occasionally breaks. It was so sad and touching. To me it rivals Walter Huston singing Kurt Weill's "September Song".

Sean Connery asked me to see a tape of his *Macbeth*. He had played the title role for Canadian television before he became famous in films. Sean had the strength and stature needed for the part; yet he played it with a combination of sensitivity and vulnerability. His was the only Macbeth I've ever found moving. Now he and I, plus his agent Richard Hatton, became excited about making a film version. Sean came to my house daily to work on the screenplay. His conceptions were brilliant, and he devised an amazing opening. Only the witches were a problem. In Vevey, Charlie became fascinated and preoccupied with a new movie idea. After the treatment he had received with *Countess*, a lesser mortal would have retired into a deep depression. Not Charlie. Now close to eighty, he was determined to fight back. In many ways Charlie was like the Tramp: there was the same refusal to be defeated, the same hope and promise that tomorrow would be a better day. Besides, he needed creative work in order to survive.

Sitting on the veranda, he watched birds fly across the lawn, and became intrigued by the movement of their wings. This was the genesis of his last film, *The Freak*. Soon he built an entire script about a young girl, found on the tip of Chile, who is born with wings and can fly. Even now when I think of the story I'm stirred.

Natives take a pilgrimage to see this miracle; when they behold the girl they begin praying. They feel she's an angel descended from Heaven. Word spreads. Two conmen from England hear about the girl, kidnap her and bring her to London. She falls into the hands of an evangelist, who exploits the "angel" during his revivalist meetings.

But she escapes, flies over London and lands in front of the Opera House in Covent Garden, where they are performing *Swan Lake*. To get away from the villains, she enters the stage door, finds herself on stage and becomes one of the swans. She suddenly takes off and begins flying over the dumbstruck audience.

Charlie wrote a small part for himself, as a drunk in Covent Garden, who weaves along the street and thinks he's seeing things when this apparition flies over his head. He devised exciting chases all over the English countryside; the entire British Army searches for the girl, afraid that she could contaminate the populace with rabies. In the climax, she flies into a country mansion during a costume party.

The mood changes. The girl is captured and put in a cage while the English courts decide whether she's an animal or a human being. Every time I read the ending, I wept; I was convinced it would have the same effect on an audience. To me it was Charlie's best film since *City Lights*. When I saw *E.T.* with Oona, I said to her *The Freak* was a combination of *E.T.* and *The Elephant Man*. She agreed.

I felt *The Freak* could be Charlie's greatest triumph. Would they dare to say this was old-fashioned too? As Irving Berlin said, when they called *Annie Get Your Gun* old-fashioned. "Sure it's old-fashioned. It's an old-fashioned *smash*." The girl with wings was to be played by Charlie's daughter, Victoria. He always said "This girl has genius," and was determined to make her a star. His daughter, Josie, was cast in a co-starring role.

We began making wings at Shepperton Studios and made tests of Vicky. The wings took months to perfect, and every so often, Charlie and I drove to Shepperton to check on their progress. Oona, Charlie and I went to see Stanley Kubrick's *2001 – A Space Odyssey*. Charlie wanted to study the flying sequences. Oona and he were both amazed by the film's brilliance.

Now I was to find the financing. Charlie wanted to put in his own money but I wouldn't allow it. I felt, at his age, he shouldn't have this extra burden. During the day I went over the budget with him at the Savoy. Usually Charlie was very alert when I would discuss costs but this time, I found him beginning to fall asleep. I couldn't adjust to the fact that he was getting older.

Sometimes he would say to me as we were out walking, "Slow down, Buddy, I'm an old man." But to me, I had fixed in my mind, the Charlie I knew in the past, who was brimming with life and vitality, leaping up from his seat like a firefly, every two minutes, as he directed at the Circle. I wouldn't allow myself to think that he had grown older; it was too painful. I was going to find the money and Charlie was going to make another film. That's the way it was and that's the way it was going to be.

In Vevey, Charlie continued to refine the script of *The Freak*. During lunch one day, Oona showed him an article in the *New Yorker* regarding the arrival of Twiggy and her manager, Justin de Villeneuve, in New York. Charlie got such a kick out of the way these two cockneys wowed America. He thought Twiggy extraordinarily beautiful.

Vicky also became enamored of her, decided she was overweight for the film and refused to eat. She suddenly became thinner than Twiggy. But Oona and Charlie soon put a stop to that.

Our *Macbeth* had to be called off because Roman Polanski beat us to it with his own version. By now Sean and I were fast friends. We talked about entering into partnership. I was very keen; except for Charlie, there is no one I would have enjoyed working with more. Sean is decent, conscientious and doesn't ever behave like a movie star. He still

ABOVE: STORYBOARD SKETCHES FOR THE FREAK: THE "FREAK" DEMONSTRATES HER FLYING AGILITY AND FLIES INTO SOMEONE'S HOME.
OPPOSITE LEFT: MORE STORYBOARD SKETCHES: THE "FREAK" ESCAPES AND FLIES OVER LONDON.
OPPOSITE, RIGHT: CHARLIE ADJUSTING VICKY'S WINGS AT SHEPPERTON STUDIOS.

had other films to make; one in Russia, another for Irvin Kershner and one for Marty Ritt. But we optimistically forged ahead.

In Vevey Charlie drew diagrams showing how the flying for *The Freak* could be achieved simply. He would say "They're making too much out of this flying business. We used these tricks years ago. It's all done with mirrors; the wires won't show." Then he would go over to his medicine cabinet with a pencil in his hand (to represent the girl). Holding the pencil horizontally in front of the cabinet door mirror, he'd shift the door from left to right. As you looked into the moving mirror, the pencil seemed to travel. The illusion worked.

EMI offered to put in half the money for certain territories: Charlie wanted to put in the other half. But I was still against this. Then two executives from United Artists, Charlie's former company, flew over to discuss the film, as Charlie wouldn't allow his script to be sent to New York. The executives (they shall remain nameless) came, with their wives in tow.

As ever, Charlie was the perfect host. He showed them around the grounds. There was a marvelous lunch. Afterwards we sat on the veranda as I read them the script. My tongue became leaden like an actor on his first night. Charlie began directing me. "No, no, no, you're

not reading that right," he said. "I'm not an actor," I replied, "You read it." "No, no, you carry on." I did so, but Charlie continued directing me.

Eventually my nerves disappeared and the script came alive. Charlie agreed that the executives could take the script back to New York for further study. Their response would be coming shortly.

Weeks passed. And more weeks passed. No word. Then one day, a package arrived at my house. It was the script. There was no letter inside; only a slip of paper – "With the compliments of —————— ———"

I was furious. If they weren't interested they could've at least had the decency to write a letter of regret to the man who had helped create United Artists. And simple good manners called for a thank you note for the lunch and afternoon spent with Oona and Charlie. Today, those two executives are hopping from one studio to another.

Sean wanted to proceed with our partnership at once. But I felt Charlie was depending on me and I couldn't let him down. "But I can't walk out on him," I said. "Let me finish the film and I'll be free." But Sean wanted a decision immediately. "You're going to work with me," he told me. "I've got a future ahead of me. Charlie is eighty – I'm still a young man." I was in another one of my quandaries.

I needed time to think – I had to be alone. I left London and booked

into a small hotel in the country. No one knew where I was. Two days later I received a call from Sean – I still don't know how he found me – "Come back immediately," he said firmly, "you're going to make up your mind." I did. I told Sean that I couldn't possibly let Charlie down. He was stunned. There was no turning back now, for either of us.

It was nearing Christmas. I went to Vevey with a story board for *The Freak*. I had made a breakthrough with financing and was anxious to tell Charlie. Oona stopped me in the hallway. "There's no picture," she said. I looked at her amazed. "I have to make the decision. He'll never survive this picture. If *The Freak* was an easy film I would let it go ahead. But you know how impatient Charlie is on the set. Can you imagine what he would be like waiting for the special effects people to get the flying right? If it was the prisoner film or a simple comedy, I wouldn't object. But this picture would kill him." That was that. *The Freak* was off.

No Sean and now no Charlie. Afterwards I learned that Charlie would have been pleased if I'd accepted Sean's proposal. Oona felt terrible. C'est la vie, I thought. If only Sean could have been more patient and waited a few more weeks, all would have been different. I run into him from time to time. We're still friends and I was thrilled at

his recent Oscar. I always felt he was an underrated actor.

Vicky had been kept on tenterhooks waiting for *The Freak* to commence. When she was told it had been canceled, she left for Paris. There she met a young French actor, Jean-Baptiste Thierrée. Soon afterwards they were married and fulfilled a lifetime's dream – they started a circus – Le Cirque Imaginaire. It was difficult at first but what a sensation they've become throughout the world.

Charlie didn't know that Oona had called off *The Freak*, and he was still talking about making it. But after my upsets about the film, and with Sean, I was now looking for another project. Syd and I began working on a screenplay about Nazi Germany. When Charlie heard about it, though, he was upset. He insisted he had told me the story years ago, and that it was his. He wanted it as a vehicle for himself.

I honestly didn't remember where the story had come from; and I didn't care. I had always been generous with ideas and would always make suggestions just to get his juices going. If he wanted the story, he could have it.

But Charlie's feathers were ruffled; he would accept no explanation. Not only that, but soon afterwards he was to take away some valuable film rights which he had given Sydney and me.

I was stunned. Through hell and high water I had stood behind Charlie. I had been loyal and devoted – and now, because of a stupid misunderstanding, he wanted nothing more to do with me. It was as if I had been excommunicated by the Pope.

Friends told me that this was evidence that he was getting older. I still couldn't accept it. Charlie always guarded his material jealously; but I had proved my trustworthiness again and again. I guess the real problem was that Charlie had to work – he needed to make a new film but now was physically unable. Oona tried her best to resolve our difficulties, but she too was stymied.

During this period I met Berniece, a Welsh girl. I had had one disastrous marriage years before and I wasn't looking for any further entanglements; my career needed sorting out first. But Berniece was a live-wire and refused to let me be depressed. She kept me working on film projects; Brian Clemens's script, the *Hot Cold War Man*, which Ken Russell was set to direct, as well as John Keane's *Big Maggie*, and an original, *Two Blue Dots*.

June 18th, 1970 was the British General Election. On the 19th I received a call from Harrods Estate Offices. Someone had heard about my house being close to the Houses of Parliament and was interested in seeing it with the possibility of renting. That suited me since Berniece and I were thinking about going to California and didn't want to leave the house unoccupied.

While I was out, my secretary showed the house to a woman called Marcia Williams and her sister. Then I received another call from Harrods; the women, I was told, were representatives of an interested party. "Who is it?" I asked. The man refused to reveal any names. I told him, "I'm not renting my house to anyone whose name can't be revealed. Besides, if I was renting I'd want a month's rent in advance, a deposit and references." They'd get back to me.

Ten minutes later, Harrods called again. A nervous voice told me that I must be sworn to secrecy. I was more confused than ever. The interested party turned out to be the Right Honourable Harold Wilson! Yesterday he had been Prime Minister, today he was homeless. I told Berniece who wanted our house. "Rent it to him," she cried. The Harrods representative asked me if Lord Goodman would be a good enough reference. I hastily told them to forget the references – being Prime Minister was good enough for me.

Wilson had been so sure that Labour would win that he had sold his house in Hampstead Garden Suburb; he and his family now had no place to live. (I was always amazed that in England if the Prime Minister loses the Election he must move out of Downing St the next day).

Within two weeks Harold and Mary Wilson, their son Giles, and their housekeeper, Mrs Pollard, moved in. Berniece and I were now homeless, so with Wilson's consent, we took up temporary residence in our basement. It was like a circus outside the house, with television cameras and reporters. The front page of the *Daily Mail*, quoting Charlie, called it the "most beautiful house in London".

Berniece and I soon became friendly with the Wilsons. When Mrs Pollard cooked, she always brought us some of her delicious roast beef or lamb. They had no pretensions. All of Wilson's official papers from Downing St were stored in my garage, in large Kelloggs cornflakes boxes. Every day he'd be down there rummaging through them, preparing for his memoirs.

Once I helped him. Among the files I found pictures of Wilson with Richard Nixon. "I met him at the White House," he commented as he looked at the photo, "and he promised me faithfully he wouldn't bomb Cambodia. While I was flying back to London, Cambodia was bombed. When I returned, I was in hot water."

Mr Wilson invited me to the opening of the new Parliament. As he was dressing, he couldn't find his black pinstriped suit. Then he saw me dressed and ready to go in my own black pinstriped suit, and accused me of wearing his. I showed him the label inside my jacket with my name. He was still skeptical as he scurried round the house, searching in all the wardrobes and boxes. Finally, I was reprieved; Mary found his black pinstriped suit.

Knowing my connection with Charlie, Wilson said to me one day, "I tried to get Chaplin a knighthood but they wouldn't let it go through." I never asked him who "they" were. But Wilson seemed determined, if he were ever Prime Minister again, to rectify the situation. Wilson stayed in my house for about eight months, then found a place nearby.

Through Oona's efforts and my own, my relationship with Charlie finally healed. In Vevey, I told Charlie what Wilson had said to me about the knighthood – how he had tried and "they" wouldn't let it go through. I also told Charlie that I had never asked Wilson who "they" were. Charlie was intrigued and asked me to repeat the conversation several times. I think he, too, was curious about who "they" were.

Charlie was now eighty-two. Some sixty years ago, when he was in San Francisco with the Karno troupe, he went to a fortune-teller. She had predicted that he would soon enter another profession, enjoy world-wide success, have three marriages, and die at the age of eighty-two. Charlie was convinced that although the fortune-teller was wrong about the number of marriages, she was right about his success; and he was sure this was to be the year of his death. Oona had a hard time pacifying him throughout the next twelve months.

Charlie had just signed a deal to release his old films and was busy preparing a new score to accompany *The Kid*. He was invited to Hollywood to accept a special Oscar. At Isow's restaurant in Soho, Charlie was adamant; he would not return to America. As an inducement, the Academy agreed to feature a twenty-minute telecast showing clips from his major movies.

I didn't think he should go to the Academy Awards ceremony. Where were the Academy governors when he was refused his re-entry permit? Through the years, there had been no statement from them protesting his treatment. William Wyler and Samuel Goldwyn were the only ones who had the courage to speak up; Graham Greene and David Lean did the same in England. But there were no other voices. Not that Charlie ever wanted anyone to speak out in his defense. Then he decided to accept an invitation to attend a tribute at Lincoln Center in New York, but still would not give a definite answer about returning to California for the Oscar ceremony.

Emotional cheering greeted him in New York. It was a hero's welcome. At Lincoln Center there was total chaos. Everyone jostled to get a glimpse of Charlie. Wherever he went he was greeted with affection. Someone came up to him and said, "Charlie, we love you!" He replied ruefully, "They loved Kennedy too . . ."

At the last minute, Charlie agreed to attend the Oscar ceremony. In California, Carol and Walter Matthau threw a lavish outdoor Sunday lunch party for him on their vast Pacific Palisades lawn. Cary Grant, Rosalind Russell, Groucho Marx, and Martha Raye were all there to welcome Oona and Charlie home.

The next night he received his special Academy Award amidst tumultuous applause. The Academy members gave him a standing ovation. Sydney and I watched the event on television with my sister and brother-in-law Dave at their home.

The Oscar ceremony took place on April 16th, Charlie's birthday. He was now eighty-three. The fortune-teller was wrong. Thank God. Oona and Charlie could now relax.

Wilson gets 'the most beautiful house in London'

By GORDON GREIG

Mr Wilson's new house in Vincent Square

MR HAROLD WILSON is moving into what has been described as 'the most beautiful house in London.'

It is No. 14 Vincent Square, Westminster, near the Houses of Parliament.

Among Mr Wilson's neighbours: Mr Richard Crossman, his former Cabinet colleague and new editor of the New Statesman, who has a flat at No. 9; and Mr Duncan Sandys, former Tory Minister who lives at No. 86.

Mr Wilson and his wife will make No. 14 their temporary home. They have taken a lease on the house, with its basic furniture and fittings, and will move in during the

CHARLIE LOVED MY HOUSE; HE CALLED IT "THE MOST BEAUTIFUL HOUSE IN LONDON". OF COURSE IT WASN'T — BUT THE *DAILY MAIL* LATCHED ON TO THE NOTION.

TOP: VICKY, NOW MARRIED, WITH HER DAUGHTER AURELIA — AND A DELIGHTED CHARLIE.
BOTTOM: ONE WEEKEND WE DRAGGED THE WINGS OUT OF THE BASEMENT AND BEGAN REHEARSING THE FILM ON THE LAWN. HERE'S VICKY WEARING THE WINGS, WITH CHARLIE AND ME IN THE BACKGROUND.

In London, two weeks before shooting was to begin on Brian Clemens's *The Hot Cold War Man*, Ken Russell abandoned the project and left me holding the bag. I moved into television, produced several shows, and simultaneously began packaging various movie scripts.

Oona called from Vevey, asking me to do her a big favor. Could Eugene, their second son, now eighteen, stay with me in London? His continuous playing of pop music was preventing Charlie from working and Eugene didn't know what he wanted to do career-wise. Eugene stayed with Berniece and me for two years while I sorted out various jobs for him. Finally he was admitted to the Royal Academy of Dramatic Art and enrolled in their stage-management course. Charlie and Oona were pleased. He was beginning to find himself.

It was now Charlie's eighty-fifth birthday, and I threw him a small party at my house. At first, Oona thought it would be too much of a strain for Charlie, but then she changed her mind. I got presents for everyone – John Cleese and his wife, Don and Ella Stewart, John Daly of Hemdale, John Terry of the National Film Finance Corporation and Peter Noble of Screen International and his wife Marianne. The gifts all had to do with Charlie: posters of his films, and copies of his autobiography. Charlie happily autographed everything. John Cleese was particularly pleased with his *Great Dictator* poster. He said it was his favorite Chaplin film.

Richard Hatton, Michael Crawford's agent, telephoned me. Crawford was starring in the musical *Billy* in the West End, and had set his heart on Charlie seeing the show. Crawford and I tried everything to entice him. Crawford arranged for Charlie to have the Royal Box (where there was a connecting bathroom), and dinner would be brought to him during the intermission. But it was now becoming progressively more difficult for Charlie to go to the theater. Much to his regret he had to decline.

Charlie never lost his enthusiasm for *The Freak*, and kept insisting he was going to make it. The wings were now stored in his basement. But they were fetched out one weekend when Vicky and Jean-Baptiste came. To please Charlie, Vicky put on the wings; Charlie began rehearsing and composing set-ups for the film on the lawn. Jean-Baptiste photographed the rehearsals. Afterwards, Charlie, Josie, Vicky and I read the script aloud. Charlie got excited. He was ready to roll up his sleeves and start working. "We're going ahead with the film," he said

to me. Then he turned to Oona. "Work out Jerry's deal." Oona and I smiled at each other knowingly.

On March 4th, 1974, Harold Wilson became Prime Minister once more. He invited Berniece and me to 10 Downing Street, and introduced me to his guests as his landlord.

Later that year, Oona called and told me in confidence that the British Ambassador to Switzerland had just phoned Charlie. Wilson wanted him to accept a knighthood. "They" had now let it go through. At first Charlie had refused, saying, "How would it look for the Tramp to be called Sir Charlie?" Then he received another call, this time from Downing Street. The Prime Minister, the caller said, and everyone else in the Cabinet would be so disappointed if he turned down the honor. Charlie said he'd give them an answer within twenty-four hours.

The next day he accepted. I didn't let onto Oona that I already knew about the knighthood. I too was sworn to secrecy.

Berniece convinced me that since the bottom had fallen out of the British film industry, it would be best to move to Los Angeles. At the Savoy we said our goodbyes to Oona and Charlie.

In California, our friend Reed Sherman, an actor and singer, found us temporary accommodation. It was a typical Hollywood apartment house, Spanish in style, with a swimming pool in the center. Every tenant was in showbusiness. You'd see them sitting around the pool reading *Variety* or the *Hollywood Reporter*. There were agents, actors, singers, disc jockeys, writers, directors; you could never be lonely.

When I awoke the first morning, I saw from my balcony a dark-haired body-builder coming out of the next apartment. I said to myself, "I wouldn't want to meet him in a dark alley." I thought perhaps he was a stuntman – every morning big hulks would take him to a gym to work out. I was told later he was an actor; he'd just written a script and was hoping to get it filmed.

Finally we were introduced. His name was Sylvester Stallone, and he turned out to be a pussycat. We became friends; and he told me all about his script – a prizefighting story called *Rocky*. He was determined to play the lead himself, and although he was broke and companies had offered big money for the property, he refused to sell.

Reed Sherman and I took offices at the Goldwyn Studios, where Mary Pickford and Douglas Fairbanks had once made their films for United Artists. Reed and I began working on a Western – *The Day the Sun Died*. Reed was shrewd, and always came up with new ideas.

Next door was the production office of Mae West's new film *Sextette*. On learning that I had worked with Chaplin, Mae sent a message to me through one of her musclemen she kept in her employ. She had great respect for Chaplin, she said, and was "a fan". I thanked the muscleman.

In London, Charlie received his knighthood from the Queen at Buckingham Palace on March 4th, 1975. Oona was present. As he walked towards the Queen to be knighted, the orchestra played the theme from *Limelight*. When the Queen left the ceremony, she smiled and waved at Oona: Oona was thrilled. Afterwards, Charlie held a reception at the Savoy, with Prime Minister Harold Wilson, Marcia Falkender, Ella and Don Stewart, plus some of the children. Newspaper cartoonists had a field day depicting the Tramp being knighted. I think Charlie savored every minute of it.

Sylvester gave me several of his original scripts to read. One was based on the life of Edgar Allan Poe, another on political corruption in Tammany Hall: another one – the best – concerned a bodyguard. They all tingled with excitement; Stallone had original concepts, and his dialogue was funny and penetrating. I made certain suggestions, and Sylvester always had an open mind. Sometimes he would go over the top with enthusiasm. One day he said to me: "I have more respect for you than anyone else in this town." I'm sure he hadn't met that many people yet.

I gave him an original script to read by Andrew Bergman (who wrote *Blazing Saddles* and *Fletch*) and Richard Walter. He loved it and wanted to play the lead. It was about a Jewish comic in the Catskill Mountains. I couldn't quite see Sylvester as a Jewish comic, but once he told me he ate only kosher chicken I began to re-think.

Charlie was to receive a Fellowship from the British Academy of Film and Television Arts; they also wanted him to open their new headquarters at 195 Piccadilly. It was becoming difficult for Charlie to travel, but he was finally persuaded to come by a warm and enthusiastic letter from Richard Attenborough. Charlie, now in a wheelchair, accepted his Fellowship on March 10th, 1976. The Queen, Prince Philip and Princess Anne were present; the evening concluded with the screening of extracts from *The Gold Rush*.

Sylvester's decision to hold firm paid off. Irwin Winkler and Robert Chartoff finally agreed to make *Rocky* with Sylvester in the lead. Filming went like clockwork. Sylvester kept me informed of its progress, and told me how he'd supervised most scenes. He insisted the film be made his way.

Berniece and I were invited to the first preview at MGM. I couldn't believe what I saw; the audience went wild. I wrote to Oona and Charlie about the film. *Rocky*, I felt, was the best American movie I'd seen since *Limelight*.

Back home, immediately after the showing, Sylvester looked both exhausted and exhilarated. "You're going to be the biggest star in town."

I said. He was in a complete daze; he couldn't believe the reception.

Rocky duly became the talk of Hollywood. The following week, there was another showing at the Academy Theater. I liked it even better the second time. I wrote again to Oona and Charlie: "Sylvester is really going to make it big. He said to me the other day, 'A year ago I was eating mice for lunch. Who could've thought this would happen to this guinea?' "

Oona wrote back wanting to know all about Sylvester: how old he was, and what he had done before. My enthusiasm was catching. She also said Charlie was putting music to some of his older films; she was happy he was doing it, since work was so important to him. Then she

On March 4th, 1975 Charlie was knighted by the Queen. He was now Sir Charles Chaplin. Here, after the reception at the Savoy, the family gathers. Left to right: Annie, Josie, Charlie, Oona, Christopher, Geraldine and Jane.

Top and bottom: Every twenty-five years in Switzerland the Fête des Vignerons (Wine Festival) takes place. Both pictures show Oona, Vicky and her son James mingling with the crowd (1977).

stated that he had recently woken up at four in the morning and was talking aloud: " …and they are *beautiful*," he said, " …and I'll never make them again …" He was talking about his films.

During this period I kept writing Oona long letters full of trivia and nonsense. I knew she was housebound, and I wanted to give her news from the outside world.

Rocky opened to sensational business. Everyone was offering Sylvester the most coveted roles. He had his heart set on playing *Superman*. But Richard Donner, the director, turned him down; he wanted a clean-cut, all-American type. Sylvester thought the description fitted him like a glove.

After seven years, Berniece and I parted. I returned to London. Sylvester asked if I could arrange for him to meet Charlie; he would fly over in an instant. I said I'd try; meanwhile he organized a 16mm print of *Rocky* to be sent to Oona and Charlie. I went immediately to Switzerland. Michael Chaplin met me at Geneva airport. As we drove to Vevey, Michael warned me that his father had changed considerably. I felt Oona wanted to prepare me.

Although Charlie had altered, to me he was still the same Charlie. While I was in London, Sylvester wrote reminding me how much he would love an "audience with the great maestro himself". I asked Oona. "It's up to you," she said. But I felt Sylvester's trip should be delayed until Charlie was feeling more like his old self.

The print of *Rocky* arrived. Charlie, Oona and the children saw it in the living-room. Charlie loved the film. He had always been a fight fan. As he watched he kept murmuring, "Excellent … excellent." Since Sylvester was such a fan of Charlie's, I only wish he could have been there to witness his reaction.

The Knie Circus was in Vevey. During the day, Oona, Charlie and I walked in the town square and visited the animals. Oona never left Charlie's side. She carried on as though he was his old self. The next night, we all went to the Circus. It was Charlie's twenty-fourth consecutive visit, and it was to be his last. Since we still had the *Rocky* print, Eugene showed it at midnight to the Knie children. *Rocky* now became the talk of Vevey.

I haven't seen or heard from Sylvester since that period. His success has been phenomenal. It must be difficult to keep your sanity when you go from "eating mice for lunch" to twenty million dollars per film up front. When I first saw *Rocky*, I felt, along with some critics, that Sylvester captured a Chaplin quality. Today (*Rambo* notwithstanding), the thing I liked most about Sylvester was not only his enthusiasm, but his genuine admiration for Charlie.

I wanted Charlie to see more films, to keep up his interest and enthusiasm. In London, I arranged, through Stanley Kubrick, for Charlie to see *Barry Lyndon* – his latest film. Oona told me that as Charlie watched the picture he commented. "Beautiful … beautiful." *Rocky* and *Barry Lyndon* were to be the last two films that Charlie ever saw.

Oona invited me to spend Christmas at Vevey. I was in the middle of shopping when I received a call from my sister. My father didn't have much longer to live; she advised me to fly to Los Angeles immediately. By the time I arrived, my father had died. My sister told me that his last words were about me; he didn't want to die yet, he said, because "what will happen to Jerry?" To my father I was still his little boy.

Below: CHARLIE IN A WHEELCHAIR WATCHING THE BIRDS, OVERLOOKING LAKE GENEVA. THIS IS ONE OF THE LAST PHOTOS OF CHARLIE.

After the funeral, I stayed onto comfort my mother and sister. Three days later, on Christmas Day, 1977, my mother woke me. A neighbor had called her to say she'd heard on the radio that Charlie Chaplin had died. I couldn't believe it. I wouldn't believe it.

I tried calling Oona. As it was Christmas, it was impossible to make connections. Finally I got through. "Oh Jerry," Oona said. "I've been trying to call you. I didn't want you to hear the news on the radio. You knew him better than anyone else." She began to weep. The funeral would be held in two days' time. I had to go. I told my mother I would return immediately. She understood.

The death of my father and Charlie within a few days of each other left me alone and bereft. Because of the holidays, it took me two days to reach Vevey. Swiss soldiers were guarding the Manoir. I arrived one hour before the funeral. It was held in a small village near Corsier. I saw dear Charlie laid to rest.

Telegrams flooded in for Oona from all over the world:

"Dearest Oona, we will always remember so great and gentle a man. He will remain with you, in love, for the rest of your life."
Sophia and Carlo Ponti.

"We would like you to know that last night's performance of the San Francisco Ballet Company at the War Memorial House was dedicated to the memory of Charles Chaplin. The audience of more than 3,000 joined the dedication with two minutes of silence."
Director of the San Francisco Ballet.

"Heartbroken."
Truman Capote.

"We all cry with you. We all loved him."
Arthur Rubenstein.

"Sincere condolences for you and your family."
François Mitterand.

"Dear Oona, although our association with Charlie was not a long one, our lives were made much richer for the experience. Our deepest sympathies."
Kit and Jay Kanter.

"The city lights are not so bright now."
The American Ambassador in Bern.

"Sincere condolences, dear Oona. You gave Charlie the best life in the entire world. My deepest affection goes to you and your family."
Georges Simenon.

"He will always be remembered by all French people who loved the work of your husband."
Valéry Giscard d'Estaing.

"Your husband has left an enduring legacy to delight filmgoers of the future . . . We understand your great loss. It is shared by us all."
The Museum of Modern Art.

"An incalculable loss is felt with the passing of 'Charlie'."
Adolfo Suarez, President of Spain.

Before leaving for London, I saw Oona in her study. She broke down. It was the first time I was witness to her tears. She always displayed such reserve. I asked if I could call my mother. "Yes," she replied, "and I would like to speak to her too." It was so like Oona to think of my mother's sorrow in the midst of her own. The two widows spoke and comforted each other.

For three months Oona never left the Manoir. During this period, Charlie's body was stolen. The kidnappers demanded ransom money, but Oona would not submit to blackmail. She knew this would have been Charlie's wish. In the 1930s, when the Lindbergh baby was kidnapped, Charlie left instructions that if he were ever abducted, blackmail money should not be paid. He was adamant about this.

When Oona came out of seclusion, she visited London. While we were dining, word reached her that Charlie's body had been found, in a cornfield some twenty miles outside Vevey. The kidnappers were apprehended and jailed. Oona, ever considerate, was concerned about them: "They're so young to spend all that time in jail."

The farmer who owned the cornfield placed a cross with a Derby and cane to commemorate the spot where Charlie's body had lain.

ABOVE AND LEFT: THE FIELD WHERE CHARLIE'S BODY WAS FOUND. THE FARMER PUT UP A CROSS AND A CANE TO MARK THE SPOT.

AFTER **9** THOUGHTS

CHARLIE

The years I worked with Charlie were the most exciting times of my life. Sure, there was tension. But it was exquisite tension. Charlie never displayed temperament. He just wanted the best from himself and expected that from others. He cared. I liked that.

He'd say to me, "Jerry, you must never lose your enthusiasm." He enjoyed how excited I became when he improvised or devised a new funny sequence. When I had the Circle, he liked the way I managed it and shared my delight whenever I discovered a new writer.

Charlie was always curious; never blasé. That was the secret of his eternal youth. In London, when we went to pantomimes and music-halls together, we would behave like kids. He'd love to peer through restaurant windows and count the number of customers. "If it's full, it must be good!" he'd say.

Sometimes he took Oona and me to dingy hovels. There was one place on Leicester Square he discovered – a garish, neon-lit joint. But he was right about their food; they had marvelous T-bone steaks. One of his favorite London restaurants was Blooms, in the East End. Sometimes, I'd buy a take-away order of corned beef sandwiches, chopped liver, potato latkas and hot horseradish sauce, and we'd have a feast at their hotel, or my house in Vincent Square. We were really living it up!

Charlie never forgot his roots. In London he'd enjoy disappearing among the crowds; he'd hop on a bus and watch the passing parade

through the window. Of course, he enjoyed the other side of life – the limousines, the luxury – but he remained unaffected by his fame. He never thought he should be treated any differently from anyone else.

In Los Angeles he showed *The Great Dictator* for a charity performance. I was invited to the theater on Wilshire Boulevard. When I arrived the pavement was choked with people, and the lines stretched around the block. As I walked around the corner, I saw Oona and Charlie lined up with all the others. "What are you doing, standing in line for your own picture?" I said. I quickly took them out of the queue and rushed them towards the box-office. We were immediately escorted in. But Charlie always refused to take advantage of his position.

Once in London, Oona found a new restaurant she wanted to try. She called for a reservation, but was disappointed to learn that there was no room. I immediately called the restaurant and told them the table was for Mr and Mrs Charles Chaplin. Charlie stood beside me, gesturing not to mention his name; he was embarrassed. I turned to him, "What's the good of being Charlie Chaplin, if you can't even get a table in a restaurant!" Naturally in two seconds there was space.

Although Charlie was wealthy he was never ostentatious. His childhood years had made an indelible impression on him; besides he'd worked too hard to squander his money. Sydney, his eldest son, on the other hand, was different. To him, money was meant to be spent. Charlie was appalled. "Easy come, easy go," he would say. And Syd would answer, "I can't help it, I was born with a silver spoon in my mouth. If he'd been born like me, maybe he'd be a big spender too!" Yet, without advertising the fact, Charlie looked after many old-timers and actresses, and kept them on his pay roll throughout their lives.

On special occasions Oona and Charlie enjoyed nothing better than celebrating alone with a bottle of champagne and a tin of the finest caviar. But he'd always say, "If you did this every day, the fun would soon be gone." He did things in moderation.

Charlie contemplating his fan mail.

Ben Turpin.

Charlie had many likes and dislikes regarding actors, actresses, and entertainers. Yet he never lost his enthusiasm for Al Jolson. He thought that seeing Jolson in person was the highest theatrical experience in his life. "It was electrifying how he moved the audience," Charlie said. "When he came down the ramp and bent on his knees and sang 'My Mammy' – it sent shivers down your back." He enjoyed Lucille Ball, too – thought her very funny and extremely talented.

Charlie himself was never jealous of other silent comedians. Although he was inherently modest, when it came to pantomime he knew he was in a class by himself. But there was one comic who made him nervous. He thought him very funny: It was Ben Turpin, the cross-eyed comic.

In the 1920s, there was a comic-strip that Charlie thought had genius – *Krazy Kat*. And why shouldn't he? Krazy Kat had the same anarchistic attitude to life as the early Tramp.

Charlie liked one of the most disliked people in Hollywood – Harry Cohn, President of Columbia Pictures. He couldn't stand the pretensions of some producers who talked about making pictures for "art", and also upstarts who knew better than anyone else what was wrong with Hollywood. Cohn let it be known that he was in the entertainment business to make a buck, and that was that. Charlie liked that about him. He wasn't a phony.

Charlie had a boat, the *Panacea*. On weekends, he and Oona would sail off to Catalina Island and come back revitalized after swimming in the Pacific. He told me how, in the old days, a young girl used to swim up to the *Panacea* and shout, "Charlie, why don't you put me in the pictures?" It was Carole Lombard.

Charlie was always able to tell when certain actors were succumbing to their new-found wealth. He'd say, "They're beginning to act like insurance salesmen!" The vitality, spark and energy that first brought them into the limelight was gone – and it had nothing to do with age. Charlie never became like this.

When certain actresses won Academy Awards and everyone raved about their talents, he'd look at them coldly and say "Even if they were good, I wouldn't like them!" Something about their personalities rubbed him the wrong way.

Charlie was always aware of the public. While at the Manoir in 1954, a friend visited him and brought him a record of a new singer called Elvis Presley. Charlie hadn't heard of him. "This man has made a sensation in the States." his friend said. "I can't understand it. He wiggles his hips and sings and people go mad." "If he's made such an impact," Charlie replied, "he *must* have something. You can't fool the public."

In New York, Oona and Charlie saw Arthur Miller's *Death of a Salesman* and found it moving. In London they enjoyed Irene Worth in *Waters of the Moon*; Lionel Bart's *Oliver*; Olivier's *Othello*; Vanessa Redgrave in *As You Like It* (and in her film *Isadora*), and Harold Pinter's *The Caretaker*. I recommended they see *Trelawny of the Wells* at the National Theatre. They loathed it. I didn't recommend anything after that.

After Christmas, when the children were young, Oona and Charlie usually brought them to London for a week, and then it was pantomime time. Tommy Steele, Ken Dodd, Danny La Rue, the Crazy Gang – we saw them all. After a while, Oona declined to go, and eventually so did the children. They preferred watching English TV in the hotel. So Charlie and I went by ourselves; we never tired of them.

If Charlie were around today, I think he would have admired

Top: Oona and Charlie (shielding his nose from the sun) on their boat, the Panacea.
Below right: Charlie and Oona.

Spielberg's *E.T.*, Hanif Kureshi's *My Beautiful Laundrette* and Dennis Potter's *The Singing Detective*, plus the talents of Eddie Murphy, Daniel Day Lewis, Robin Williams, Jessica Lange, William Hurt, Debra Winger, Jeff Bridges, Holly Hunter, Jeff Daniels, Steve Martin and Michael Gambon. In English music-halls, I think he would have enjoyed the new comic, Michael Barrymore.

I never saw Charlie depressed. I saw him anxious, tense, but never down. I was always amazed how, in the face of adversity, he was able to pick himself up and get on with living. For him, each new day was a day full of challenge and promise. "Don't wish your life away," he'd say when Oona or I were eagerly awaiting some big event, "enjoy the moment."

Charlie may not have been very tall, but when he came into a room he seemed to tower over everyone else. Even if you didn't know who he was, you'd be aware you were looking at a man of importance.

People often asked me what he was like in real life. "See his films and you'll know," I'd reply. Everything he did on the screen was a facet of himself. I think that's why people all over the world identified with him.

Charlie never gushed over his children, although he was delighted with them. As they grew older, none of them was able to pull the wool over his eyes. But he always encouraged his children to follow their hearts. When Josie was sixteen, she decided she wanted to become an opera singer. Charlie backed her up completely.

Jane had ambitions to be an actress, and had to audition for a part in a play. Charlie asked her why she was so nervous. She told him about the audition. "All good actors get nerves." he said. "But what if I fail?" Jane wailed. "Failure, is unimportant." Charlie replied, "But it takes courage to make a fool of yourself. Keep trying and you'll eventually gain confidence. You must take risks in life. Then you'll succeed."

Charlie was a shrewd and careful business man, but when he was creating, nothing else mattered. Business was cast aside. Yet when the moment arrived for him to visit his bankers, he was able to shift hats. In front of my eyes he suddenly became all business – sober, humorless and suspicious. Gone was the fun-loving Charlie I had been working with a few hours before.

Charlie was like the actor/managers at the turn of the nineteenth century – writing, directing, presenting, and starring in their own vehicles. He simply transferred what was common in the theater to films.

After meeting Ingmar Bergman in Sweden, Charlie gave an interview to the *Herald Tribune,* and said he never missed an Ingmar Bergman film. By mistake, the paper printed it as "an *Ingrid* Bergman film". She was thrilled, and in subsequent interviews she quoted Charlie as saying he never missed one of her films. Charlie was too much of a gentleman to refute the lady.

RIGHT: CHARLIE ENCOURAGING JOSIE AT THE PIANO.
BELOW RIGHT: CHARLIE TAKING HIS NEW-BORN FOR A STROLL.

When Charlie and I were discussing the title music for *The Adding Machine*, he suggested that I write it myself. I was taken aback. "You know the feeling of your film better than anyone else," Charlie said. "Express that feeling in music and write it." Charlie felt nothing was impossible in this life if you had the desire.

Charlie was sometimes contradictory. When he heard that Tommy Steele, without permission, had filmed his childhood for TV, he was outraged and said he was going to sue. Then he was shown a tape of the programme in Vevey, and Oona found him watching it in tears. He loved it. That ended the lawsuit.

Another example: Charlie always said he didn't believe in psychoanalysis. He felt one's personality – the thing that made an individual unique – would be destroyed. Yet, in *Limelight*, he tries to discover what is behind the paralysis in Terry's legs, and begins analyzing her.

Still another example. Although Charlie admired the latest fashions, he always maintained that the best-dressed women in the world were to be found in Butte, Montana – a small mining town. He remembered seeing well-groomed girls walking in the streets in Butte when he was touring with Karno. Oona and I would laugh. "They must have been hookers," I said. Charlie became furious. "I don't care what they were. They were still the best-dressed women in the world." The girls of Butte, Montana, should be very flattered.

Charlie often said that he would never have achieved such worldwide success if he had stayed in England. There, he was up against a social barrier that impedes advancement. Americans never ask "Where do you come from? Are you public school?" They are only interested in what you can do and how well you do it.

In the late 1940s and 1950s, Charlie was outraged that the American film industry wasn't prepared to unite and take a stand against political witch-hunters. Instead, out of fear, the studio heads capitulated. "They have the most powerful instrument in their hands – the motion picture," Charlie said. "They should have used it to expose these bastards. Instead, they sold out and became weak and mealy-mouthed."

"What this country needs now," he'd say to me, "is a Will Rogers." Rogers, who was killed in a plane crash in 1935, was the well known homespun American humorist/philosopher who, while twirling a lasso, poked fun at politicians and made the whole country laugh. "He would take the wind out of those buffoons," Charlie would say. And that's what Charlie was soon to do himself in *A King in New York*.

In spite of how he was eventually treated during the witch-hunts, Charlie never lost his affection for America. "After all," he used to say, "that's where I met Oona."

Charlie kidding around . . .

CHARLIE AT ONE TIME WANTED TO PORTRAY
NAPOLEON. HE NEVER DID — BUT THE
DESIRE NEVER LEFT HIM.

RIGHT: CHARLIE AS NAPOLEON AT THE
GEORGE INN, LONDON.

FAR RIGHT: CHARLIE AS NAPOLEON AT SAN
SIMEON WITH PRINCESS BIBESCO.

BOTTOM LEFT: CHARLIE AS NAPOLEON
SURVEYS AFRICA.

BOTTOM RIGHT: CHARLIE AS THE EMPEROR
VISITS A ROMAN RUIN IN SWITZERLAND
WITH MICHAEL.

CHARLIE IN HIS SAUNA IMPROVISING A
HORROR FILM.

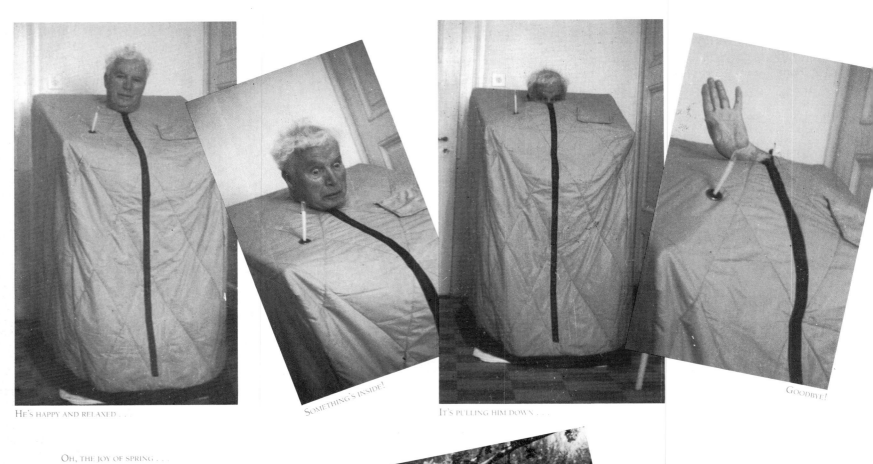

HE'S HAPPY AND RELAXED . . .

SOMETHING'S INSIDE!

IT'S PULLING HIM DOWN . . .

GOODBYE!

OH, THE JOY OF SPRING . . .

PANSIES ARE IN BLOOM . . .

OH, THE HELL WITH IT!

OONA

To me, Oona and Charlie were one. I always thought of them, and loved them, as a couple.

One day at the Circle, Charlie said to me, "You know, Oona is very fond of you. She's a very private person and has few friends. You should take this as a compliment." I did.

I was in my early twenties when I first met them at our living-room theater, where we were performing *The Adding Machine*. After the performance, all the actors surrounded the great Charlie but I was just as intrigued by Oona – her smile, her gentleness, her warmth and modesty.

In all the years I've known her, I've never asked her about her life before she knew Charlie. I would never invade her privacy. But from snatches of conversation, heard from friends, I gathered bits and pieces. She had an older brother Shane, to whom she was devoted. Her father, the playwright Eugene O'Neill, had married an actress called Carlotta Monterey after his divorce from Oona's mother, the novelist Agnes Boulton. When Oona wrote to her father, the possessive Carlotta would destroy her letters. She kept O'Neill isolated and prevented Oona from seeing him.

I remember, when I lived in Brooklyn, reading in the papers that Oona had been voted Debutante of the Year in New York. I also heard that she once acted in a stock company production of Rogers and Hart's *Pal Joey*.

When they were both in their teens, Oona and her close friend, Carol Marcus (now Matthau), went to Los Angeles. I understand that Oona had a difficult time, living in a small room on the wrong side of the tracks with little money. Shortly afterwards, through Minna Wallis, an agent, Oona was presented to Charlie for the part of a young Irish girl in his proposed film; *Shadow and Substance*. They fell in love and married. To this day, that's all I know about Oona's background.

"I ONLY HAVE EYES FOR YOU." CHARLIE IS
REFLECTED IN OONA'S SUNGLASSES.

Right: Oona and Geraldine doing yoga.

Right: Oona and Geraldine doing yoga.

Whenever Charlie and I were together – whether working on the set, or on a script or just taking long walks – we looked forward to Oona joining us. She was always so gay, so full of life; she brought more laughter into our working relationship.

No one relates a story better than she, and what a joy it is to receive one of her letters; they're full of humor and news. All her friends have encouraged her to write but she dismisses the idea.

My relationship with Charlie sometimes had its ups and downs, Oona usually saw to it that any problems were quickly resolved. She would always try to understand the other person's point of view.

One night in Los Angeles, as we were taking a drive, Oona and Charlie were discussing their children. I remarked that when I was a child, I used to ask my mother whom she loved more – my father or me – and she replied, "Your father will always come first in my life." Charlie latched onto that and turned to Oona; "That's the way you must be," he said.

But Oona didn't have to be told. Charlie came first, last and always in her life. When he grew older, she never left his side. As she said, "When I was young, he looked after me. Now it's my turn to look after him."

Oona adored all her children and showered them with love and devotion. Even if she had only ten minutes to spend with them, she would give them her complete attention. That's what counted. When Michael was eight, Oona noticed one day that he seemed very down. She was disturbed and asked what was bothering him. He couldn't articulate his feelings. I shall never forget the way she said, "Oh my darling!" as she enveloped him in her arms. He was soon feeling better.

In the 1970s, Charlie had just finished putting a new score to his 1921 classic, *The Kid*. As Oona, Charlie and I watched the film, Charlie rhapsodized about the performance of his young co-star, Jackie Coogan. Oona quickly chimed in: "Michael was a much better actor than Coogan." She was referring to Michael's performance in *A King in New York*.

Left: Oona and Michael. *Below:* Oona and Josephine.

"He was very good," Charlie said flatly, "but not like Coogan." But Oona wasn't having it. She stuck to her guns: "Coogan could never have said all those lines like Michael!" She defended her son to the end. The matter was dropped. There were no winners.

Charlie and Oona radiated happiness. It was a pleasure to be in their company. One evening in London, after working late, editing *The Adding Machine*, I went to Trader Vic's, knowing I would find them there. At first I couldn't see them, then I spotted them in a dark corner, gazing into each other's eyes like two young lovers. It was touching.

Sometimes Charlie would refer to Oona as "the missus" or "the old lady". To Charlie these expressions were terms of endearment. Although Oona was thirty-five years younger than he, he used to say jokingly "This woman took away the best years of my life!"

When I was a child my mother used to drag me to Kleins in Manhattan to buy me a suit, Kleins was the cut-rate department store on Fourteenth Street, where immigrants shopped for bargains. On the walls of the shop were large signs warning people against shoplifting, written in every language – Spanish, Italian, German, Yiddish, Greek, and Chinese. I mentioned this to Oona. To my surprise, she said, "Before I knew Charlie, that's where I used to buy *my* clothes. In fact the dress I was married in I bought at Kleins!"

Oona should have been an editor for a publisher. She is a voracious reader with excellent literary tastes. She devours everything. She loves Philip Roth, Graham Greene, V. S. Pritchett, Saul Bellow, Bernard Malamud, Norman Mailer, Anita Brookner, the poetry of Philip Larkin; among the classics, her favorite is Jane Austen.

Charlie had great admiration for the Jewish people, although he was not Jewish himself. Originally he was against Zionism, but when he discovered the horrors of the holocaust, he was all out for the State of Israel – a homeland for the Jews.

Recently, Oona told me about a trip she took to New York. At Kennedy Airport, the Flight Captain approached her. "Lady Chaplin, may I ask you a question?" "Of course," Oona replied. She couldn't imagine what he wanted. "Was your husband Jewish?" he asked. For a moment she was taken aback. Then she replied "Yes."

"But Charlie told me he wasn't," I said to Oona. "You must always say 'Yes' if people ask you." Oona explained; "It's a big mistake to deny it, otherwise you could be playing into the hands of anti-Semites." This was Charlie's attitude too. "Anyway," she went on, "he was part Jewish, wasn't he?" Then she laughed. "Oh, I really don't know, but who cares? . . . What does it matter?"

Oona has never altered through all the years I've known her. She remains loyal and steadfast with all her friends. Her closest friend is Carol Matthau (Walter's wife). They've known each other since their

teens. Even today, there's a bond between them. Both would drop everything at a moment's notice, no matter where they were, if either of them needed the other's help. I, too, am one of the lucky ones.

There has always been a certain mystery and reserve about Oona which makes her fascinating. Her children feel it too.

So many people seem to be drawn to her. While touring Europe, Michael Jackson said the one person he wanted to meet was Oona Chaplin.

From just seeing her photos in the papers, people have asked me what she is like in person. "She seems so nice," they say. All I can reply is "She's as nice as she looks!"

As Charlie would say, "You can't fool the public."

Today, Oona is fortunate to have her children. They help fill the gap in her life. They are like part of my family too. When they visit London, many of them stay at my house.

Geraldine, the eldest daughter, has the dazzling Chaplin smile. She is now an established actress, best remembered for her roles in *Dr. Zhivago* and *Nashville*. She has enormous enthusiasm for life and is a great weaver of tales. Today she lives in Madrid with her son and daughter.

Michael, the eldest son, worked for me on *The Adding Machine*. He is intelligent, intuitive and a fine writer. There's a remarkable resemblance between him and his grandfather, the young Eugene O'Neill. He now lives on a farm in the South of France with his wife, Patricia, and their seven children. I think he now appreciates the difficulties of being a father.

Josephine Chaplin was born in Santa Monica, California, while Charlie was directing *Caligula*. She's effervescent, resourceful and an accomplished actress; recently she played Ernest Hemingway's first wife in a TV mini-series. But she also enjoys the role of housewife and is a superb cook. She lives in the South of France and has three sons.

Victoria Chaplin has the largest blue eyes you ever saw. Charlie chose Vicky for the leading part in his last film project. *The Freak*, but when it was abandoned she decided she didn't want to be an actress,

Right: Jane with her new baby.
Far right: Michael and Josephine.
Below: Geraldine.
Center right: Josephine and her baby.

Bottom left: Christopher, the newest Chaplin talent.
Bottom center: Eugene.
Bottom right: Annie.

despite many offers. Instead, she followed her heart, and started a circus with her multi-talented husband, Jean-Baptiste Thierree.

Le Cirque Imaginaire has been acclaimed in London, Italy, France, Belgium and the United States. To quote *The Boston Globe*, " …it's magnifique, it's also charming, funny, clever, magical … non-stop delight." They have two children, the lovely Aurelia, sixteen, and James, fourteen. In the circus, James performs somersaults and cartwheels just as his grandfather did in Karno's music-hall. How proud Charlie would have been of Vicky and Jean-Baptiste, and their Cirque Imaginaire.

Eugene lives with his wife Bernadette and three children in the Manoir grounds. He graduated from the Royal Academy of Dramatic Art as a stage manager, worked in the Montreux recording studios, and is now the proprietor of a video shop in Vevey. If you ever get at odds with him, he has only to flash that marvelous smile of his and all is forgiven.

Jane is unpredictable and fiery. She has written two screenplays and has directed a short film that was shown at the London Film Festival. She lives with Ilya Salkind, the film producer, and they have a son.

Annie Chaplin is bewitching. She is always on the move, and has broken many a heart in many a country. But she is most interested in her career and has completed three films. She recently received glowing notices from the Paris critics for her stage performance in Sam Shepherd's *Buried Child*.

Christopher, the youngest, is a dead ringer for the young Charlie. He majored in philosophy, then studied to be a concert pianist. But when the Muses called he decided he really wanted to act. He has one film to his credit – *Where is Parsifal?* – and has performed in Dostoevsky's *Notes from the Underground* and other fringe productions in Britain. Like Charlie, this young, shy boy suddenly becomes another person when on stage – energetic, funny, and mesmerizing.

Charlie had two other children from a former marriage, Charlie Chaplin Jr and Sydney Earl Chaplin. To be named Charlie Chaplin Jr must have been very difficult to live with. But Charlie Jr was a sweet and gentle man who adored his father. He appeared in two Circle productions, *The Adding Machine* and *The Time of Your Life*. In 1968 he hit his head on the bathtub and died, leaving a widow, Susan, and Charlie's first grandchild.

Sydney Chaplin is known at his mother's home as Tommy, the name she originally intended for him. Sydney performed at the Circle

for five years and then achieved great success on Broadway. But after the in-fighting on *Funny Girl*, he swore he would never perform in New York again – and he hasn't. I'm devoted to him. He's been a good and loyal friend. Today he owns the booming 'Chaplin's' restaurant in Palm Springs, California, and has a son Stephan.

LEFT: CHRISTOPHER IN HIS NEW APARTMENT IN PIMLICO.

ABOVE: SYDNEY.
BELOW LEFT: CHARLES CHAPLIN JR WITH HIS BABY AND CHARLIE AND OONA.

BELOW RIGHT: OONA AS SHE IS TODAY, SURROUNDED BY MICHAEL'S TWO DAUGHTERS DOLLY (UPPER LEFT) AND CARMEN (LOWER RIGHT) AND VICTORIA'S DAUGHTER AURELIA (LOWER LEFT).

OONA EMBRACING CHARLIE. OH, THOSE
WONDERFUL EYES OF HIS...

As for myself, at the time of writing I am producing, with Simon Callow, a film based on Penelope Fitzgerald's novel, *At Freddie's*. Simon is the brilliant English director, author and actor who first performed the role of Mozart in Peter Shaffer's *Amadeus* at the National Theatre.

As I look back, I can think of many happy periods in my career – working with the wonderful Andrews Sisters, Maxene, Patti and LaVerne, Universal Studios and the Circle Theatre. I was most pleased to read an article in the June 1961 *Theatre Arts* magazine by Patterson Greene, the eminent Los Angeles theater critic. He wrote that the entire theater movement in Los Angeles started in a Hollywood living-room. Before that there were only talent showcases and tired roadshows. But it was the Circle Theatre that was the beginning of making Los Angeles a theater town.

Years ago, when I met André Previn, he said to me, "The Circle Theatre was like an oasis for all of us – it was the only place to go at that time in Los Angeles."

But my association with Chaplin brought me the most satisfaction. We worked as a team. On the studio floor, I knew instinctively what he wanted. Watching us together on the *Countess* set, the novelist Penelope Gilliatt said in the *Observer,* was like watching a doctor in the operating theater with his assistant, shoving the right instruments in to his hands without having to say a word.

Since his birth on April 16th, 1889, Chaplin's impact throughout the world has been felt on painters, writers, actors, composers, dancers and politicans; the list is endless. And his influence on the motion picture industry has been innovative and far-reaching.

Before Charlie, comedy had no real structure. It was a series of chases and gags. He brought it body, form and, most of all, character. He was the first to construct a comic sequence, add complications and milk the situation, until it reached its logical conclusion. The motion picture industry owes him an enormous debt.

Today, the young know the figure of the Tramp, but they are not acquainted with his films. And they should be! Schools should screen Charlie's works as part of cultural studies, alongside musical appreciation and the history of art.

Chaplin's films elevate the spirit and enrich the soul. Television does not do them justice: they should be shown on at least a 16mm movie screen, where the viewer can behold his incredible eyes, the nuance of his gestures and the stillness of his figure.

Charlie's very presence on the screen has given hope, optimism, romance and happiness, to people all over the world.

I am proud to have worked with him, and to have known him as a friend.

I miss him.

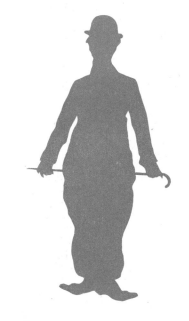

Page numbers in italics refer to captions

ACKNOWLEDGEMENTS

When I was a child, I went to my mother tearfully one day and said, "I have no friends." She replied, "In order to have friends you must *be* a friend." I have never forgotten her words.

Here, I would like to acknowledge some of the people who, through their friendship, have contributed to this book.

First and foremost, I am indebted to Oona Chaplin for allowing me to have any Chaplin still I desired. Those wonderful pictures helped make the book. I would also like to thank Oona's daughter Victoria Chaplin who, while in London with her "Le Cirque Imaginaire", jogged my memory; her daughter Aurelia, who made perceptive observations; Jane Chaplin, who talked with me at length about her mother and father; and Christopher Chaplin, Oona and Charlie's youngest son, on whom I tried out many of my anecdotes about his father. He would say afterwards, "I wish I'd been born then. You had all the fun."

All my friends, through their kindness, warmth and devotion through the years, have in some way made this book possible.

Carol and Walter Matthau. If I ever need them, at the drop of a hat they will beeee there. Carol is extraordinaryy: gifted, beautiful and talented (a great Blanche Dubois). It's no wonder she has been Oona's closest friend since childhood. And Walter, although he underplays his kindness, is as good-natured as they come. Norma and Larry Storch. Norma was a lovely actress at the Circle and has been married for many years to the inimitable comic, Larry Storch. Through highs and lows they have always stood by me, and never wavered in their loyalty. Philip and Marilyn Langner. I introduced them and they have lived happily ever after.

The taped reminiscences I made of some of the original Circle players proved invaluable. We had so many laughs, talking about old times together . . . Bill Schallert, Leah Waggner, Bob Burns, Naomi Stevens, Robert Sherman, Earle Herdan, Julian Ludwig, Ruth Conte and Sydney Chaplin – all helped me to recall events at the Circle. I thank them all. And a special thanks to Lillian Ross for allowing me to quote from her *New Yorker* article of 1978, about Charlie rehearsing at the Circle.

Geoff Brown meticulously indexed all my anecdotes, so that I was easily able to find any story. Besides that, he researched events and carefully filed all the photographs (what a job!) and was my constant sounding board. I can't sing his praises highly enough.

I have many other acts of kindness to record. David Robinson, the London *Times* film critic and author of the definitive biography, *Chaplin – His Life and Art*. He spent many hours helping me with the shape of the book, going through the photos and insisting that I include stories about Ella Stewart and Constance Collier. Christopher Maclehose, the Collins/Harvill publisher, along with his wife Kookla. They also advised me on how to approach the book, and steered me in the right direction for its publication. Petra and Jeremy Lewis. Jeremy is an editor at Chatto & Windus, but it was his wife, Petra, who persuaded me to start the first chapter with a summary of Chaplin's life and career. "A lot of the young today don't know his background." I would also like to thank Charles Walker of Peters, Fraser & Dunlop – my agent – the very best; the novelist Diana Farr, who throughout the writing kept in touch and offered wise counsel; and Cathy Brown – Geoff's wife – for not complaining when Geoff gave up many a weekend.

The manuscript was read by the novelist Charles Webb, when he and his wife Gretchen stayed with me. Charles teaches creative writing in California. I profited greatly from his expertise.

As for Bloomsbury, my publishers, I couldn't have had a happier association. They are a relatively new group who overnight became a strong force in English publishing. They were always a joy to deal with, even when, close to publication, I altered some of the text; they took it all in their stride. But when it came to the selection of the photographs, we all became nervous wrecks. I was told to eliminate some of the 1,500 photographs I had submitted; the narrowing-down process turned us all into nail-biters. But David Reynolds, with his good editorial sense and taste, kept us all sane. When I first met the shrewd and enthusiastic Chairman, Nigel Newton, and the gracious Liz Calder, I knew I was in the right hands; then there was Miren Lopategui, who edited the book – she made editing a pleasure; and Penny Phillips, assistant editor, who was always super-efficient and on the ball. Roger Yelland, the production director, was instrumental in seeing that many of the best photographs were retained and given their proper due; while Simon Jennings, Roy Williams and Laurence Bradbury, the designers, I feel excelled themselves with this book.

A special thanks to Pam Paumier, Oona Chaplin's business manager, who stayed with me many hours as I selected the Chaplin stills in her Paris office; Markku Salmi of the British Film Institute, who also supplied many photos; and Gene Young of Little, Brown in New York, who was the first to realize the book's potential and gave me wise guidance.

And those marvelous secretaries, who toiled through the night, typing and retyping the manuscript: Brenda Watkinson – she should get a job with the British Museum translating hieroglyphics; Rachel Wyndham, who brought me into the twentieth century with a word processor; and Sue Brice, who gave birth to her baby at the same time I finished the book.

I wouldn't have survived without the kindness of John and Ellen Ann Hopkins. John is the superb American novelist. Through the Hopkins' generosity my life was opened up – their friends became mine. Clare and David Astor, Clare and "Kipper" Asquith. They forced me to get away for weekends during the writing and to enjoy the English countryside. (I'm a city boy: "Trees? What's that?") Keith Allison and Charles Humphreys, my close friends and solicitors. They have always kept me on the straight and narrow.

I am also grateful to the film producer Sandy Lieberson. We went through much together and he has been forever loyal; the film historians Kevin Brownlow and David Gill; Leslie Hardcastle, the director of the National Film Theatre and the guiding light behind the new Museum of the Moving Image. It was his vision that brought fresh vitality and excitement to London's South Bank. Faisal Kasim, also of the National Film Theatre, who encouraged me to "stick with it". David Gothand, the English impresario who put the Riverside Studios on the map; Hanif Kureishi, the screenwriter of *My Beautiful Laundrette*; Barbara and David Stone, Otto Plaschkes, Wilt Melnick and the novelist William Watson; the screenwriters Andrew Bergman, Richard Walter and Brian Clemens; Richard Heft, my collaborator on *Hung Jury*; and Pierre ("Superman") Spengler and his wife, Agnes. And, finally, John Kohn, and Arthur Cohn, the brilliant European film producer from Basel.

There are countless other friends I would like to thank. Denis Betro, a fine musician and working colleague, who is reliable, trustworthy and loyal; my cousins, Michael and Carol Tolan; the writer Anna Kythreotis; the novelist James Thackera and his wife Davina; Mary and Bruce Lansbury, Rose and Edgar Lansbury, Yvonne and Gordon Hessler, Baroness Nora David, Sandra Marsh and John Heyman; and Chas. Green, John Baldwin, Jean and Eric Mahoney, Brian Pordage and Julian Bailey – all working colleagues. And John B. Keane, the Irish playwright (*Big Maggie*), the novelist Penelope Fitzgerald, Kendall Duesbury, Carlos and Rosemary Tufnell, Sarah Harrison, Cas Narizanno, Maureen Stapleton, Steve Linnett, Gil Kane, Bill and Jane McClure, Robert and Linda Vaughn, Barbara Eden, Stu Whitman, John Hunter, Robert Hussong, Rosemary Anne Sisson, Sy Litvinoff, Andrew Sinclair, Rhoda and Bernard Bergman, Claire and Al Sachs, Marlon Brando, Alan and Tracy Sussman, Sir John Terry, David Tringham, Dr H.S. Klein and Harry Fine. Lady Margaret Colston, Dorothy and Sam Henry, Sally and Pascal Ricketts, Peter and Jenny Mitchell and Geraldine and Charlie Burt – all good neighbors. Gary McCloy, Michel and Luki Rossier, Pepi and Herbert Luft, who through the years have never lost their enthusiasm for Chaplin, me or the Circle. They talk about the Circle as though it were yesterday. David Knight, Jerry Pam, Des O'Connor, John and Peggy Schuster, Liz and Michael Pemberton, Vanessa and Jay Benedict, Howard Brandy, George and Marios Leondiou, the superb London restaurateurs ("Seafresh"), and Barbara Steele.

I live near the Westminster Hospital in London and have good friends there. They have all been most helpful. Doctors Peter Emerson, Timothy Evans, Andrew Morgan, Richard Hartley, Mark Johnson and Albert Feranti. Plus Barbara Copland, Selina Essiedu and Pat Andrews.

Last but not least, my family. My sister Helen and my brother-in-law Dave always gave me support, devotion and love. And they continuously gathered up old Circle pictures from Bill Schallert, Naomi Stevens, cardboard boxes and agents.

And my nephew, Dr Robert Weinstein, whom I constantly interrupted at his practice in Santa Monica with long-distance phone calls from London, asking him to look for more photos. (When we were filming *Limelight* I was living at my sister's house near Culver City. At seven o'clock every morning Charlie would pick me up in his car on his way to the studio. Robert, who was then eight, would stand on the sidewalk waiting for Charlie Chaplin to arrive. They would always wave to each other).

On my mother's side, they are all professional people. My uncles, nieces, nephews and cousins are all doctors, lawyers and teachers. So when I return to California I have it made! So I wish to thank Susan and Jeff Brand, Carol and John Karp, Debbie and Dr Arthur Bakal, Ziva Weinstein, Sally, Raymond and Mac Allex, Leah London, Drs David and Arnold London, my cousins Harold and Norman London and Norman's sons Rik (Billy Joel's manager), Ronnie and Mark, and my cousins Shirley, Kitty, Rose and Marsha – the laugher.

And on the East Coast, on my father's side, ranging from Brooklyn and Long Island to New Hampshire – Irving, Elaine, Karen, Howard, Alan, Leonard, Bea, Aaron, Jackie, Keith, Esther, my kind Aunt Rose and Donald – all Epsteins! Plus my other Aunt Rose and Joe Ginsberg. God bless them all. If I left anyone out, forgive me.

And finally I'm grateful to my darling absent-minded mother, for giving my sister and me her sense of humor.